2-14

SPOTLIGHT 2013

QUITO

BEN WESTWOOD

Contents

QUITO

Ecuador's capital is a city that scales many heights, not least in terms of elevation. The second-highest capital in the world after Bolivia's La Paz, Quito sits at 2,850 meters above sea level in a valley hemmed in by mountains, including the twin peaks of Volcán Pichincha. Quito's dramatic geographical position has led to its long thin shape: spread out over 50 kilometers long, but just eight kilometers wide.

Quito (pop. 1.6 million) is an intriguing mix of old and new: colonial squares and concrete office blocks, traditional markets and modern malls, indigenous artisans and fashion-conscious professionals—and this diversity allows visitors to have the best of both worlds. The *centro histórico* (historic center) delivers a delightful trip back in time to the colonial era with narrow cobbled streets, elegant plazas,

and spectacular churches. New Town, on the other hand, looks firmly forward and is so cosmopolitan that parts of it are nicknamed *gringolandia*. With a vibrant cultural scene, great nightlife, a vast array of hotels, travel agencies, and the country's best range of restaurants, it's no surprise that Ecuador's political capital is also its tourism hub.

Much of the population of Ecuador's second-largest city lives in *barrios* (neighborhoods) or shantytowns, either up the slopes of the mountains or spread north and south of the city center. The people themselves are historically more conservative than in the rest of Ecuador; the capital has always clung to traditional, conservative values, in contrast to the outward-looking merchants of Guayaquil. However, a new generation, a large student

HIGHLIGHTS

◖ La Compañía: The epitome of gaudy golden grandeur, this extravagant chapel is the most dazzling of all Quito's many beautiful colonial churches (page 13).

◖ La Basílica del Voto Nacional: The tallest church in Ecuador with its armadillo gargoyles is a striking sight, and even more spectacular are the views from its spires over Old Town (page 18).

◖ Casa de la Cultura: From Valdivia figurines to giant *bahía* statues and a majestic Inca sun mask, this is easily Ecuador's best museum (page 20).

◖ Capilla del Hombre: Oswaldo Guayasamín's final work, the Chapel of Man, is an awe-inspiring and humbling tribute to the indigenous peoples of the Americas (page 24).

◖ Mitad del Mundo and Museo de Sitio Intiñan: Take the obligatory photo with a foot in each hemisphere (supposedly), then test out the real Equator a few hundred meters away at nearby Museo de Sitio Intiñan (pages 53 and 54).

◖ Mindo: This sleepy town, nestled in the cloud forest, teems with toucans, hummingbirds, quetzals, and butterflies. Adrenaline seekers can fly across the forest canopy on zip-lines or plunge down the river rapids (page 59).

© AVALON TRAVEL

LOOK FOR ◖ TO FIND RECOMMENDED SIGHTS, ACTIVITIES, DINING, AND LODGING.

population, and modern businesses have all injected a healthy dose of open-mindedness. Most importantly, visitors will find Quiteños helpful, welcoming, and justifiably proud of their city.

Quito's residents have plenty to be proud of: In 1978 it was the first city in the world to receive World Heritage Site status from UNESCO. Although there have been problems with upkeep, in recent years a multimillion-dollar regeneration program has left the city in better shape than ever. A new feeling of cleanliness and security pervades Old Town,

with an increased police presence and a burgeoning cultural and nightlife scene. Interior patios have been tastefully renovated, and street artists have replaced beggars and hawkers. New Town is also increasingly well-kept, although it has some way to go to solve its security problems.

HISTORY

According to a pre-Inca legend, the city of Quito was founded by Quitumbe, son of the god Quitu, in honor of his father. The valley that would eventually cradle Ecuador's capital was originally occupied by the Quitu people, who united with the Cara from the north to form the Shyris nation around A.D. 1300. In 1487 the Incas took over and turned the city into an important nexus of their northern empire, known as the Quitosuyo. Within 100 years the empire fell to infighting, leaving room for the newly arrived Spanish to start almost from scratch.

The city of San Francisco de Quito was founded by Sebastián de Benalcázar on December 6, 1534, and named in honor of fellow conquistador Francisco Pizarro. Benalcázar quickly set about appointing government officials, distributing land to his men, and constructing churches. Originally, Quito consisted only of the present-day section known as Old Town, bounded by the Plaza de San Blas to the north, the Pichinchas to the west, and the Machangara ravine to the east. An art school was founded in 1535 and helped the city become a center of religious art during the colonial period, with its own style, the Quito School.

Since its founding, Quito has been an administrative rather than a manufacturing center. A population boom in the mid-20th century, aided by the discovery of oil, brought thousands of immigrants who spread their homes and businesses into today's New Town, as well as farther south of Old Town and west up the slopes of Pichincha. By the mid-1980s, these makeshift *suburbios* housed as much as 15 percent of the city's population and had acquired most of the services that the older areas took for granted. An earthquake in 1987 damaged numerous structures and left others in ruins, and the eruption of Guagua Pichincha in 1999 showered Quito in ash but otherwise left the city unscathed. Today, the city is officially home to about 1.8 million residents, but the real number is likely higher.

CLIMATE

Quito is famed for its springlike climate, and most of the year daytime temperatures fluctuate 10–21°C. As you would expect in a city at an elevation of 2,850 meters, cloud cover and the time of day have a big effect on the temperature. Mornings tend to be chilly, but it can heat up considerably around midday, when you will likely take off the sweater. Don't leave it in the hotel, though, as temperatures drop quickly on rainy afternoons and in the evenings. Locals say that the city can experience all four seasons in a single day, and that isn't far off the mark.

The dry season in the capital lasts June–September, with July–August seeing the least precipitation. This is also the warmest time of year. A shortened dry season runs December–January, which is also the coldest time of year. The most rain falls February–April and, to a lesser extent, October–November. Afternoons tend to be rainier, so sightseeing early is a good idea.

More of a consideration than the weather is the elevation, which will leave you breathless and light-headed for a couple of days. Dizzy spells, headaches, and fatigue can also occur. It is best not to overexert yourself and to minimize caffeine and alcohol in favor of plenty of water and light food. After two or three days, you'll be used to the elevation.

ORIENTATION

Quito extends over 50 kilometers north–south, and about eight kilometers across. Luckily for first-time visitors, the capital is easily divided into zones: one for historical sights (Old Town); one for visitor services, restaurants, and accommodations (New Town); and then everything else. The city's long, narrow geography makes it quite easy to get around.

A new system of street numbers was implemented in Quito in 2000, with letters prefixing the normal hyphenated numbers (e.g. "Foch E4-132"). Most addresses also give the nearest cross street, so the full address would be "Foch E4-132 y Cordero."

Old Town

Quito's historical heart sits at the northern flank of El Panecillo (Little Bread Loaf) hill, whose statue of the Virgin is visible from most of the neighborhood. This area, also called Quito Colonial or *centro histórico* (historic

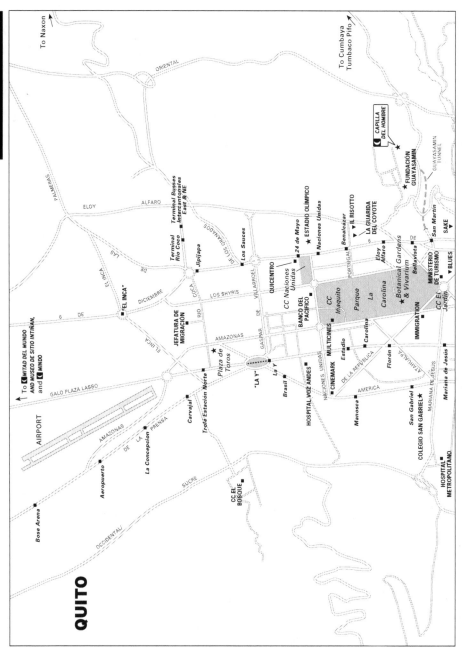

QUITO

To Naxon

ORIENTAL

To Cumbaya
Tumbaco Pifo

CAPILLA
DEL HOMBRE

FUNDACION
GUAYASAMIN

GUAYASAMIN
TUNNEL

PALMERAS

ELOY

ALFARO

Terminal Busses
Intercantonales
East & NE

24 de Mayo

ESTADIO OLIMPICO

Naciones Unidas

Benalcazar

IL RISOTTO

LA GUARIDA
DEL COYOTE

San Martin

SAKE

Terminal
Rio Coco

Jipijapa

DE LOS GRANADOS

Los Sauces

QUICENTRO

Naciones
Unidas

PORTUGAL

Eloy
Alfaro

Bellavista

DE

Botanical Gardens
& Vivarium

MINISTERIO
DE TURISMO

DE

"EL INCA"

DICIEMBRE

COCA

LOS SHYRIS

VILLARROEL

CC Naciones
Unidas

BANCO DEL
PACIFICO

CC
Iñaquito

Parque
La
Carolina

BLUES

CC EL
Jardin

EL INCA

6

DE

RIO

AMAZONAS

JEFATURA DE
MIGRACION

GASPAR

DE

Carolina

IMMIGRATION

LAS

MULTICINES

Estadio

DE LA REPUBLICA

Floron

ATAHUALPA

Mariana de Jesus

To MITAD DEL MUNDO
AND MUSEO DE SITIO INTIÑAN,
and MINDO

GALO PLAZA LASSO

Plaza de
Toros

"LA Y"

La Y

Brasil

HOSPITAL VOZ ANDES

NACIONES UNIDAS

CINEMARK

AMERICA

Manosca

San Gabriel

Mariana de Jesus

AIRPORT

AMAZONAS

DE LA PRENSA

Carvajal

Trole Estación Norte

COLEGIO SAN GABRIEL

HOSPITAL
METROPOLITANO

Aeropuerto

La Concepcion

SUCRE

Bose Arena

OCCIDENTAL

CC EL
BOSQUE

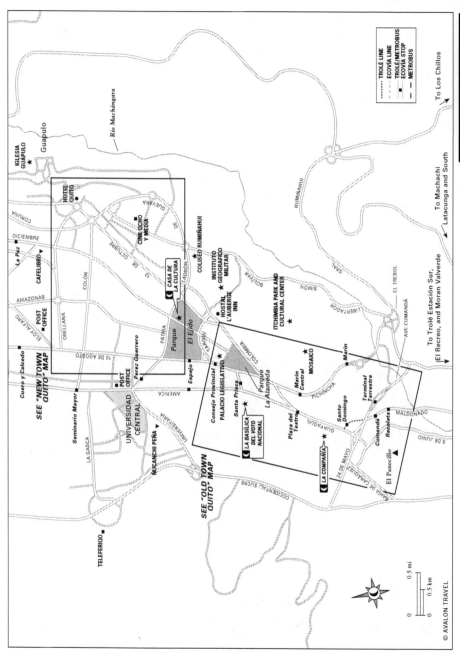

TROLE LINE
ECOVIA LINE
TROLE/METROBUS
ECOVIA STOP
METROBUS

To Los Chillos

To Machachi
Latacunga and South

To Trolé Estación Sur,
El Recreo, and Moran Valverde

IGLESIA GUAPULO
Guapulo

Río Machángara

HOTEL QUITO

CORUÑA
DICIEMBRE
La Paz
CAFELIBRO
CINE OCHO Y MEDIA
GUEVARA
12 DE OCTUBRE
COLON
CORUÑA

CASA DE LA CULTURA
COLISEO RUMIÑAHUI
INSTITUTO GEOGRAFICO MILITAR
LADRON
DE
BOLIVAR

POST OFFICE
AMAZONAS
ELOY ALFARO
ORELLANA
PATRIA
Parque El Ejido

ITCHIMBIA PARK AND CULTURAL CENTER
HOSTAL L'AUBERGE INN

10 DE AGOSTO
Perez Guerrero
POST OFFICE
Espejo
AMERICA
YAGUACHI
COLOMBIA

RUMIÑAHUI
GRAL

SOWIS
LIBERTADOR
EL TREBOL
AVE CUMANDA

SEE "NEW TOWN QUITO" MAP

Cuero y Caicedo
Seminario Mayor
LA GASCA
UNIVERSIDAD CENTRAL
UNIVERSITARIA
ÑUCANCHI PEÑA

Santa Prisa
Consejo Provincial
PALACIO LEGISLATIVO
Parque La Alameda
Marin Central
MOSACO
Marin
PICHINCHA
Terminal Terrestre

TELEFERICO

SEE "OLD TOWN QUITO" MAP

OCCIDENTAL/SUCRE

LA BASILICA DEL VOTO NACIONAL
Plaza del Teatro
GUAYAQUIL
Santo Domingo
Cumanda
Recoleta
MALDONADO

LA COMPAÑIA
24 DE MAYO
BAHIA DE CARAQUEZ
El Panecillo
6 DE JUNIO

0   0.5 mi
0   0.5 km

© AVALON TRAVEL

center), is roughly bordered by 24 de Mayo to the south and Parque La Alameda to the north. Most of the sights are situated within a few blocks of the central Plaza de la Independencia, the original core of the city.

Steep, narrow streets characterize this part of Quito, and cars barely fit in lanes designed for horse and foot traffic. Wrought-iron balconies hang over ground-level storefronts selling household wares, clothing, and shoes.

Most visitors come for the outstanding churches, convents, museums, and plazas that are key to Quito's status as a UNESCO World Heritage Site. Other visitors are content to wander the cobbled streets that evoke Ecuador's colonial past.

There are many wonderful viewpoints to take in Old Town's impressive skyline—from the gothic spires of the Basílica to the top of El Panecillo or the green spaces of Parque Itchimbía.

New Town

Northeast of Old Town, Parque La Alameda and El Ejido form a buffer between past and present. New Town is a world away from the colonial cobbled streets of the historic center. The Mariscal Sucre area is the hub and aptly nicknamed *gringolandia* for its abundance of hotels, restaurants, tour operators, shops, Internet cafés, bars, and discos. This area, enclosed by Avenidas Patria, Orellana, 10 de Agosto, and 12 de Octubre, is alive with backpackers and also doubles as the city's main area for nightlife, heaving with partyers on weekends. North and east of La Mariscal are quieter neighborhoods such as La Floresta and González Suárez as well as Quito's largest park, Parque Carolina. To the east, high above this park, is one of the highlights of the city, artist Oswaldo Guayasamín's famous work, La Capilla del Hombre (Chapel of Man).

Other Neighborhoods

The section of Quito north of New Town hosts much of the capital's industry and sparkles with shiny high-rises that house a large part

© QUITO TURISMO

La Basílica del Voto Nacional

of the city's businesses. These areas are of less interest to visitors. Modern shopping centers and chic restaurants cater to the middle and upper classes that live in this area or in the fast-growing Valle Los Chillos and Tumbaco valleys, both to the east, which also have growing expat retirement communities. The dramatic beauty of the steep old neighborhood Guapulo spills down below Avenida 12 de Octubre and the lofty Hotel Quito. More residential neighborhoods occupy the lower slopes of Pichincha west and north of New Town.

SAFETY

Unfortunately, this most dramatic and historic of South American cities is not without its problems. Quito has rising crime rates, and although you shouldn't be alarmed, bear in mind that there is more crime against visitors here than in any other region of Ecuador. The high concentration of foreigners sadly has led to an increased number of criminals targeting them, so you must take precautions.

One of the diciest areas is the visitor-filled Mariscal Sucre neighborhood of New Town, sometimes simply called "La Mariscal." Increased police presence has recently improved the situation, but the neighborhood still harbors many thieves. Walking alone at night should be avoided; take a taxi to and from your hotel, preferably booked in advance. Don't get into an unmarked cab, and check for the orange license plate and registration number on the side of the vehicle, as "express kidnappings" (a robbery using a vehicle) have been reported.

Watch for pickpockets and bag-slashers on public transport and in Old Town in general. Pay particular attention in crowded areas and when exiting tourist spots like churches. Keep all bags and cameras in front of you, and don't leave your wallet in your back pocket. Don't go into any parks after dark. Beware of people "accidentally" spilling liquids on you and other diversionary tactics.

The trolleybus services (Trole, Ecovia, and Metrobus) are perhaps the worst for pickpockets, and it is guaranteed there will be several thieves on crowded services. It's simple: either keep your valuables well-hidden, or don't take them on the bus at all. Better yet, if you're going sightseeing, take a taxi. A ride from New Town to Old Town costs just $2–3.

The area around El Panecillo is not safe, so take a taxi to get there and back (the driver will usually wait for about $8 round-trip). At the *teleférigo* (cable car), assaults and muggings have been reported on the hike to Rucu Pichincha, although there are now police patrols on the weekend. Do not attempt this climb alone, and ideally don't take valuables.

PLANNING YOUR TIME

If the elevation doesn't make your head spin, the amount to see in Quito probably will. Quito can be a little overwhelming, and you simply can't see it all in a couple of days. You might even consider getting straight on a bus and going down in elevation to a quieter town (Otavalo, Mindo, or Baños) to get your bearings if you've just arrived in South America.

If you only have a couple of days here, spend one each in Old Town and New Town. Start at **Plaza Grande** and take in the cathedral, the presidential palace, **La Compañía,** and Plaza San Francisco before enjoying the views over the city at **El Panecillo** or **La Basílica.** In New Town, don't miss the **Museo del Banco Central,** the **Guayasamín Museum,** and the **Capilla del Hombre.** You may have time to visit the Equator at the **Mitad del Mundo,** or take an extra day to combine this with a hike to **Pululahua** for a little bird-watching and crater-viewing. The *teleférigo* (cable car) ride west of New Town offers the most spectacular views over the city at 4,000 meters.

Most visitors stay in New Town, mainly because there are so many visitor amenities. However, staying in Old Town is increasingly possible and offers a more authentic experience. It really depends on what you want: to hook up with kindred spirits for tours and to socialize at night, stay in New Town; for quieter and more cultural experiences, stay in one of the historic hotels in Old Town. Wherever you stay, it's only a short cab or bus ride between the two districts.

Sights

Quito's Old Town is what makes the city famous, containing a huge number of colonial churches and religious buildings set around elegant plazas. The walls and ceilings are decorated with elaborate paintings and sculptures, and altars are resplendent with gold leaf.

Flash photography is prohibited in most churches and historical museums to protect the fragile pigments of the religious paintings and statues. Keep in mind that opening hours fluctuate regularly; those provided here are the latest available. Several churches are currently undergoing extensive renovation work, but all are open.

OLD TOWN

Quito's Old Town is cleaner, safer, and a joy to wander around following a multimillion-dollar regeneration in the past decade. Gone are the beggars and street vendors, replaced with police and horse-drawn carriages carting visitors around churches, which are beautifully lit at night. A system called Pico y Placa regulates traffic congestion by restricting the entry of certain license-plate numbers at peak hours. It has improved the traffic situation, although the narrow streets still struggle to accommodate Quito's cars. Cars are prohibited completely 9 A.M.–4 P.M. Sunday, making it the most pleasant day for sightseeing.

The municipality of Quito has put together excellent **guided maps** to historic walks through Old Town, available at tourist offices. Even better are the **multilingual tours** given by municipal police from the tourist office.

Plaza Grande and Vicinity

This ornate 16th-century plaza is the political focal point of colonial Quito. Officially called the Plaza de la Independencia, it features a winged statue to independence atop a high pillar. The surrounding park is a popular gathering place with regular music, mime, and dance performances.

On the plaza's southwest side, the **Catedral**

is actually the third to stand on this site (mass 6–9 A.M. daily). Other visits are available through the museum located on Venezuela (tel. 2/257-0371, 9:30 A.M.–4 P.M. Mon.–Sat., $1.50). Hero of independence Antonio José de Sucre is buried here. Behind the main altar is the smaller altar of Nuestra Señora de Los Dolores, where, on August 6, 1875, president Gabriel García Moreno drew his last breath after being attacked with machetes outside the presidential palace. He is now buried here also, as is the country's first president, Juan José Flores.

Next door, formerly the main chapel of the cathedral, the **Iglesia El Sagrario** (10 A.M.–4 P.M. Mon.–Fri., 10 A.M.–2 P.M. Sat.–Sun.) was begun in 1657 and completed half a century later. The walls and ceiling of the short nave are painted to simulate marble—even the bare stone is speckled black-and-white. Impressive paintings and stained glass windows decorate the center cupola. Bernardo de Legarda, the most outstanding Quiteño sculptor of the 18th century, carved and gilded the baroque *mampara* (partition) inside the main doorway.

A long, arched atrium to the northwest lines the front of the handsome **Palacio Presidencial** (10 A.M.–5 P.M. Tues.–Sun., free tours when the government is not in session), also known as El Carondelet. The ironwork on the balconies over the plaza, originally from the Tuileries Palace in Paris, was purchased just after the French Revolution. Current president Rafael Correa opened the doors of the palace to daily visitors in 2007, and it's worth making a line for the guided tours of the interior that leave every hour or so.

The **Palacio Arzobispal** (Archbishop's Palace) on the northeast side leads to a three-story indoor courtyard housing a number of small shops and eateries. Cobbled courtyards, thick whitewashed walls, and wooden balconies make it worth a look. The plaza's colonial spell is broken only by the modern **City Hall** to

President Rafael Correa has opened up the Palacio Presidencial to the public.

© BEN WESTWOOD

the southeast. The church of **La Concepción** (10 A.M.–4 P.M. Mon.–Fri., 10 A.M.–2 P.M. Sat.–Sun.) stands at the corner of Chile and García Moreno. The attached convent is Quito's oldest, dating to 1577, and is closed to visitors.

At the corner of Benalcázar and Espejo, the **Centro Cultural Metropolitano** (tel. 2/295-0272, 9 A.M.–4:30 P.M. daily) houses the collection of the **Museo Alberto Mena Caamaño** (tel. 2/295-0272, ext. 135, 9 A.M.–5 P.M. Tues.–Sun., $1.50), which includes colonial and contemporary art and a set of wax figures depicting the death throes of patriots killed in 1810 by royalist troops. The cultural center also includes lecture rooms, the municipal library, and gallery space for temporary art exhibits.

◖ La Compañía

La Compañía (9:30 A.M.–5 P.M. Mon.–Fri., 9:30 A.M.–4 P.M. Sat., 1:30–4 P.M. Sun., $3) is one of the most beautiful churches in the Americas and certainly the most extravagant.

Seven tonnes of gold supposedly ended up on the ceiling, walls, and altars of "Quito's Sistine Chapel," which was built by the wealthy Jesuit order between 1605 and 1765. The church has been restored from the damage caused by the 1987 earthquake and a raging fire in 1996. It is a glorious example of human endeavor but at the same time borders on opulence gone mad.

Even the outside is overwhelming, crammed with full-size statues, busts, and sculpted hearts. The interior has eight side chapels, one of which houses the guitar and possessions of Quito's first saint, Santa Mariana de Jesús—her remains are under the main altar. Some of the more expensive relics, including a painting of the Virgin framed with gold and precious stones, are locked away in a bank vault between festivals. One of the more eye-catching objects in La Compañía is a painting depicting hell, where sinners—each labeled with one of the deadly sins—receive excruciating punishments.

Across Sucre from La Compañía is the **Museo Numismático** (tel. 2/258-9284,

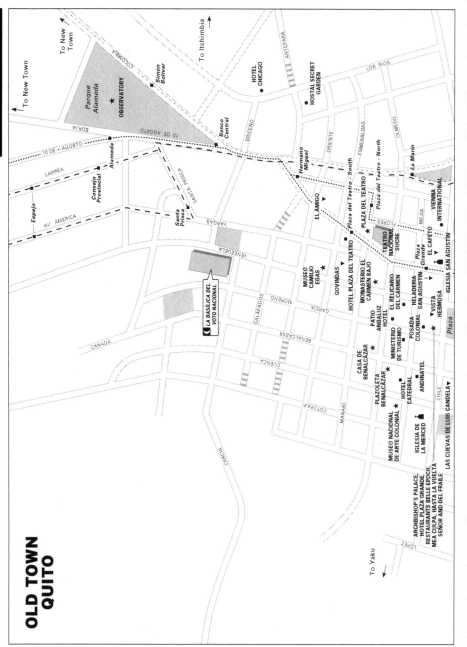

OLD TOWN
QUITO

To New Town

To New Town

To Itchimbia

COLOMBIA

Parque
Alameda

OBSERVATORY ★

Simón
Bolívar ★

Banco
Central

10 DE AGOSTO

HOTEL
CHICAGO ●

HOSTAL SECRET
GARDEN ●

LOS RÍOS

ANTEPARA

10 DE · AGOSTO

LARREA

Alameda

Consejo
Provincial

Espejo

AV. AMERICA

Santa
Prisca

SANTA PRISCA

BORJA

BRICEÑO

ORIENTE

ESMERALDAS

OLMEDO

Hermano
Miguel

La Marín

VARGAS

VENEZUELA

EL AMIGO ▼

Plaza del Teatro - South

Plaza del Teatro - North

Plaza DEL TEATRO

VIENNA ▼
INTERNATIONAL

FLORES

MEJIA

MUSEO
CAMILIO
EGAS ★

GOVINDAS ▼

HOTEL PLAZA DEL TEATRO ●

MONASTERIO EL
CARMEN BAJO ★

TEATRO
NACIONAL
SUCRE

EL CAFETO ▼

Plaza
Grande

GARCIA

MORENO

GALÁPAGOS

EL RELICARIO
DEL CARMEN ▼

HELADERIA
SAN AGUSTIN ▼

IGLESIA SAN AGUSTIN

CANADA

LA BASÍLICA DEL
VOTO NACIONAL

BENALCÁZAR

PATIO
ANDALUZ
HOTEL ●

MINISTERIO
DE TURISMO ●

POSADA
COLONIAL ●

VISTA ▼
HERMOSA

Plaza

CUENCA

CASA DE
BENALCÁZAR ★

PLAZOLETA
BENALCÁZAR ★

HOTEL
CATEDRAL ●

ANDINATEL ■

CHILE

LAS CUEVAS DE LUIS CANDELA ▼

COTOPAXI

MANABI

MUSEO NACIONAL
DE ARTE COLONIAL ★

IGLESIA DE
LA MERCED ✚

CARCHI

ARCHBISHOP'S PALACE,
HOTEL PLAZA GRANDE,
RESTAURANTS BELLE EPOCH,
MEA CULPA, HASTA LA VUELTA
SEÑOR AND DEL FRAILE

LÓPEZ

To Yaku

To New
Town

QUITO

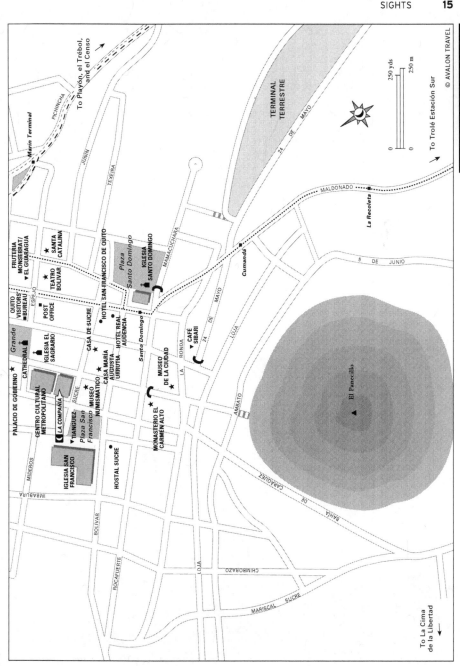

© AVALON TRAVEL

9 A.M.–1 P.M. and 2–5 P.M. Tues.–Fri., 10 A.M.–1 P.M. and 2–4 P.M. Sat.–Sun., $1), which traces the history of Ecuador's various currencies, from shell currency to the adoption of the U.S. dollar. An inflation chart shows just how bad the economic situation used to be, before dollarization stabilized it in the last decade. Also housed here is the national music library, where there are often free concerts in the evenings. On the opposite side of García Moreno from the museum is the **Casa de María Augusta Urrutia** (García Moreno 760, between Sucre and Bolívar, tel. 2/258-0107, 10 A.M.–6 P.M. Tues.–Sat., 9:30 A.M.–5:30 P.M. Sun., $2), a wonderfully preserved 19th-century mansion. Doña María passed away in 1987, and her house is a virtual window on the past, with three inner patios and luxurious accoutrements from all over the globe, as well as a gallery of Victor Mideros's paintings.

Heading east on Sucre brings you to the **Casa de Sucre** (Venezuela 513 at Sucre), once home to Simón Bolívar's southern counterpart. The building has been preserved in its original state from the early 1800s, and the collection focuses on military history.

Plaza San Francisco and Vicinity

Turn right up the hill past La Compañía to one of Ecuador's most beautiful squares. This wide cobbled expanse is a highlight of the city, dominated by the wide facade of the **Iglesia San Francisco** (8 A.M.–noon and 3–6 P.M. daily), the oldest colonial edifice in the city and the largest religious complex in South America. It was begun on the site of an Inca royal house within weeks of the city's founding in 1534. The first wheat grown in Ecuador sprouted in one of its courtyards, and Atahualpa's children received their education in its school.

Two white spires flank a glowering stone facade, which sets the perfect mood for the interior. Inside, it's easy to imagine yourself in the 16th century, with the musty odor drifting up from the creaking wooden floorboards. Thick encrustations of gold cover almost every surface, and seeing the carved roof alone is worth a visit. Notice how many of the design motifs

© BEN WESTWOOD

Plaza San Francisco is one of Quito's most beautiful squares.

come from indigenous cultures, including the smiling and frowning faces of sun gods, repeated several times, and harvest symbols of flowers and fruit. At the time of this writing, the altar of the church was still undergoing a long and painstaking multiple-year restoration. Don't miss the choir rooms upstairs at the back of the church, adorned by statues of monks and the original wooden ceilings (enter through the museum).

To the right of the main entrance, the **Museo Fray Pedro Gocial** (tel. 2/295-2911, 9 A.M.–5:30 P.M. Mon.–Sat., 9 A.M.–12:30 P.M. Sun., $2) houses one of the finest collections of colonial art in Quito, dating from the 16th–19th centuries. Guided tours are included in English, Spanish, and French. A highlight is the seven-meter-high portrait of the Franciscan family tree on the stairs leading up to the choir room. On the other side, the **Capilla de Catuña** (8 A.M.–noon and 3–6 P.M. daily) also has colonial art on display. The story goes that this chapel was constructed by an indigenous man named Catuña who promised to have it completed in a certain amount of time. When it became obvious that he wasn't going to come close to his deadline, he offered his soul to the devil in exchange for help getting the job done. Catuña finished but had a sudden change of heart, begging the Virgin Mary to save him from his hasty agreement. Sure enough, a foundation stone was discovered missing during the inauguration, negating his deal with the devil.

The Tianguez café and gift shop downstairs is a great place to overlook the plaza with a coffee and a snack.

Plaza Santo Domingo and Vicinity

Down the hill southeast of Plaza San Francisco is the elegant Plaza Santo Domingo. A statue of Sucre pointing to the site of his victory on the slopes of Pichincha decorates the square. Crowds often surround performance artists in front of the **Iglesia Santo Domingo** (7 A.M.–noon and 3–6 P.M. daily), which was

begun in 1581 and finished in 1650. Four clock faces and an off-center tower decorate the stone facade. Despite the stained glass behind the altar, the decoration, much of which was completed in the 19th century, is a little muddled, although the baroque filigree of the Chapel of the Rosary to one side is stunning. The attached **Museo Fray Pedro Bedon** (tel. 2/228-2695, 9 A.M.–4:30 P.M. Mon.–Fri., 9 A.M.–1 P.M. Sat.–Sun., $1) has obligatory tour guides to take you through the reserved chapels.

Nearby is one of the best-preserved colonial streets in Old Town. Also called Calle Juan de Díos Morales, **La Ronda** was nicknamed for the evening serenades (*rondas*) that once floated through its winding path. The narrow lane is lined with painted balconies, shops, tiny art galleries, and cafés. It's reached most easily via Guayaquil, sloping down from the Plaza Santo Domingo. This used to be a dangerous area, but an extensive regeneration has

© BEN WESTWOOD

The historic street, La Ronda, has been completely regenerated with bars, cafés, and live music.

left it safe and one of the most popular evening haunts for Quiteños and visitors to soak up the atmosphere with a drink and some traditional music. It is well guarded and completely a pedestrian-only zone.

Museo de la Ciudad and Monasterio El Carmen Alto

Just up from La Ronda is Museo de la Ciudad (García Moreno and Rocafuerte, tel. 2/228-3882, 9:30 A.M.–4:30 P.M. daily, $3). One of Old Town's best museums, it traces the history of the city from precolonial times to the beginning of the 20th century. It is set in the old Hospital San Juan de Díos, founded at the order of King Philip in 1565. The collection includes Inca burials, photographs, clothing, religious and scientific artifacts, scale models of the city at different periods, and a large painting depicting Francisco de Orellana's descent of the Amazon. Tours in English, French, Italian, and German can be arranged for an extra charge.

The Monasterio El Carmen Alto, opposite the museum at Rocafuerte and García Moreno, was the home of Santa Mariana de Jesús from 1618 to 1645. Abandoned children were once passed through a small window in the patio to be raised by the nuns; adjacent, there is a small store that allows visitors to purchase cookies, chocolate, honey, creams, and herbs (9–11 A.M. and 3–5 P.M. Mon.–Fri.). The church is only open for 7 A.M. mass. The **Arco de la Reina** (Queen's Arch) over García Moreno marks the original southern entrance to Quito's center and once sheltered worshippers from the rain.

NORTH AND EAST OF PLAZA GRANDE
Iglesia de la Merced and Vicinity

The entrance to one of Quito's most modern churches, Iglesia de la Merced (6:30 A.M.–noon and 12:30–6 P.M. daily), completed in 1742, is on Chile, just up from the corner of Cuenca. The 47-meter tower houses the largest bell in town. Enter the high-vaulted nave, decorated with white stucco on a pink background, from the Plaza. The church is dedicated to Our Lady

of Mercy, whose statue inside is said to have saved the city from an eruption of Pichincha in 1575. To the left of the altar is the entrance to the **Monasterio de la Merced,** housing Quito's oldest clock, built in London in 1817; a new clock face was recently installed. There are many paintings by Victor Mideros depicting the catastrophes of 1575.

Across Mejía is the **Museo Nacional de Arte Colonial** (Cuenca and Mejía, tel. 2/228-2297, 9 A.M.–1 P.M. and 2–4 P.M. Tues.–Fri., 10 A.M.–2 P.M. Sat., $2), home to Quito's finest collection of colonial art. Works by renowned artists Miguel de Santiago, Caspicara, and Bernardo de Legarda make up part of the collection, which has been extensively renovated.

A few blocks away, the colonial mansion and beautiful courtyard of **Casa de Benalcázar** (Olmedo 962 at Benalcázar, tel. 2/228-8102, 9 A.M.–1 P.M. and 2–5 P.M. Mon.–Fri., free) is worth a visit. It was built in 1534, the year of Quito's refounding.

◖ La Basílica del Voto Nacional

Walk eight blocks northeast from Plaza Grande on Venezuela for the best view of Old Town from within its boundaries. Even though construction began in 1892, the Basílica (9 A.M.–5 P.M. daily, $2) is still officially unfinished. However, its two imposing 115-meter towers make this the tallest church in Ecuador. Notice that the "gargoyles" are actually a menagerie of local animals, including armadillos. After appreciating the stained glass and powerful gilt statues in the nave, ride the elevator up to take in the fantastic views. Climb up unnerving stairs and metal ladders to the roof on the northern steeple or, even more unnerving, a higher point on the east tower. Tread carefully.

Iglesia San Agustín and Vicinity

East of Plaza Grande, the Iglesia San Agustín (Chile and Guayaquil, 7 A.M.–noon and 1–6 P.M.) contains no surface left unpainted, including the likenesses of saints that line the arches against a pastel background. A black Christ occupies a side altar. The adjoining **Convento y Museo de San Agustín** (Chile and

Flores, tel. 2/295-5525, 9 A.M.–12:30 P.M. and 2:30–5 P.M. Mon.–Fri., 9 A.M.–1 P.M. Sat., $1) features a feast of colonial artwork on the walls and surrounds a palm-filled cloister. Ecuador's declaration of independence was signed in the *sala capitular* on August 10, 1809; don't miss the incredible carved benches and altar. Many of the heroes who battled for independence are buried in the crypt.

Plaza del Teatro and Vicinity

This small plaza at Guayaquil and Manabí is surrounded by restored colonial buildings, including the **Teatro Nacional Sucre,** one of Quito's finest theaters. The gorgeous building, erected in 1878, also has a wonderful restaurant called Theatrum on the second floor above the lobby. The theater hosts frequent plays and concerts, including opera, jazz, ballet, and international traveling groups. Tucked in the far corner is the renovated **Teatro Variedades,** reborn as an elegant dinner theater. Next door is the popular **Café Teatro.**

Enter the **Monasterio El Carmen Bajo** (Venezuela between Olmedo and Manabí, 8 A.M.–noon daily, free) through huge wooden doors that date to the 18th century. Whitewashed stone pillars support a two-story courtyard inside, surrounded by nuns' quarters and schoolrooms.

Teatro Bolívar

Scorched by a fire in 1999, only two years after an extensive restoration, the opulent Teatro Bolívar (Pasaje Espejo 847 y Guayaquil, tel. 2/258-3788, www.teatrobolivar.org) is being restored yet again. The 2,200-seat theater was built in 1933 by a pair of American theater architects, and it incorporates elements of art deco and Moorish styles. The theater is on World Monuments Watch's 100 Most Endangered Sites list and is currently open during restoration. Your ticket price will help fund the ongoing work, and you can make an additional donation.

Santa Catalina

The newly opened **Convent Museo Santa Catalina** (Espejo and Flores, tel. 2/228-4000, 8:30 A.M.–5 P.M. Mon.–Fri., 8:30 A.M.–12:30 P.M. Sat., $1.50) is housed with the church of the same name. The remains of assassinated president Gabriel García Moreno rested here secretly for many years before being buried under the cathedral. Many of his personal effects are on display, and his heart is buried in the private chapel. There is also a wide-ranging display of religious art and artifacts. A guided tour is included in the price and is recommended because the collection is spread among many rooms.

ABOVE OLD TOWN
El Panecillo

Old Town's skyline is dominated by a 30-meter statue of the Virgin of Quito on the hill at the southern end. The close-up view of the Virgin with a chained dragon at her feet is very impressive, and although she's nicknamed the "Bailarina" (Dancing Virgin), she's actually preparing to take flight. You can climb up inside the base (9 A.M.–5 P.M. Mon.–Sat., 9 A.M.–6 P.M. Sun., $1) to an observation platform for a spectacular view of the city. Note that the neighborhood on the way up is dangerous so take a taxi and ask the driver to wait. The area at the top of the hill has security until 7 P.M. A taxi ride costs about $3–4 one-way, $8 round-trip including a short wait.

Itchimbía Park and Cultural Center

The old Santa Clara market building—imported from Hamburg in 1899 and brought to the highlands, by mule, in sections—has been transported from Old Town and rebuilt in all its glass-and-metal glory on top of a hill to the east. The structure is now a cultural center (tel. 2/295-0272, ext. 137, 9 A.M.–5 P.M. daily, $1) hosting occasional exhibitions, but the more common reason to come here is the view. The vicinity is more pleasant than El Panecillo, if not quite as spectacular, and not as hair-raising as climbing the Basílica. The center is surrounded by a 34-hectare park that is being reforested and laced with footpaths. It is beautifully lit up at night, and the views are great by day too. Just below on Samaniego is the restaurant Mosaico, along with several happening new spots for drinks and elite elbow-rubbing that justify their prices every evening at sunset. A taxi from Old Town costs $3.

La Cima de la Libertad

In the foothills of Pichincha to the west of Old Town stands this military museum and monument to Sucre's decisive victory over the royalist forces at the Battle of Pichincha on May 24, 1822. At the **Templo de la Patria,** an expansive mosaic of the independence struggle by Eduardo Kingman competes with the view of the city and snowcapped volcanoes on clear days. The **Museo de las Fuerzas Armadas** (tel. 2/228-8733, 9 A.M.–5 P.M. Mon.–Fri., 10 A.M.–4 P.M. Sat.–Sun., $1) displays a modest collection of historical military tools and weapons as well as a scale model depicting the battle. Not many visitors make it up here; there are occasional buses, or take a taxi from Old Town (from $5).

BETWEEN OLD TOWN AND NEW TOWN
Parque la Alameda

Ornamental lakes and a monument to Simón Bolívar hold down opposite ends of this triangular park. In the center stands the oldest **astronomical observatory** in South America, inaugurated in 1864 by then-president García Moreno. If you've visited observatories in North America and Europe, it may come up short, but it's still worth a visit. The beautiful old building also houses a museum (tel. 2/257-0765, 9 A.M.–noon and 2:30–5:30 P.M. daily, $1) filled with books, photos, and antique astronomical tools, including a brass telescope that still works. Visitors can sometimes view the stars on clear nights; call ahead for a schedule and information on occasional astronomy lectures. Many of the large trees found here were planted in 1887, when the park began as a botanical garden.

Palacio Legislativo

Just north of Parque la Alameda at Gran Colombia and Montalvo, drop by when this arm of Ecuador's government is out to lunch and you can peek through the fence to see Oswaldo Guayasamín's infamous 1988 mural titled *Imagen de la Patria.* The huge work, depicting and protesting injustice in Latin America, caused a stir during its unveiling at a formal ceremony of ambassadors and dignitaries. An evil-looking face with a helmet labeled CIA caused the U.S. ambassador to storm out of the room. Copies of the mural are available in the Guayasamín Museum.

◖ Casa de la Cultura

On the northern edge of Parque El Ejido, this curved glass building looks rather like a convention center, but don't let that dissuade you from visiting the best collection of museums in Ecuador. The Casa de la Cultura (tel. 2/222-3392, www.cce.org.ec, 9 A.M.–5 P.M. Tues.–Fri., 10 A.M.–4 P.M. Sat.–Sun., $2) was remodeled in 2005. The centerpiece of the complex is **Museo del Banco Central,** a world unto itself and easily Ecuador's most impressive museum. The collection includes more than 1,500 pieces of pre-Inca pottery, gold artifacts, and colonial and contemporary art, all labeled in English and Spanish.

The first hall is the massive **Sala de Arqueología,** which contains archaeology from Ecuador's long line of indigenous cultures: Figurines from the Valdivia, animal-shaped bottles from the Chorrera, one-meter-high statues known as *gigantes de la bahía* (bay giants), and Manteña thrones are just a few of the vast array of pieces.

A vault downstairs protects a dazzling collection of gold pieces: masks, breastplates, headdresses, and jewelry, many decorated with motifs of cats, serpents, and birds. The highlight is the majestic Inca sun mask, the symbol of the museum.

Upstairs is the **Sala de Arte Colonial,** which contains a massive 18th-century altar and a large collection of paintings and polychrome carvings from the Quito School. There are adjacent rooms dedicated to republican and contemporary art, the highlight being several paintings by renowned artist Oswaldo Guayasamín. The Casa also contains collections of furniture and musical instruments.

The **Agora,** a huge concert arena in the center of the building, hosts concerts (admission cost varies by event). There's also a *cine* showing art and cultural films most evenings.

The old building on 6 de Diciembre, facing the park, houses occasional exhibits and a bookshop that sells its own publications. Next door is the **Teatro Prometeo,** open for evening performances.

Parque El Ejido

Avenidas Patria, 6 de Diciembre, 10 de Agosto, and Tarquí form the wedge filled by Quito's most popular central park. It's all that remains of the common grazing lands that stretched for more than 10 kilometers to the north. The park played its part in one of the most infamous moments in Ecuador's history when liberal president Eloy Alfaro's body was dragged here and burned following his assassination. These days, the most heated things get is during a game of *Ecuavolley* (the local version of volleyball) in the northwest corner of the park most evenings and weekends; a children's playground takes up the northeast corner. You can also often see people playing an Ecuadorian version of a French game of *boules.* On weekends, the area near the arch at Amazonas and Patria becomes an outdoor arts and crafts market; paintings line the sidewalk along Patria, and Otavaleños and other artists sell textiles, antiques, and jewelry.

NEW TOWN

New Town is where most visitors, particularly backpackers, stay in Quito and go out in the evenings. The commercial artery of this sector is **Avenida Amazonas,** and the busiest area lies just off the avenue in the blocks around Plaza Foch. Here you'll find all the visitor amenities: hotels, restaurants, bars, Internet cafés, banks, shops, and travel agencies. It's not nicknamed *gringolandia* for nothing, and the contrast with Old Town is striking; this sector has a decidedly international feel, which may or may not suit you. On the plus side, you can meet plenty of kindred spirits in the bars and cafés, and the nightlife is particularly raucous Thursday–Saturday. The biggest concentration of quality international cuisine in Ecuador is also here, and there are several 24-hour coffee shops for night owls. However, if you want to escape the hordes of foreign visitors and have a more authentic Andean experience, you may be tempted to spend your time elsewhere.

Museo Jacinto Jijón y Caamaño

The family of a prominent Ecuadorian archaeologist donated his private collection of colonial art and archaeological pieces to the Universidad Católica after his death. Now it's on display at the Museo Jacinto Jijón y Caamaño (tel. 2/299-1700, ext. 1242, 9 A.M.–4 P.M. Mon.–Fri., $0.60), located within the university compound on the third floor of the main library building. Enter off 12 de Octubre near Carrión—ask the guard to point you in the right direction. Nearby in the Central Cultural block is the extensive **Weilbauer** collection.

Museo Amazónico

The small **Abya Yala** complex (12 de Octubre 1430 at Wilson, tel. 2/396-2800) contains a bookstore with the city's best selection of works on the indigenous cultures of Ecuador. Shops downstairs sell snacks, crafts, and natural medicines, while the second floor is taken up by the small but well-organized Museo Amazónico (8:30 A.M.–12:30 P.M. and 2–5 P.M. Mon.–Fri., $2). Guided tours are available in Spanish to take you past stuffed rainforest animals, stunning Cofán feather headdresses, and real Shuar *tsantsas* (shrunken heads). The pottery depicting lowland Kichwa gods, each with its accompanying myth, is particularly interesting, as are photos of oil exploration and its environmental impact.

Mindalae Ethnic Museum

Run by the Sinchi Sacha Foundation, which promotes indigenous cultures, fair trade, and responsible tourism, the Mindalae Ethnic

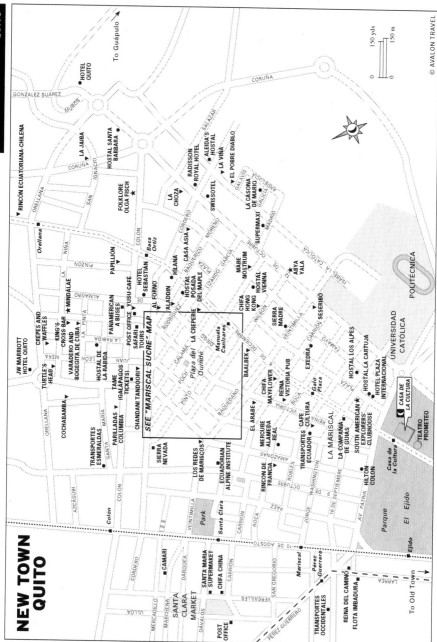

NEW TOWN QUITO

© AVALON TRAVEL

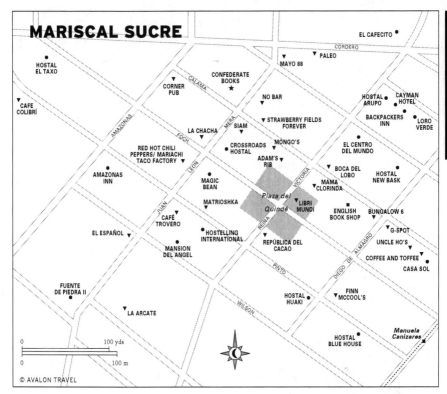

MARISCAL SUCRE

© AVALON TRAVEL

Museum (Reina Victoria and La Niña, tel. 2/223-0609, 9:30 A.M.–5:30 P.M. Mon.–Sat., $3) has five floors with comprehensive collections of ethnic clothing, artifacts, and ceramics from all regions, plus a shop and a restaurant.

NORTH OF NEW TOWN
Parque La Carolina

If you want to escape the concrete of New Town without actually leaving the city, the nearest place to do so is Quito's largest park, which stretches from the intersection of Orellana and Eloy Alfaro almost one kilometer east to Naciones Unidas. It's popular with early-morning joggers, and the *laguna* has two-person paddleboats for rent.

Natural history is the focus of the dusty **Museo de las Ciencias Naturales** (Rumipamba 341 at Los Shyris, tel. 2/244-9824, 8:30 A.M.–4:30 P.M. Mon.–Fri., $2), at the east end of the park. Here the Casa de la Cultura administers displays on zoology, botany, and geology, including a huge collection of dead spiders and an anaconda skeleton. Fans of creepy-crawlies will enjoy the **Vivarium** (Amazonas 3008 at Rumipamba, tel. 2/227-1820, 9:30 A.M.–5:30 P.M. Tues.–Sun., $2.50), with more than 100 live reptiles and amphibians. The collection includes poisonous and constrictor snakes from the Oriente. You can have your photo taken with a six-meter-long python ($3) if that appeals. If you're more into flora than fauna, visit the **Jardín Botánico** (between Ciencias Naturales and Shyris, 9 A.M.–5 P.M. daily, $3), which showcases Ecuador's vast array of flora, including some 500 species of orchids in the greenhouses.

For a modern shopping experience, there are three large **shopping malls** surrounding the park: El Jardín (Avenida de La República and Amazonas), Iñaquito (Amazonas and Naciones Unidas), and Quicentro (Naciones Unidas and Avenida de Los Shyris).

Note that Parque Carolina, like most of Quito's parks, is not safe after dark.

Museo Fundación Guayasamín

East of Parque Carolina, up a steep hill in the Bellavista neighborhood, the former home of Ecuador's most famous artist has been converted into the Museo Fundación Guayasamín (Bosmediano 543, tel. 2/244-6455, 10 A.M.–5 P.M. Mon.–Fri., $3). Pre-Columbian figurines and pottery fill the first building, while Oswaldo Guayasamín's paintings and an impressive collection of colonial art wait farther on. Guayasamín's large-scale paintings are alternately tender and tortured but are always deeply emotive. The balcony

outside has a café. In the gift shop, ask to see the many unique pieces of jewelry designed by the master himself. The artist is buried beneath the Tree of Life in the gardens of his house just above the museum.

To get to the museum, take a bus bound for Bellavista from Parque Carolina (marked "Batan–Colmena") or hail a taxi ($2).

Capilla del Hombre

You can't see everything in Quito, but whatever you do, don't miss Oswaldo Guayasamín's masterwork. Completed three years after his death in 1999 by the Guayasamín foundation, the Chapel of Man (Calvachi and Chavez, tel. 2/244-8492, www.capilladelhombre.com, 10 A.M.–5:30 P.M. Tues.–Sun., $3) is dedicated to the struggles endured by the indigenous peoples of the Americas before and after the arrival of the Spanish.

Huge paintings fill the open two-story building, which is centered on a circular space beneath an unfinished dome mural portraying the millions of workers who died in the silver

Iglesia de Guápulo dates from the 17th century.

© QUITO TURISMO

the *teleférIqo* (cable car)

© QUITO TURISMO

Guápulo

Take the precipitous Camino de Orellana down the hill behind the Hotel Quito—or the footpath from the park and playground—to reach this hillside neighborhood. Narrow cobbled streets are lined with shops, cafés, and homes, including lavish walled-in residences favored by ambassadors, a world away from Quito's New Town. At the center is the 17th-century plaza fronting the beautiful **Iglesia de Guápulo,** built between 1644 and 1693 on the site of an even older convent. The sparkling church can be seen from far above and houses a collection of colonial art, including crucifixes and a pulpit carved by Juan Bautista Menacho in the early 18th century.

Telefériqo (Cable Car)

Quito's most dizzying tourist attraction is the *telefériqo* (cable car) ride (tel. 2/225-0825, 10 A.M.–7 P.M. Sun.–Thurs., 10 A.M.–10 P.M. Fri.–Sat., $4), which climbs up the slopes of Pichincha. Completed in 2005, it departs from above Avenida Occidental, where a tourist center with restaurants, a café, and a small theme park has been built. The 2.5-kilometer ride takes about 10 minutes. After a big rush of visitors in its first year, the *telefériqo* has recently lost popularity, but the breathtaking views over the city and the Andes from 4,050 meters make it worth the trip. It's busiest on the weekend, when there is also more security. From the top, you can hike three kilometers to Rucu Pichincha, but don't do this walk alone because robberies have been reported. *Telefériqo* shuttles run from Río Coca y 6 Diciembre (Ecovia) and Estación Norte (Trole).

mines of Potosí, Bolivia. Other works cover topics both heartening and wrenching, from the tenderness of a mother and child's embrace in *La Ternura* to the gigantic *Bull and Condor,* symbolizing the struggle between Spanish and Andean identities. In the center of the ground floor burns an eternal flame. Guided tours are offered in English and Spanish.

Visitors receive a discount on entrance fees if they visit both the chapel and the Guayasamín museum in the same day, although this is only possible Tuesday–Friday. The chapel is a 10-minute walk up the hill from the museum.

Entertainment and Events

Quito has a thriving nightlife scene centered around Plaza Foch, Reina Victoria, and Calama in Mariscal Sucre. These blocks heave with locals and visitors Thursday, Friday, and Saturday evenings. Historically, things don't really get going until after 11 P.M., but a new law prohibits alcohol sales after midnight Monday–Thursday and after 2 A.M. Friday–Saturday. This has compelled young people to go out earlier, although many establishments stay open later regardless. Most of the dance clubs and discos include a small cover charge (usually $3–5), which includes a drink. Many bars have happy hours 5–8 P.M. to bring in the crowds earlier, and several have ladies nights with free drinks before 10 P.M. After hours, there are a couple of cafés that stay open 24 hours, but late-night alcohol sales are officially banned. Most bars, discos, and even many restaurants are closed on Sundays.

Note that as well as being the most popular nightlife spot, at night Mariscal Sucre is also the most risky area for foreign visitors. Walk just a couple of blocks away from the main drag and the police presence is replaced by groups of thieves looking for an opportunity. You can reduce the risk by taking a taxi to and from your hotel, even if it's only a few blocks away. Don't take valuables, credit cards, or more cash than necessary (you're unlikely to spend more than $30, unless it's a big celebration).

NIGHTCLUBS AND DISCOS

By far the most popular spot in Mariscal is the American- and British-run **Bungalow 6** (Calama and Almagro, tel. 8/519-4530, 8 P.M.–midnight Mon.–Thurs., 8 P.M.–2 A.M. Fri.–Sat., cover $5). Recently expanded to three floors, this friendly place is where Quito's college crowd mixes on the dance floor with backpackers. It gets very busy downstairs on the weekend after 11 P.M., but there's always a quieter spot upstairs for a drink. Ladies night is Wednesday.

Elsewhere, the discos in Mariscal are

decidedly hit and miss. If you're looking for total mayhem, try out the meat market of **No Bar** (Calama and Juan León Mera, tel. 2/245-5145, 8 P.M.–midnight Mon.–Thurs., 8 P.M.–2 A.M. Fri.–Sat., cover $5). Somewhere among the gyrating bodies is a pool table.

For a more Latin American experience, **Seseribó** (Veintimilla and 12 de Octubre, tel. 2/256-3598, 9 P.M.–2 A.M. Thurs.–Sat., cover $5–10) has been offering *pura salsa* for more than a decade. It occasionally has live music too. Another popular *salsateca* is **Mayo 68** (Lizardo García 662 at Juan León Mera, tel. 2/290-6189, 9 P.M.–2 A.M. Thurs.–Sat.).

One of the few late-night bars in Quito is **Blues** (República 476 at Pradera, tel. 2/222-3206, www.bluesestodo.com, 10 P.M.–6 A.M. Thurs.–Sat., cover $7–15), spinning a mix of electronic and rock with international DJs and live rock bands on Thursdays to a style-conscious crowd.

BARS, PUBS, CAFÉS, AND *PEÑAS*

Quito's sizable expat population from Europe and North America can't do without their draft beer, and a few decent pubs have been doing great business in the city for years. Perhaps the best ales can be found at the **The Turtle's Head** (La Niña 626 at Juan León Mera, tel. 2/265-5544, 4 P.M.–midnight Mon.–Thurs., 4 P.M.–2 A.M. Fri.–Sat.), a few blocks from the main drag. Even though the Scottish owner has moved on, the legacy of microbrew beers lives on. They also have pool, darts, and food. Nearby **King's Cross Bar** (Reina Victoria and La Niña, tel. 2/252-3597, 5 P.M.–midnight Mon.–Thurs., 5 P.M.–2 A.M. Fri.–Sat.) sometimes features a good selection of ales.

One block from the center of the Mariscal scene, Irish-run **Finn McCool's** (Almagro N24-64 at Pinto, tel. 2/252-1780, www.irishpubquito.com, 5 P.M.–midnight Mon.–Thurs., 5 P.M.–2 A.M. Fri.–Sat.) has developed into the most popular expat pub, attracting a multinational crowd for pool, foosball, and pub food. The **Reina Victoria Pub** (Reina Victoria 530 at Roca, tel. 2/222-6369, 5 P.M.–midnight Mon.–Thurs., 5 P.M.–2 A.M. Fri.–Sat.), located in a 100-year-old house, is west of the main drag. Although it has seen better days, the quiet British- and American-run pub atmosphere is ideal for relaxing with an ale and a plate of English fish-and-chips in front of the fireplace. The aptly named **Corner Pub** (Amazonas and Calama, tel. 2/290-6608, 2 P.M.–midnight Mon.–Thurs., 4 P.M.–2 A.M. Fri.–Sat.) is a newer bar that has quickly become popular with expats and visitors. For a trip back to the 1960s, visit Beatles bar **Strawberry Fields Forever** (Calama and Juan León Mera, tel. 9/920-0454, 5 P.M.–midnight Mon.–Thurs., 5 P.M.–2 A.M. Fri.–Sat.), adorned with memorabilia, a menu of cocktails named after Beatles songs, and a *Yellow Submarine*–themed restroom. It attracts a creative Bohemian crowd and is a welcome break from the Mariscal madness.

Jazz and the occasional singer or poetry reader attracts an arty crowd to **Café Libro** (Leonidas Plaza and Wilson, tel. 2/223-4265, www.cafelibro.com, noon–2 P.M. and 5 P.M.–midnight Mon.–Sat.). Well-stocked bookshelves and photos of writers decorate this literary place. **Ghoz Bar** (La Niña 425 at Reina Victoria, tel. 2/255-6255, www.ghoz.com, 5 P.M.–midnight Mon.–Thurs., 5 P.M.–2 A.M. Fri.–Sat.) is Swiss-run and offers darts, pool, foosball, and pinball upstairs. On the first floor, there's a wide selection of quality beers, board games, and a kitchen that whips up a good set meal—Swiss food, of course—for $4–7.

Elsewhere in Mariscal, there are plenty of attractive restaurants that double as great places for a drink. Standing out from the crowd is the colorful glass-encased **Boca del Lobo** (Calama 284 at Reina Victoria, tel. 2/254-5500, 5 P.M.–midnight Mon.–Thurs., 5 P.M.–2 A.M. Fri.–Sat.). Chic and stylish with rather surreal decor and an eclectic Mediterranean menu, it's a great place to indulge. **La Bodeguita de Cuba** (Reina Victoria 1721 at La Pinta,

tel. 2/254-2476, noon–4 P.M. and 5 P.M.–midnight Mon.–Fri., noon–midnight Sat.–Sun.) is a Cuban restaurant with live music Thursday–Saturday.

Gay bars are harder to find and in a conservative culture, the Internet is probably the best source of information; www.quitogay.net has useful recommendations. The best-known are **Bohemio** (Baquedano and 6 de Diciembre, tel. 2/221-4127, 10 P.M.–3 A.M. Fri.–Sat.), also known as El Hueco, and **Matroishka** (Pinto and Juan León Mera, tel. 2/227-5617, 8 P.M.–midnight Wed.–Thurs., 8 P.M.–2 A.M. Fri.–Sat.). Take a taxi to and from these bars.

There is a certain herd mentality to going out in Mariscal, and it's not for everyone. If you want a quieter evening, head to La Floresta, where ◖ **El Pobre Diablo** (Isabel la Católica E12-06 at Galavis, noon–3 P.M. and 7 P.M.–midnight Mon.–Thurs., 7 P.M.–2 A.M. Fri.–Sat.) is still one of the best places for live music in Quito. There are bands playing a range of jazz, blues, and world music several times a week, particularly on Wednesdays and Saturdays. The diverse cocktail menu, fusion food, and sophisticated crowd make for a great atmosphere. In the neighborhood of Guápulo is **Ananké** (Camino de Orellana 781, tel. 2/255-1421, 6 P.M.–midnight Mon.–Sat.), a funky little spot with great views from both floors by day, and DJs and chill-out rooms upstairs by night. The pizzas are a specialty, and there's also a branch on Almagro at Pinto in Mariscal.

Live folk music happens at **Ñucanchi Peña** (Universitario 496 at Armero, tel. 2/225-4096, 9 P.M.–midnight Wed.–Thurs., 9 P.M.–2 A.M. Fri.–Sat.).

Alternatively, Quito's Old Town also has a few good spots to go out. The best are along the regenerated **La Ronda,** which is lined with restaurants, cafés, and bars, several of which offer live music on the weekend. One of these is **Café Sibari** (La Ronda 707, tel. 2/228-9809, 11 A.M.–midnight Mon.–Sat.) which has performances every night.

Wherever you go out, you cannot help but notice that Ecuadorians' dancing skills leave the rest of us looking like we have two left feet. You can do something about this—take the plunge and get some classes at one of these **dancing schools: Academia Salsa and Merengue** (Foch E4-256, tel. 2/222-0427), **Ritmo Tropical Dance Academy** (Amazonas N24-155 at Calama, tel. 2/255-7094, ritmotropical5@hotmail.com), **Tropical Dancing School** (Foch E4-256 at Amazonas, tel. 2/222-0427), and **Son Latino** (Reina Victoria N24-211 at Lizardo García, tel. 2/223-4340). Prices at all of these schools start at about $6 pp per hour for one-on-one or couples lessons.

CINEMA

There are plenty of cinemas around the city showing mainstream releases a few months after they appear in the United States. Most showings are available in English with Spanish subtitles or dubbed into Spanish; check the language before buying your ticket. The *El Comercio* newspaper has a daily cinema schedule. Cinemas include **Multicines** (in the CC Iñaquito, Naciones Unidas and Amazonas, tel. 2/226-5061 or 2/226-5062; at the CC **El Recreo** on Maldonado in south Quito, www.multicines.com.ec) and **Cinemark** (Naciones Unidas and América, tel. 2/226-0301, www.cinemark.com.ec); ticket prices are $4.

For a more artistic lineup, look to **Ocho y Medio** (Valladolid N24-353 at Vizcaya, tel. 2/290-4720), an alternative theater in La Floresta neighborhood. Pick up its monthly program at many hotels and restaurants.

THEATERS AND CONCERTS

The *El Comercio* newspaper runs information on theater performances and music concerts.

When possible, buying advance tickets is a good idea. The **Casa de la Cultura** (6 de Diciembre N16-224 at La Patria, tel. 2/290-2272, www.cce.org.ec) is the city's leading venue for theater, dance, and classical music. The colorful, indigenous-themed **Jacchigua Ecuadorian Folklore Ballet** (tel. 2/295-2025, www.jacchiguasecuador.com) performs here at 7:30 P.M. Wednesday. Another good option for ballet and contemporary dance is Ballet Andino Humanizarte at **Teatro Humanizarte** (Leonidas Plaza N24-226 at Lizardo García, tel. 2/222-6116).

Quito has several excellent theaters. The 19th century **Teatro Sucre** (Plaza del Teatro, tel. 2/257-0299, www.teatrosucre.com) is Ecuador's national theater and one of the best. The **Teatro Bolívar** (Espejo 847 at Guayaquil, tel. 2/258-2486, www.teatrobolivar.org) is still under restoration following a devastating fire but should return to its former glory in the near future following substantial government investment.

The **Teatro Politecnico** (Ladrón de Guevara and Queseras) is the best place for classical music, hosting the National Symphony. The **Patio de Comedias** (18 de Septiembre 457 at Amazonas, tel. 2/256-1902) is a good spot to catch a play Thursday–Sunday in a more intimate atmosphere.

Quito's biggest rock and pop concerts take place at the **Coliseo Rumiñahui** and **Estadio Olímpico.** Many big-name acts from North and South America play at these prestigious venues. A good website for tickets to upcoming events is Ecutickets (www.ecutickets.ec).

Shopping

CRAFTS AND GALLERIES

New Town has the richest pickings for shoppers—almost every block in the Mariscal district has some sort of crafts shop or sidewalk vendor. Take your time, shop around, and compare quality. There are also a few standouts in Old Town.

Hungarian-born Olga Fisch came to Ecuador to escape the war in Europe in 1939. She became a world-renowned expert on South American crafts and folklore; during her lifetime, she was sought by the Smithsonian Institution and collectors worldwide for her advice. **Folklore Olga Fisch** (Colón E10-53 at Caamaño, tel./fax 2/254-1315, www.olgafisch.com, 9 A.M.–7 P.M. Mon.–Sat.) was her house until her death in 1991. The first floor is filled with gorgeous but pricey ceramics and textiles from all over the continent. Out back in what was once a storeroom is a restaurant called El Galpon. There are outlets of Fisch's shop in the Hilton Colón, the Swissôtel, and the Patio Andaluz in Old Town.

La Bodega (Juan León Mera and Carrión, tel. 2/222-5844) has been in business for over 30 years and stocks high-quality artisanal works that include adorable ceramic Galápagos creatures and jewelry. For suede and leather, try **Aramis** (Amazonas N24-32 at Pinto, tel. 2/222-8546), where they can make clothes or handbags to order.

Mindalae (Reina Victoria 17–80 at La Niña, tel. 2/223-0609) is also operated by the non-profit Sinchi Sacha Foundation. It houses a shop selling indigenous crafts and a small restaurant. The **Camari Cooperative** (Marchena and 10 de Agosto, tel. 2/252-3613, www.camari.org) provides a place for indigenous and fair-trade groups from throughout Ecuador to sell their crafts. The store features a wide selection with good prices and quality.

Excedra (Carrión 243 at Tamayo, tel. 2/222-4001) serves as an art gallery, folklore and antique outlet, and tea room. It's an offbeat little place with a nice selection of crafts.

Beautiful, high-quality wool textiles for less money than you'd think are the specialty at **Hilana** (6 de Diciembre 1921 at Baquerizo Moreno, tel. 2/250-1693).

The most popular place to buy paintings is **Parque El Ejido Art Fair** (Patria and Amazonas), open all day Saturday–Sunday. Most paintings for sale are imitations of more famous works, but there's a good range and excellent value. Haggling, of course, is advised.

Professional browsers could spend hours on Juan León Mera and Veintimilla, where half a dozen highbrow crafts and antiques stores and art galleries cluster within two blocks of Libri Mundi. Try **Galería Latina** (Juan León Mera N23-69, tel. 2/222-1098, www.galerialatina-quito.com) for Tigua hide paintings and other quality works; or stop by the weekend arts-and-crafts market in the park by Avenida Patria. **Galería Beltrán** (Reina Victoria 326, tel. 2/222-1732) has a good selection of paintings by Ecuadorian artists.

In Old Town, one of the best options is **Tianguez** (underneath the Iglesia San Francisco, Plaza San Francisco, tel. 2/223-0609, www.tianguez.org, 9 A.M.–6 P.M. daily), which is run by the Sinchi Sacha Foundation, a nonprofit set up to help support the people of the Oriente. The store, which also has an outdoor café on the Plaza San Francisco, features an excellent selection of quality handicrafts from around the country for surprisingly low prices. Profits from the masks, ceramics, Tigua hide paintings, jewelry, and weavings go to fund their programs to benefit indigenous communities.

Hugo Chiliquinga (Huachi N67-34 at Legarda, tel. 2/259-8822) is considered by many to be the best guitar maker in Ecuador. He makes and sells guitars, but he may have a waiting list, since he has an international reputation.

BOOKS

Libri Mundi (Juan León Mera N23-83 at Wilson, tel. 2/223-4791, www.librimundi.com,

8:30 A.M.–7:30 P.M. Mon.–Fri., 10 A.M.–6 P.M. Sat.) is probably the best bookstore in Ecuador. Along with a wide range of titles in Spanish, it sells new and a few used English, German, and French foreign books at a markup. Libri Mundi also has branches in the Plaza del Quindé, Centro Comercial Quicentro, and in Cumbayá.

For great deals on secondhand books, have a free cup of tea at the friendly English-run **English Bookshop** (Calama and Almagro, 10 A.M.–6:30 P.M. daily). **Confederate Books** (Calama 410 at Juan León Mera, tel. 2/252-7890, 10 A.M.–6 P.M. Mon.–Sat.) also has a wide range of used books. **South American Explorers** (Jorge Washington and Leonidas Plaza, tel./fax 2/222-5228, quito-club@saexplorers.org, www.saexplorers.org, 9:30 A.M.–5 P.M. Mon.–Fri., 9:30 A.M.–noon Sat.) has a good selection of guidebooks and a book exchange.

MAGAZINES AND NEWSPAPERS

Foreign magazines fill the shelves at **Libro Express** (Amazonas 816 at Veintimilla, tel. 2/254-8113, 9:30 A.M.–7:30 P.M. Mon.–Fri., 10 A.M.–6 P.M. Mon.–Sat). Street vendors all along Amazonas also stock a few foreign publications. Bookshops in expensive hotels sell foreign magazines and newspapers, but be sure they don't try to mark up the newspapers over the printed price.

SPORTING EQUIPMENT

If you're looking for a mask and snorkel (or even a wetsuit) for your Galápagos trip, you'll find them—along with a whole store full of modern sporting equipment—at **KAO Sport** (Ed. Ecuatoriana, Almagro and Colón, tel. 2/255-0005 or 2/252-2266). Other KAO branches are located in many of the city's *centros comerciales*.

JEWELRY AND ACCESSORIES

Marcel G. Creaciones (Roca 766, between Amazonas and 9 de Octubre, tel. 2/265-3555, fax 2/255-2672) carries a good selection of Panama hats. For exclusive jewelry designs, stop by the **Museo Fundación Guayasamín** (Bosmediano 543, tel. 2/244-6455, 10 A.M.–5 P.M. Mon.–Fri.) or **Ag** (Juan León Mera 614 at Carrión, tel. 2/255-0276, fax 2/250-2301). Many small leather-working shops in New Town can make custom clothes, boots, bags, and other accessories for surprisingly reasonable prices; try **Zapytal** (Pinto 538 at Amazonas, tel. 2/252-8757).

MARKETS

Vendors have been moved off the streets, making driving and walking around the city much easier, if a little less colorful. For street-side shopping in Old Town, go to Ipiales (clothing and shoes), Calle Cuenca between Mejía and Olmedo (crafts and bazaar items), San Roque (food and furniture), and Plaza Arenas ("recycled" stolen goods, clothes, and hardware). Note that there are a lot of pickpockets, so watch your wallet, and ideally don't take valuables and cameras when you go to a market.

On weekends, the north end of **Parque El Ejido** becomes an outdoor art gallery with a selection of paintings, sculpture, and jewelry. **La Mariscal** artisan market in New Town occupies half of the block south of Jorge Washington between Reina Victoria and Juan León Mera. Just about every indigenous craft in Ecuador makes an appearance daily. Quality is variable, and haggling is obligatory.

Local produce is the main draw to New Town's **Mercado Santa Clara** (biggest market on Wed. and Sun.), along Ulloa and Versalles just south of Colón. Every Friday, a fruit and vegetable market fills Galaviz between Toledo and Isabel La Católica, where children sell baskets of spices and wealthy shoppers hire elderly basket carriers to tote the day's purchases.

Boutiques, supermarkets, and movie theaters find a home in Quito's many *centros comerciales* (malls). Close your eyes and you could be in North America. Major malls include **El Bosque** (Al Parque and Alonso de Torres), **El Jardín** (República and Amazonas), **Iñaquito** (Amazonas and Naciones Unidas), **Multicentro** (6 de Diciembre and La Niña), **CC Nu** (Naciones Unidas and Amazonas), and **Quicentro** (6 de Diciembre and Naciones Unidas); and in the south, the **El Recreo** trolley terminus and **Quitumbe** bus terminal.

Sports and Recreation

CLIMBING AND MOUNTAINEERING
Climbing Companies

A few of the many tour companies in Quito specialize in climbing—they have the experience and professionalism to get you back down in one piece should anything go wrong. Prices for these climbing tours vary from $70 per person for easier climbs, such as the Pichinchas, to $190 per person for a two-day ascent of Cotopaxi.

Andean Face (Pasaje B 102, Jardines de Batán, tel. 2/243-8699, www.andeanface.com) is a Dutch-Ecuadorian company specializing in climbing. The **Compañía de Guías** (Jorge Washington 425 at 6 de Diciembre, tel. 2/255-6210, tel./fax 2/250-4773, guisamontania@accessinter.net, www.companiadeguias.com) is a guide cooperative whose members speak English, German, French, and Italian. **Ecuadorian Alpine Institute** (Ramírez Dávalos 136 at Amazonas, Of. 102, tel. 2/256-5465, www.volcanoclimbing.com) has well-organized, professionally run climbs and treks, and spans all experience levels. **Safari Tours** (Edificio Banco de Guayaquil, 11th Fl., Reina Victoria y Colón, tel. 2/255-2505, fax 2/222-3381, tel./fax 2/222-0426, www.safari.ec) has highly recommended climbing trips to any peak in the country, plus a range of other tours. **Sierra Nevada** (Pinto 637 at Cordero, tel. 2/255-3658 or 2/222-4717, fax 2/255-4936, www.hotelsierranevada.com) is a small, dependable operator that also offers rafting, the Galápagos, and Amazon trips.

Climbing and Camping Equipment

Quito has by far the best selection of outdoor gear merchants in the country. Everything from plastic climbing boots and harnesses to tents, sleeping bags, and stoves is readily available, although not always of the highest quality or best state of repair. Needless to say, check all zippers, laces, and fuel valves before you head off into the wild. Large-size footgear (U.S. size 12 and up) may be hard to locate. Gear is both imported (at a high markup) or made in Ecuador.

For climbing gear for sale or rent, try **Altamontaña** (Jorge Washington 425 at 6 de Diciembre, tel. 2/255-8380) or **Antisana Sport** (tel./fax 2/246-7433) in the El Bosque Shopping Center, also good for large-size hiking boots. Other places to buy camping gear include **Camping Cotopaxi** (Colón 942 at Reina Victoria, tel. 2/252-1626), **The Explorer** (Reina Victoria 928 at Pinto, tel. 2/255-0911), and **Los Alpes** (Reina Victoria 2345 at Baquedano, tel./fax 2/223-2326). **Equipos Cotopaxi** (6 de Diciembre N20-36 at Jorge Washington, tel. 2/225-0038) makes its own sleeping bags, backpacks, and tents for less than you'd pay for imported items. The various **Marathon Sports** outlets in the Centros Comerciales El Bosque, El Jardín, Iñaquito, San Rafael, and Quicentro stock light-use sportswear at decent prices.

BIKING

The **Aries Bike Company** (Av. Interoceanica Km. 22.5, Vía Pifo, La Libertad, tel. 2/238-0802, www.ariesbikecompany.com) offers 1–14-day biking and hiking tours all over Ecuador. The guides speak English, Dutch, and Spanish.

Biking Dutchman (Foch 714 at Juan León Mera, tel. 2/254-2806, www.bikingdutchman.com) runs well-reviewed day trips to Cotopaxi, Papallacta, and the Tandayapa-Mindo area. The 30-kilometer descent down Cotopaxi is guaranteed to raise your blood pressure. There are two-day trips to Cotopaxi and Quilotoa as

TOUR COMPANIES

Quito has more tour companies than ever, and many of them are excellent. For a price, they offer expertise and local knowledge that you can't find elsewhere and provide a rewarding experience that would be difficult to replicate independently. Taking a guided tour also takes the worry out of traveling: Accommodations, food, and logistics are all sorted out for you. Bear in mind that not all operators in Quito have good reputations: Some overcharge and are underqualified. The following are recommended for their quality, professionalism, and value.

- **Dracaena** (Pinto E4-353 and Amazonas, tel./fax 2/254-6590, www.amazondracaena.com) is best known for its 4-5-day Cuyabeno trips.

- **Enchanted Expeditions** (De Las Alondras N45-102 at Los Lirios, tel. 2/334-0525, fax 2/334-0123, www.enchantedexpeditions. com) covers the entire country, with a focus on the Galápagos – the boats *Cachalote* and *Beluga* receive frequent praise.

- **Metropolitan Touring** is the largest tour operator in the country and was the first to organize high-quality Galápagos trips

in the 1960s. Since then, the company has branched out to include just about every kind of tour in Ecuador, including hacienda stays, community visits, city and market tours, and train trips. It has branch offices throughout the country, including a main one in Quito (De los Palmeras N45-74 at Las Orquideas, tel. 2/298-8200, www.metropolitan-touring.com). Information and bookings are available in the United States through Adventure Associates (13150 Coit Rd., Suite 110, Dallas, TX 75240, U.S. tel. 800/527-2500, U.S. fax 972/783-1286, www.adventure-associates.com).

- **Nuevo Mundo Travel and Tours** (18 de Septiembre E4-161 at Juan León Mera, tel. 2/250-9431, www.nuevomundotravel. com) was started in 1979 by a founder and former president of the Ecuadorian Ecotourism Association. Its tours and facilities are therefore among the most environmentally conscious in Ecuador – the company doesn't even advertise some of them to minimize impact on the destinations. Along with the usual Galápagos and Oriente tours, several unique options include shamanism

well as the upper Amazon, and tours of up to eight days are offered.

Once every two weeks on Sunday, a long north–south section of road through Quito is closed to cars and open only to cyclists, skateboarders, skaters, and walkers.

RAFTING AND KAYAKING

Yacu Amu Rafting (Foch 746 at Juan León Mera, tel. 2/290-4054 or 2/254-6240, fax 2/290-4055, www.yacuamu.com) is the leader in white-water trips out of Quito. The year-round day trips down the Toachi and Blanco Rivers offer more rapids per hour than anywhere else in Ecuador ($79 pp Toachi, $89 pp Quijos)—plus cold beer at the end of every trip. Two-day trips cost from $219 pp, and five-day trips on the Upano are offered

August–February. Customized itineraries are possible, as are kayak rentals and kayak courses.

HORSEBACK RIDING

Sally Vergette runs **Ride Andes** (tel. 9/973-8221, www.rideandes.com), offering top-quality riding tours through the highlands. From the foothills of Imbabura to cattle roundups near Cotopaxi, the trips use local horse wranglers, support vehicles, and healthy, happy animals. Guests stay in some of the country's plushest haciendas along the way. The options range from $98 pp for two people on a one-day tour to an eight-day circuit of Cotopaxi for $1,860 pp. You must have some riding experience for the longer tours, but it's worth it to experience the scenery from atop a horse.

Astrid Müller of the **Green Horse Ranch**

programs and one-month Spanish courses combined with environmental studies.

- **RainForestur** (Amazonas N4-20 at Robles, tel./fax 2/223-9822, www.rainforestur.com) has received praise for its Cuyabeno trips and rafting in Baños, but there's also a full slate of other options.

- **Safari Tours** (Foch E4-132 at Cordero, tel./fax 2/222-0426, tel. 2/255-2505, fax 2/222-3381, www.safari.com.ec) is one of the most frequently recommended operators in the country and can take you just about anywhere in Ecuador to climb, hike, bird-watch, camp, or mountain bike. Safari has a complete Galápagos database and can book last-minute spaces or make reservations online.

- **Sangay Touring** (Amazonas 1188 and Cordero, tel. 2/255-0180, www.sangay.com) is a British- and Ecuadorian-run agency that has been offering tours around the country since 1992. Sangay recently split off a sister company, Guide2Galapagos (www.guide-2galapagos.com) to handle island bookings.

- **Surtrek** (Amazonas N23-87 at Wilson, tel. 2/223-1534, fax 2/250-0540, www.surtrek. org) offers a wide range of Galápagos and Amazon tours as well as trekking, climbing, cycling, and rafting.

- **Tropic Journeys in Nature** (Republica E7-320 at Almagro, tel. 2/222-5907, in the U.S. tel. 202/657-5072, www.tropiceco.com) is run by Andy Drumm, a fellow of the Royal Geographic Society and the president of the Amazon Commission of the Ecuadorian Ecotourism Association. These trips have won awards for socially responsible tourism and are especially strong in the Oriente, where they introduce travelers to the Huaorani, Cofán, and Achuar.

- **Via Natura** (Av. Del Parque Oe7-154, CC Dicentro, 3rd Fl., tel. 2/600-5011, www.vianatura.com) offers tours to the Galápagos on the yacht *Monserrat* and at the Casa Natura hotel in Puerto Ayora. Additionally, personally tailored tours are offered throughout Ecuador, with everything from boutique luxury to ecotourism and adventure tours.

(tel. 8/612-5433, www.horseranch.de) offers riding trips starting in Pululahua Crater from $75 pp for one day, $195 pp for two days, and up to $1,620 pp for a nine-day tour in the highlands and cloud forests. These are for people of all experience levels, and the prices include food, accommodations, and transportation to and from Quito. Multilingual guides accompany all trips.

SPECTATOR SPORTS

Watching a **soccer** match (called *fútbol* or football outside the United States) in Ecuador is quite an experience. Witnessing the fervor of the fans firsthand can be exhilarating. The best place to go in Quito is the **Estadio Atahualpa** (6 de Diciembre and Naciones Unidas) when the national team plays. Take the Ecovia to the Naciones Unidas stop to get there. The Casa Blanca, which is the stadium of Liga de Quito, the city's most successful club, has home games several times per month. Buy tickets ahead of time at Casa Blanca at the "Y" junction, and take the Metrovía bus to the Ofelia terminal. **Bullfights** are held year-round on publicized dates at the **Plaza de Toros** (Amazonas and Juan de Azcaray), just south of the airport; Take the trolley north to La Y. The festival of the founding of Quito during the first week of December is an especially popular time for bullfights. Smaller evening bullfights are sometimes held at the remodeled Plaza Belmonte near San Blas.

CITY TOURS

The **tourist information office** (tel. 2/257-0786, 9 A.M.–2 P.M. daily) on the Plaza Grande in Old Town offers four daily tours ($6–15 pp) of Quito's municipal highlights, as well as two nightly tours (6–9 P.M., $8–20 pp). The pricier tours include admission fees and transportation.

What better way to enjoy newly spruced-up Old Town than in **horse-drawn carriages,** which depart from the Plaza Grande next to the Government Palace 6 P.M.–midnight daily. It's best in the evening when there is less traffic.

CLASSES
Art and Dance
The **Academia Superior de Arte** (Jorge Washington 268 at Plaza, tel. 2/256-4646, class locations may vary) offers drawing and painting courses as well as tai chi and martial arts classes.

Overcome your inhibitions on the dance floor by signing up for Latin and Caribbean dance classes—including salsa, merengue, *cumbia,* and *vallenato*—at the following recommended schools: **Academia Salsa and Merengue** (Foch E4-256, tel. 2/222-0427), **Ritmo Tropical Dance Academy** (Amazonas N24-155 at Calama, tel. 2/255-7094, ritmotropical5@hotmail.com), **Tropical Dancing School** (Foch E4-256 at Amazonas, tel. 2/222-0427), and **Son Latino** (Reina Victoria N24-211 at Lizardo García, tel. 2/223-4340). Prices at all of these schools start at about $6 pp per hour for one-on-one or couples lessons.

Learning Spanish
Ecuador is quickly becoming one of the best places to learn Spanish in Latin America. Not only do Ecuadorians—at least those who live in the mountains—speak slowly and clearly in comparison to their quick-talking, slang-tossing neighbors, but competition among dozens of schools keeps prices low and quality up—and it's a great place to travel.

Dozens of Spanish schools in Quito offer intensive Spanish instruction. With such intense competition, it's worth your while to shop around for one that fits your needs perfectly. Tuition usually includes 4–7 hours of instruction per day, either in groups or one-on-one (four hours daily is usually plenty). Costs range $6–9 per hour. An initial registration fee may be required, and discounts are often possible for long-term commitments. Make sure to get a receipt when you pay, and check to see if any extras are not included in the hourly rate. South American Explorers (SAE) members often receive discounts of 5–15 percent.

Many schools draw business by offering extras such as sports facilities and extracurricular activities. Some will house you (for a fee) or arrange for a homestay with a local family (typically $10–25 per day for full board, $9–15 for lodging only). Don't sign any long-term arrangements until you're sure of both the school and the family.

The following schools have received many positive reviews:

- **Amazonas** (Ed. Rocafuerte, 3rd Fl., Jorge Washington 718 at Amazonas, tel./fax 2/250-4654, www.eduamazonas.com)
- **Bipo and Toni's** (Carrión E8-183 at Plaza, tel. 2/255-6614, www.bipo.net)
- **Cristóbal Colón Spanish School** (Colón 2088 at Versalles, tel./fax 2/250-6508, www.colonspanishschool.com)
- **Guayasamín Spanish School** (Calama E8-54 near 6 de Diciembre, tel. 2/254-4210, www.guayasaminschool.com)
- **Instituto Superior de Español** (Darquea Terán 1650 at 10 de Agosto, tel. 2/222-3242, www.instituto-superior.net)
- **La Lengua** (Ed. Ave María, 8th Fl., Colón 1001 at Juan León Mera, tel./fax 2/250-1271, www.la-lengua.com)
- **Simón Bolívar** (Foch E9-20 at 6 Diciembre, tel. 2/254-4558, www.simon-bolivar.com)
- **South American Language Center** (Amazonas N26-59 at Santa María, tel. 2/254-4715, www.southamerican.edu.ec)

Accommodations

As Ecuador's capital and tourism hub, Quito has an enormous range of accommodations, from bargain basement to lavish luxury. Most are found in New Town, although Old Town has more historic hotels.

Reservations are a good idea at busy times, such as holidays, especially Christmas and Easter. Book by phone or fax whenever possible. A tax of up to 22 percent will be added to bills in the more expensive hotels, and a separate charge may be tacked on for paying by credit card.

UNDER $10

The constant stream of backpackers through Quito means that competition is fierce and there is a huge range of budget accommodations. Most are very good value and are concentrated in New Town. Luckily, Quito keeps most of its room-by-the-hour seedy motels separate from the main tourist areas of Mariscal and Old Town (if you must know, they are found near Parque Carolina).

New Town

French Canadian–run **El Centro del Mundo** (Lizardo García 569 at Reina Victoria, tel. 2/222-9050, www.centrodelmundo.net, $6 dorm, $8 s, $15 d) is one of the most popular backpacker crash pads and has rock-bottom prices. The small rooftop patio features cooking facilities, and the cable TV is always on in the cushion-strewn common room. Note that it gets pretty raucous on the free rum-and-coke nights. Breakfast and Internet access are included. **The Backpacker's Inn** (Juan Rodriguez E7-48 at Reina Victoria, tel. 2/250-9669, www.backpackersinn.net, $6.50 dorm, $11 s, $16 d) is a quieter budget option with simple, decent guest rooms, a laundry area, free Internet, and TV in the lounge. **Hostal New Bask** (Lizardo García and Diego de Almagro, tel. 2/256-7153, www.newhostalbask.com, $6 dorm, $16 s or d) is another quiet option with a homey

atmosphere, excellent-value guest rooms, and a small lounge.

Hostal Blue House (Pinto and Diego de Almagro, tel. 2/222-3480, www.bluehouse-quito.com, $8–9 dorm, $18 s, $24–30 d) is a very popular new backpacker hostel with a kitchen, a bar, free Internet, and breakfast included. A cozy option is **El Cafécito** (Cordero 1124 at Reina Victoria, tel. 2/223-4862, www.cafecito.net, $7 dorm, $10–15 s, $25 d), which has guest rooms above a popular café. The small and inviting **Hostal Posada del Maple** (Juan Rodriguez E8-49 at 6 de Diciembre, tel. 2/290-7367, www.posadadelmaple.com, $9 dorm, $19–21 s, $26–33 d, breakfast included) is an attractive place with balconies and a plant-filled courtyard. Breakfast is big, and there's a comfortable TV room. **Hostal Huauki** (Pinto E7-82 at Diego Almagro, tel. 2/604-3734, www.hostalhuauki.com, $6 dorm, $8–15 s, $20 d) is a little corner of Japan in a converted 1940s residence with comfortable guest rooms and a very good sushi restaurant.

Old Town

Most of Old Town's options are in the mid- and expensive range, but **Hostal Sucre** (Bolívar 615 at Cuenca, tel. 2/295-4025, $4–10 pp) bucks the trend. It's astonishing that such a cheap place is right on Plaza San Francisco with views of the square. For these prices and location, you can't expect more than cheap, shabby guest rooms, but the view and the friendly atmosphere make it a worthwhile choice.

Hidden away on a quiet street northeast of Old Town is Aussie-run backpacker favorite **Secret Garden** (Antepara E4-60 at Los Rios, tel. 2/295-6704, www.secretgardenquito.com, $9 dorm, $24–30 s and d). Set on five floors in a UNESCO World Heritage–listed building, TV is shunned for music and murals. The rooftop terrace has an impressive view, and there are big breakfasts and organic food. It's

QUITO

a great place to meet other travelers in a relaxed setting.

$10-25

You are spoilt for choice in this category in New Town. All hotels below offer guest rooms with private baths unless otherwise noted.

New Town

Hostal El Vagabundo (Wilson E7-45, tel. 2/222-6376, $13 s, $22 d) is another dependable budget option with a small café and table tennis. The **Loro Verde** (Rodriguez 241 at Almagro, tel. 2/222-6173, www.hostaloroverde.com, $15 s, $28 d, breakfast included) is as colorful and chirpy as its name ("green parrot"). On a corner of Mariscal's main artery, the **Amazonas Inn** (Pinto 471 at Amazonas, tel. 2/222-5723, $14 s, $26 d) is a friendly hotel with comfortable if compact guest rooms with cable TV.

You don't have to stay in Mariscal; a few blocks uphill from New Town is a neighborhood called La Floresta. Not to be confused with La Casona in Old Town, **La Casona de Mario** (Andalucia 213 at Galicia, tel./fax 2/223-0129 or 2/254-4036, www.casonademario.com, $10 pp) is run by a friendly Argentine in a comfortable house with a garden, a kitchen, a patio, and laundry facilities. Also in La Floresta is **Aleida's Hostal** (Andalucia 559, tel. 2/223-4570, www.aleidashostal.com.ec, $17–21 s, $30–36 d), a friendly family-run guesthouse with large guest rooms.

Old Town

The **Vienna International** (Chile and Flores, tel. 2/295-9611, $20 s, $40 d) offers good service with guest rooms around an interior patio. Just before the southbound Plaza del Teatro *trole* stop, the **Hotel Plaza del Teatro** (Guayaquil 1373 at Esmeraldas, tel. 2/295-9462 or 2/295-4293, $12 pp) is a great value. The plush reception area leads to charming if slightly worn guest rooms.

$25-50

All hotels in this category and up include breakfast in the price unless otherwise indicated.

New Town

A small rise in price brings you into the realm of charming old guesthouses with all the amenities and a healthy dose of character. **Hotel Plaza Internacional** (Leonidas Plaza 150 at 18 de Septiembre, tel. 2/252-4530, tel./fax 2/250-5075, www.hotelplazainternacional.com, $25 s, $32 d) is the attractive colonial home of two former presidents. Staff speak English, French, and Portuguese. **Hostal El Arupo** (Juan Rodriguez E7-22 at Reina Victoria, tel. 2/255-7543, $30 s, $45 d) is an attractive renovated house with colorful rooms, and nearby **Cayman Hotel** (Juan Rodriguez 270 at Reina Victoria, tel. 2/256-7616, www.hotelcayman-quito.com, $34 s, $53 d) has a similar offering with a huge fireplace, a large garden, and a good restaurant inside a renovated house. **Jardín del Sol** (Calama E8-29 at Almagro, tel. 2/223-0941, www.hostaljardindelsol.com, $30 s, $45 d) has decent guest rooms, some with balconies. The rear guest rooms are quieter.

Wooden floors and a cozy atmosphere await visitors to the **Casa Sol** (Calama 127 at 6 de Diciembre, tel. 2/223-0798, www.lacasasol.com, $48 s, $68 d), a cheery spot with a tiny courtyard owned by *indígenas* from Peguche, near Otavalo. They have a TV room and a book exchange in front of a fireplace.

Old Town

A former colonial home, the ◖ **Hotel San Francisco de Quito** (Sucre 217 at Guayaquil, tel. 2/228-7758, tel./fax 2/295-1241, www.sanfranciscodequito.com.ec, $30 s, $48 d) is the pick of Old Town's mid-range options, with a fountain and ferns filling the courtyard and a rooftop patio with great views. Tucked upstairs facing La Concepción Church is the renovated **Posada Colonial** (García Moreno and Chile, tel. 2/228-1095, $26 s, $36 d), with comfortable guest rooms that have classic decor and tall ceilings. **Hotel Catedral** (Mejia 638 at Benalcázar, tel. 2/295-5438, www.hotelcatedral.ec, $31 s, $55 d) has recently been upgraded with more comfortable guest rooms, cable TV, a sauna, and a steam room. **Hotel Real Audiencia** (Bolívar 220 at

Guayaquil, tel. 2/295-2711 or 2/295-0590, www.realaudiencia.com, $33 s, $52 d) has stylish guest rooms, black-and-white photography on the walls, and a great view of Plaza Santo Domingo.

$50-75
New Town

Thick fur rugs in front of the fireplace add to the Old World feel of **Hostal Los Alpes** (Tamayo 233 at Jorge Washington, tel./fax 2/256-1110, www.hotellosalpes.com, $67 s, $80 d). The bright and clean **Hostal de La Rábida** (La Rábida 227 at Santa María, tel./fax 2/222-2169, www.hostalrabida.com, $71 s, $91 d) has an immaculate white interior and stylish carpeted rooms. There's a fireplace in the living room and a peaceful garden out back.

[**Fuente de Piedra II** (Juan León Mera and Baquedano, tel. 2/290-0323, $56) is a place to treat yourself. This colonial-style mid-range hotel is elegantly furnished with attentive service, Wi-Fi, and a gourmet restaurant. A sister hotel is at Tamayo and Wilson.

$75-100
New Town

A nine-story building is home to the **Hotel Sebastián** (Almagro 822 at Cordero, tel. 2/222-2300, fax 2/222-2500, www.hotelsebastian.com, $82 s, $94 d, not including breakfast), which uses organic vegetables in its restaurant; the building boasts one of the best water-purification systems in the country.

[**Café Cultura** (Robles 513 at Reina Victoria, tel./fax 2/222-4271, www.cafecultura.com, $100 s, $122 d) is set in a beautifully restored colonial mansion, formerly the French cultural center. The hotel is lovingly decorated with dark wood, paintings, and a grand staircase in the center of it all. Guest rooms are individually styled, and the baths are huge, with tubs for relaxing after a hard day's sightseeing. There's a gourmet café downstairs, a small private garden out back, a library full of guidebooks, and three stone fireplaces for those cold Quito nights. Breakfast is not included in the room price.

$100-200
New Town

The lavishly decorated **Mansion del Angel** (Wilson E5-29 at Juan León Mera, tel. 2/255-7721, $150 d) has 10 beautifully appointed guest rooms with crystal chandeliers, antiques, and attentive service, plus luxurious private baths and a buffet breakfast. Book well in advance.

The huge **Hotel Quito** (González Suárez N27-142 at 12 de Octubre, tel. 2/254-4600, fax 2/256-7284, www.hotelquito.com, $111 s, $148 d, not including breakfast) boasts one of the best views in Quito, high on a hill above Guapulo. The guest rooms are rather bland, but there is plenty to keep you busy—a casino, a swimming pool, a spa, and a gourmet restaurant.

The 415 guest rooms and suites of the **Hilton Colón** (Amazonas 110 at Patria, tel. 2/256-0666, fax 2/256-3903, U.S. tel. 800/HILTONS—800/445-8667, www.hiltoncolon.com, $161 s or d, not including breakfast) tower over the Parque El Ejido, and it's probably the most popular spot for visitors who have unlimited budgets. Facilities include an excellent gym, a 10-meter pool, a reading room, a casino, and shops.

Mariscal now has its very own slice of boutique chic in the shape of the **Nu House** (Foch E6-12, tel. 2/255-7485, www.nuhousehotels.com, $145 s, $160 d). This wood-and-glass building rises high over the main plaza. Guest rooms have huge windows and dramatic color schemes, and there's a new spa.

The newest and perhaps largest luxury hotel in Quito is the **JW Marriott Hotel Quito** (Orellana 1172 at Amazonas, tel. 2/297-2000, fax 2/297-2050, www.marriott.com, $162 s or d). This glass palace contains 257 guest rooms and 16 suites, a business center, an outdoor heated pool, a health club, and a Mediterranean restaurant.

Old Town

Once a family home, **El Relicario del Carmen** (Venezuela and Olmedo, tel. 2/228-9120, www.hotelrelicariodelcarmen.com, $105 s, $135 d) has been meticulously renovated and made into a comfortable retreat for travelers who want to stay in the colonial part of the city. The abundant artwork and stained glass windows are particular highlights.

Patio Andaluz (García Moreno and Olmedo, tel. 2/228-0830, www.hotelpatioandaluz.com, $200 s or d) is the fruit of a massive project that restored a 16th-century colonial home with two interior patios, spacious guest rooms, and split-level suites. There is an excellent restaurant on the first-floor patio with carved stone pillars, and service is understandably top-notch.

OVER $200
New Town
Uphill from the Hilton Colón to the east, the **Swissôtel** (12 de Octubre 1820 at Cordero, tel. 2/256-7600, fax 2/256-8079, http://quito. swissotel.com, $250 s, $265 d) has 277 wheel-chair-accessible guest rooms and a private health club, along with Japanese and Italian restaurants, a casino, and a gourmet deli.

Old Town
Quito's first hotel and still one of its best is **Plaza Grande** (García Moreno and Chile, tel. 2/251-0777, U.S. tel. 888/790-5264, www. plazagrandequito.com, $500 s or d) on the main square. It has 15 suites, three restaurants, a ballroom, champagne and brandy bars, chandeliers, and luxurious guest rooms with the marble bathroom floors and jetted tubs.

LONGER STAYS
Most **hotels** will arrange a discount for stays of a few weeks or more. For example, the **Residencial Casa Oriente** (Yaguachi 824 at Llona, tel. 2/254-6157) offers apartments with or without kitchens for $115–140 per month with a minimum stay of two weeks. Spanish lessons are available, and English, French, and German are spoken. **Alberto's House** (García 545, tel. 2/222-4603, www.albertoshouse.com) has guest rooms with shared or private baths from $70 per week, $180 per month.

To have a more authentic cultural experience, a **family stay** is a great way to practice your Spanish and get to know Ecuadorian culture from the inside. It is often just as affordable as a budget hotel as long as you are willing to make a longer commitment. Check at the South American Explorers (SAE) Quito Clubhouse for the latest list; stays can also easily be arranged through language schools. SAE is also a reliable source of information on **apartments** for rent, or try the classified ads in the local newspapers.

Food

Quito has the widest range of international restaurants in Ecuador as well as many excellent local eateries. Here you will find the biggest diversity of world cuisine: from Asian curries to Italian pasta, Mexican fajitas to Argentine steaks, and there are plenty of cheap cafés, fast food joints and $2 set-menus for those on a tighter budget. Many restaurants outside New Town close by 9 or 10 P.M. and throughout the city many are closed on Sundays. Note also that it's surprisingly difficult to find an early breakfast in New Town as most places open at 8 A.M.

OLD TOWN
Bakeries, Cafés, and Snacks
There are plenty of cozy little bakeries to pop into between sights in Old Town. At the entrance of San Agustin Monastery is **El Cafeto** (Chile and Guayaquil, no phone, 8 A.M.–7:30 P.M. Mon.–Sat., 8 A.M.–noon Sun.), specializing in coffee and hot chocolate served with *humitas,* tamales, empanadas, and cakes. In the courtyard of the Centro Cultural Metropolitano, **El Búho** (Jose Moreno and Espejo, tel. 2/228-9877, 11 A.M.–7 P.M. Mon.– Thurs., 11 A.M.–9 P.M. Fri.–Sat., noon–5 P.M. Sun., $3–6) is a quiet spot for a snack with a range of soups, salads, sandwiches, and pasta.

Old Town has several great ice cream parlors. **Frutería Monserrate** (Espejo Oe2-12, tel. 2/258-3408, 8 A.M.–7:30 P.M. Mon.–Fri., 9 A.M.–6:30 P.M. Sat.–Sun., $2–5) serves

FOOD

MARKETS AND SUPERMARKETS

The most economical spot to buy food is the **Santa Clara Market** (Ramírez Dávalos between Carrión and Antonio de Marchena, 7 A.M.–3 P.M. Mon.-Fri., 7 A.M.–noon Sat.-Sun.), two blocks from 10 de Agosto. This place has countless small food stands and meals to go along with a few inexpensive markets.

For a more comfortable shopping experience, head to **Supermaxi,** the city's biggest supermarket, with branches at La Niña and Yanes Pinzón, one block off 6 de Diciembre, as well as in the Centros Comerciales El Bosque, Iñaquito, Multicentro, América, El Jardín, and El Recreo, among others. The biggest **Megamaxi** branch is at 6 de Diciembre and Julio Moreno. **Mi Comisariato** is in the Centro Commercial Quicentro, at García Moreno and Mejía, and at Nuñez de Vela and Ignacio San María. They're all open 9 A.M.–7 or 8 P.M. Monday-Saturday and close earlier on Sunday. The **Santa María** stores (8 A.M.–8 P.M. daily) are a little cheaper; there are two in the north on Versalles and in Centro Commercial Iñaquito, as well as in the center at Venezuela and Sucre.

extravagant helpings of fruit salad and ice cream as well as cheap lunches and sandwiches. **Heladería San Agustín** (Guayaquil 1053, tel. 2/228-5082, 9 A.M.–6 P.M. Mon.–Fri., 9 A.M.–4 P.M. Sat., 10 A.M.–3 P.M. Sun., ice cream $1.50) claims to be the oldest in the city, having made *helados de paila* sorbets in copper bowls for 150 years.

Ecuadorian

Old Town has plenty of places for cheap set meals, but quality varies widely. On Plaza Grande, there is a small food court on Chile with a range of restaurants offering well-prepared local specialties. Just down the hill from

Plaza Grande, **El Guaragua** (Espejo Oe2-40, tel. 2/257-2552, 10 A.M.–9 P.M. Mon.–Thurs., 10 A.M.–11 P.M. Fri.–Sun., entrées $3–6) is one of several restaurants offering local specialties from chicken stew to fried pork chops with beans. With live music Thursday–Saturday and 360-degree views over the colonial city, the **Vista Hermoso** (Mejía 453 at García Moreno, tel. 2/295-1401, entrées $6–10) offers pizzas, snacks, and cocktails on its rooftop terrace. Bring a jacket at night.

On Plaza San Francisco, under the arches below the monastery is the ideally situated café **Tianguez** (Plaza San Francisco, tel. 2/295-4326, www.tianguez.org, 10 A.M.–6 P.M. Mon.–Tues., 10 A.M.–11 P.M. Wed.–Sun., entrées $3–5). After browsing the eclectic gift shop, choose from traditional snacks such as tamales and well-presented entrées such as *fritada* and *llapingacho*.

International

Part of colonial Quito's recent renaissance is an upsurge in high-end eateries. For a gourmet meal, look no further than the cozy cellar setting of ◖ **Las Cuevas de Luis Candela** (Benalcázar 713 at Chile, tel. 2/228-7710, 10 A.M.–11 P.M. daily, entrées $7–10), which has been attracting Quito's wealthy patrons since the 1960s. Paella and fondue bourguignonne are just two of the specialties. **Theatrum** (Manabi N8-131, tel. 2/257-1011 or 2/228-9669, www.theatrum.com.ec, 12:30–4:30 P.M. and 7–11 P.M. Mon.–Fri., 7–11 P.M. Sat.–Sun., entrées $10–15), on the second floor of the Teatro Sucre, is another of the city's most elegant dining experiences, serving extravagantly presented gourmet dishes such as barbecued octopus, crab ravioli, and rabbit risotto in a stylish setting. **Mea Culpa** (Chile and García Moreno, tel. 2/295-1190, 12:30–3:30 P.M. and 7–11 P.M. Mon.–Fri., entrées $10–20), which overlooks the Plaza Grande, has a strict dress code, so leave your sneakers and jeans at home if you want to try out the special fare, such as ostrich with brandy and apple.

Beneath the Itchimbía Cultural Center is ◖ **Mosaico** (Samaniego N8-95 at Antepara, tel. 2/254-2871, 11 A.M.–11 P.M. daily, entrées $9–12), which is best for drinks at sunset, when the views of Old Town are unbeatable from the mosaic-inlaid tables on the terrace. Arrive early to secure a table, because this stylish spot fills up quickly with Quito's elite. The limited menu lists Greek dishes, sandwiches, and desserts. Cheesecake is a particular specialty. A taxi from Old Town is $2.

Vegetarian food is harder to come by in Old Town than in Mariscal, but **Govindas** (Esmeraldas 853, tel. 2/296-6844, 8 A.M.–4 P.M. Mon.–Sat., entrées $2–3) is 100 percent meat-free and has a wide range of lunches such as vegetable risotto and plenty of fresh yogurt and granola for breakfast.

NEW TOWN
Asian
Hundreds of inexpensive *chifas* fill the city, but most are barely adequate. **Chifa Mayflower** (Carrión 442 at 6 de Diciembre, tel. 2/254-0510, www.mayflower.com.ec, 11 A.M.–11 P.M. daily, entrées $3–7) has received good reviews from celebrity chefs and is one of seven in a small Quito chain, which includes branches in the El Bosque, El Jardín, Quicentro, and El Recreo malls. Portions of fried rice and noodles are large, and there are plenty of veggie dishes.

For sushi, expect to pay out. **Tanoshii** (in the Swissôtel, 12 de Octubre 1820 at Cordero, tel. 2/256-7600, 12:30–3 P.M. and 7–11 P.M. daily, entrées $10–20) is one of the best in town, with excellent teppanyaki and sashimi. **Sake** (Rivet N30-166, tel. 2/252-4818, 12:30–3 P.M. and 6:30–11 P.M. daily, entrées $15–25) is also very good.

Mariscal offers several restaurants offering Asian specialties that you would struggle to find anywhere else in Ecuador. For curries, you can't beat **《 Chandani Tandoori** (Juan León Mera and Cordero, tel. 2/222-1053, noon–10 P.M. Mon.–Sat., noon–5 P.M. Sun., entrées $3–5). Everything from *dopiaza* to korma, tikka masala, and *balti* is done well here, served with saffron rice or naan bread. For Vietnamese, Thai, and Asian fusion specialties, head to **《 Uncle Ho's** (Calama

and Almagro, tel. 2/511-4030, noon–11 P.M. Mon.–Sat., entrées $5–8). Choose from a wide range of rolls, soups, and curries. It's a good place for a drink too, and friendly Irish owner Kevin is usually the life and soul of the party.

For something a little different, try Mongolian barbecue at **Mongo's Grill** (Calama E5-10 at Juan León Mera, tel. 2/255-6159, noon–11 P.M. Mon.–Sat., entrées $3–8), where sizzling meat and vegetables are cooked in front of you. The buffet lunch is a particularly good value, and it's a good place for cocktails later on.

Cafés, Bakeries, and Snacks
El Cafécito (Cordero 1124 at Reina Victoria, tel. 2/223-4862, entrées $3–7) is a good option for breakfast as well as Italian and Mexican dishes later on. Candles and crayons for coloring your place mat and a fireplace add to the cozy ambience. **The Magic Bean** (Foch 681 at Juan León Mera, tel. 2/256-6181, 7 A.M.– 11 P.M. daily) is another great option for breakfast with fresh Colombian coffee, crepes, and a wide range of juices. Branches of the **Coffee Tree** (Plaza del Quindé, Foch and Reina Victoria, Plaza de los Presidentes, Washington and Amazonas, 24 hours daily) are always an option when nowhere else is open, but the food is nothing special.

The best option for breakfast and after hours is **《 Coffee and Toffee** (Calama and Almagro, tel. 2/254-3821, 24 hours daily, entrées $3–6), which serves a variety of breakfasts prepared in the open kitchen and served on sofas and armchairs. Choose from the cozy brick interior or a seat on Calama watching the world go by. There's free Wi-Fi too. Another good option for breakfasts and snacks is **El Español** (Juan León Mera and Wilson, tel. 2/255-3995, 8 A.M.–9 P.M. Mon.–Fri., 8 A.M.–6 P.M. Sat.–Sun., entrées $3–6), a chain delicatessen with great sandwiches and high-quality cured hams and cheeses.

Chocoholics should head to **República del Cacao** (Foch and Reina Victoria, tel. 2/255-3132, 9 A.M.–11 P.M. daily), where you can consume it in all its varieties: truffles, cakes, ice cream, cocktails, and hot drinks.

Burgers and Steaks

Burgers, grilled plates, and barbecue are the specialties at **Adam's Rib** (Calama and Reina Victoria, tel. 2/256-3196, noon–11 P.M. Mon.–Sat., $6–8). A similar offering is found at slightly cheaper prices at **The Texas Ranch** (Juan León Mera 1140 at Calama, tel. 2/290-6199, noon–11 P.M. Mon.–Sat., $4–7). For very cheap burgers with trimmings galore, ignore the dubious name and try **G-Spot** (Almagro and Calama, no phone, 11 A.M.–11 P.M. daily, entrées $1.50–$3).

Cuban

The cuisine of this Caribbean island has become quite popular in Ecuador. There are two good places at the north end of Mariscal. **Varadero Sandwiches Cubanos** (Reina Victoria and La Pinta, tel. 2/254-2757, noon–4 P.M. and 7 P.M.–midnight Mon.–Sat., entrées $5) has sandwiches, and things heat up at night with live music by the bar. **La Bodeguita de Cuba** (Reina Victoria 1721 at La Pinta, tel. 2/254-2476, noon–4 P.M. and 7 P.M.–midnight Mon.–Sat., entrées $4–6) is popular for its Cuban *bocaditos* (appetizers) as well as the live Cuban music on Thursday nights.

Ecuadorian

Amidst the dozens of international restaurants, a few eateries offering local specialties stand out. **La Choza** (12 de Octubre 1821 at Cordero, tel. 2/223-0839, noon–4 P.M. and 7–10 P.M. Mon.–Fri., noon–4 P.M. Sat.–Sun., $2–4) is a popular mid-price place serving appetizers such as *tortillas de maíz* and entrées like the tasty *locro de papas*. For larger portions, try **Mama Clorinda** (Reina Victoria 1144 at Calama, tel. 2/254-4362, 11 A.M.–10 P.M. Mon.–Sat.), where you can get *llapingachos* and a quarter of a chicken for $6, or try a half guinea pig (*cuy*) for $10.

French

Gallic cuisine tends to be served in the most upscale of Quito's foreign restaurants. **Rincón de Francia** (Roca 779 at 9 de Octubre, tel. 2/222-5053, www.rincondefrancia.com, 12:30–3 P.M. and 7–11 P.M. Mon.–Fri., 12:30–3 P.M. Sat., entrées $15–20) is among the best restaurants in the city. Make reservations and dress well. Specialties include oysters, steak in brandy, and fruit melba.

For a more economical dip into French fare, **La Crêperie** (García 465 at Almagro, tel. 8/222-6274, 5 P.M.–midnight Mon.–Sat., entrées $3–5) is one of the longest-running restaurants in the city, and it's often packed on Friday nights for live music. Crepes, of course, are the mainstay, but the cheese fondue ($18 for 2 people) is also hard to beat.

Italian

As the city has spread north, several classy restaurants have followed the business-lunch crowd up Eloy Alfaro. One of the best is the **Il Risotto** (Eloy Alfaro and Portugal, tel. 2/222-6850, noon–3 P.M. and 5 P.M.–11:30 P.M. daily, entrées $7–16), with a great view of the city from the main dining room northeast of the Mariscal. Good service and generous portions make the prices more bearable, as does the delicious tiramisu. For more economical pizza and pasta, try **Le Arcate** (Baquedano 358 at Juan León Mera, lunch and dinner daily, entrées $6–14), which offers over 50 varieties of wood-oven pizzas (the "Russian" has vodka as an ingredient) for $6–9. Equally good is **Al Forno** (Moreno and Almagro, tel. 2/252-7145, noon–3 P.M. and 6:30–11 P.M. Mon.–Sat., entrées $6–14) with an equally wide range of pizzas. The calzone is particularly mouthwatering. More central in Mariscal is **Tomato** (Moreno and Almagro, tel. 2/290-6201, 10 A.M.–1 A.M. daily, entrées $4–8).

Mexican

A plate of fajitas at **Red Hot Chili Peppers** (Foch and Juan León Mera, tel. 2/255-7575, noon–10:30 P.M. Mon.–Sat., entrées $5–8) will easily fill two people. It's a tiny place with a big TV and graffiti covering the walls, and it just may serve the most authentic Mexican food in town. Next door, **Mariachi Taco Factory** (Foch and Juan León Mera, tel. 2/255-3066, noon–10:30 P.M. Mon.–Sat., entrées $5–8) is busier, and they have karaoke later (which may or may not be a good thing).

Middle Eastern

Shawarma (grilled meat in warm pita bread with yogurt sauce and vegetables) is becoming more and more popular in Ecuador, and Middle Eastern restaurants are springing up left, right, and center. In Mariscal, **El Arabe** (Reina Victoria 627 at Carrión, tel. 2/254-9414, 10 A.M.–9 P.M. Mon.–Sat., 11 A.M.–7 P.M. Sun., entrées $6–8) is a long-established popular spot. The patio at **Aladdin** (Almagro and Baquerizo Moreno, tel. 2/222-9435, 10:30 A.M.–midnight daily, entrées $2–4) is always packed at night. The water pipes and 16 kinds of flavored tobacco probably have something to do with it, along with the cheap falafel and *shawarma.*

Seafood

Two restaurants stand out in this category: **Mare Nostrum** (Tamayo 172 at Foch, tel. 2/252-8686, noon–10 P.M. Tues.–Sat., entrées $8–17) claims to have "70 ways of serving fish." Boat models, suits of armor, low lighting, and dark wood beams in a castle-like building set the stage for delicious cream soups and *encocados* served in half a coconut shell. The same owners run **Las Redes de Mariscos** (Amazonas 845 at Veintimilla, tel. 2/252-5691, noon–10 P.M. Mon.–Sat., $5–8), which has an extensive wine list and specializes in large bowls of *ceviche.*

Vegetarian

Being vegetarian tends to attract quizzical looks around Ecuador, but in Quito there are several good options. **El Maple** (Foch 476 at Almagro, tel. 2/223-1503, noon–9 P.M. daily, entrées $3–5) has everything from pasta and

curry to burritos and stir-fries. Lunch is great value at $3.50.

Although there are animals on the menu, **The Magic Bean** (Foch 681 at Juan León Mera, tel. 2/256-6181, 7 A.M.–10 P.M. daily, entrées $5–7) is still a vegetarian restaurant at heart. Salads, pizzas, pancakes, fresh juices, and Colombian coffee—served inside or on the covered patio—have made this place one of the more popular gringo stopovers in New Town.

Other International

For a tangy Swiss fondue, try **Paleo** (Cordero E5-48 at Juan León Mera, tel. 2/255-3019, lunch and dinner Mon.–Sat., entrées $6–12), which also serves great raclette. **La Paella Valenciana** (Republica and Almagro, tel. 2/222-8681, noon–3 P.M. and 7:30–11:30 P.M. Mon.–Sat., noon–3 P.M. Sun., entrées $10–20) is one of the best places for a wide range of Spanish entrées and tapas.

One of the most enticing restaurants in Mariscal is the colorful, glass-encased patio of ◖ **La Boca del Lobo** (Calama 284 at Reina Victoria, tel. 2/254-5500, 5 P.M.–midnight Mon.–Sat., entrées $7–14). The decor is flamboyantly eclectic, with birdcages and psychedelic paintings, and the menu focuses on Mediterranean specialties—marvel at how many ways they can cook mushrooms. The cocktail menu is another highlight. This place attracts a higher class crowd and is also gay-friendly.

If you want the exact opposite of La Boca del Lobo (i.e., down-to-earth home cooking), try the Irish bar **Mulligans** (Calama E5-44, tel. 2/254-0876, 11 A.M.–midnight Sun.–Thurs., 11 A.M.–2 A.M. Fri.–Sat., entrées $3–6), where the order of the day is fried food such as chicken wings and fish and chips washed down by pitchers of draft beer with soccer on the big screen.

Information and Services

VISITOR INFORMATION

The **Corporación Metropolitana de Turismo** (Quito Visitors Bureau) is the best tourist information bureau in Ecuador and an excellent source of information on Quito, with maps, brochures, leaflets, English-speaking staff, and a regularly updated website. The main office is at the Palacio Municipal (Plaza de la Independencia, Venezuela and Espejo, tel. 2/257-2445, 9 A.M.–6 P.M. Mon.–Fri., 9 A.M.–5 P.M. Sat.). There are also branches in Mariscal (Reina Victoria and Luis Cordero, tel. 2/255-1566), the airport (tel. 2/330-0164), the Museo Nacional del Banco Central (6 de Diciembre and Patria, tel. 2/222-1116), and at Quitumbe bus terminal.

The Quito Visitors Bureau works with the Tourism Unit of the Metropolitan Police (tel. 2/257-0786) to provide **guided tours** of the city. These well-informed officers are clad in blue-and-red uniforms (and look rather like airline pilots). Tours of Old Town range $6–15 pp, and a tour of Mitad del Mundo costs $40.

The main office of Ecuador's **Ministerio de Turismo** (Eloy Alfaro N32-300 at Tobar, 3rd Fl., tel. 2/239-9333, 8:30 A.M.–12:30 P.M. and 1:30–5 P.M. daily), near the Parque La Carolina, is also helpful and can assist with hotel reservations. It has maps, and some staff speak English.

Outside the tourist offices, a good source of information is **South American Explorers** (SAE, Jorge Washington 311 at Plaza, tel./fax 2/222-5228, quitoclub@saexplorers.org, www.saexplorers.org, 9:30 A.M.–5 P.M. Mon.–Wed. and Fri., 9:30 A.M.–8 P.M. Thurs., 9:30 A.M.–noon Sat.). The SAE puts most of its energy these days toward paying members, making the annual fee ($60 pp, $90 per couple) a solid investment for those who plan to stay in Ecuador more than a month or travel through many countries in South America. Nonmembers can get free maps and advice here too. With branches in Ithaca (New York), Lima, Cuzco (Peru), and Buenos Aires, the club stocks a wealth of information readily accessible to members by mail, email, fax, or in person. You can store equipment, peruse the library, and help yourself to tea and coffee in the lounge. An SAE membership card entitles you to discounts at many hotels, tour agencies, and Spanish schools in Quito and around the country. The biggest perk of membership is access to countless trip reports written by members giving the lowdown on destinations throughout the continent. The SAE also has a good volunteering database.

VISAS

Tourist-visa extensions beyond the standard 90 days are the main reason most travelers end up at the **Ministerio de Relaciones Exteriores** (Carrión E1-76 at 10 de Agosto, tel. 2/299-3200, www.mmrree.gob.ec, 8:30 A.M.–1:30 P.M. Mon.–Fri.) Go early and be ready to wait. Unfortunately, you can only extend your visa on the day before or on the actual day it expires, which makes it a stressful process. If you can, go the week before to be sure of the procedure. All nontourist visa holders (student, cultural, volunteer, or work visas) must register within 30 days of arrival at the same office; otherwise you have to pay a $200 fine.

MAPS

The hike up Paz y Miño is worth it for the commanding view of the city from the **Instituto Geográfico Militar** (IGM, tel. 2/250-2091, 8 A.M.–4 P.M. Mon.–Fri.). Here you can get general tourist maps of Ecuador, as well as topographical maps for hiking. While you wait for the staff to process your map order (bring a book), consider a show at the planetarium. The IGM often closes early on Fridays, and visitors must surrender their passports at the gate to enter.

The Quito **Visitors Bureau** (Plaza de la Independencia, Venezuela and Espejo, tel. 2/257-2445, 9 A.M.–6 P.M. Mon.–Fri., 9 A.M.–5 P.M. Sat.) can supply decent maps for visitors as well as specialist walking tour maps.

CONSULATES IN QUITO

- **Argentina:** Ed. Banco de los Andes, 5th Fl., Amazonas 477 between Robles and Roca, tel. 2/256-2292, 9 A.M.-1 P.M. Mon.-Fri.

- **Bolivia:** Ed. Torres Viscaya II, 1st Fl., César Borja Lavayen and Juan Pablo Sanz, tel. 2/245-8863, 8 A.M.-4 P.M. Mon.-Fri.

- **Brazil:** Ed. España, 10th Fl., Amazonas 1429 at Colón, tel. 2/256-3141, 9 A.M.-3 P.M. Mon.-Fri.

- **Canada (Australia):** Amazonas 4153 at Unión Nacional de Periodistas, tel. 2/245-5499, 9 A.M.-noon and 2:30-5:30 P.M. Mon.-Fri., appointment required, Australians also welcome; the Australian consulate is in Guayaquil.

- **Chile:** Sáenz 3617 at Amazonas, 4th Fl., tel. 2/224-9403, 8 A.M.-5 P.M. Mon.-Fri.

- **Colombia:** Atahualpa 955 at República, 3rd Fl., tel. 2/245-8012, 8:30 A.M.-1 P.M. Mon.-Fri.

- **Costa Rica:** Isla San Cristobal N44-385 at Guepi, tel. 2/225-2330, 8 A.M.-1:30 P.M. Mon.-Fri.

- **Cuba:** Mercurio 365 at El Vengador, tel. 2/245-6936, 9 A.M.-1 P.M. Mon.-Fri.

- **Denmark:** Ed. Gabriela 3, 3rd Fl., República de El Salvador 733 at Portugal, tel. 2/243-7163, 9:30 A.M.-1:30 P.M. and 3-5 P.M. Mon.-Fri.

- **France:** 18 de Septiembre 115 at Leonidas Plaza, tel. 2/294-3840, 8:30 A.M.-1 P.M. and 3-5:30 P.M. Mon.-Fri.

- **Germany:** Ed. Citiplaza, 14th Fl., Naciones Unidas and República de El Salvador, tel. 2/297-2820, 8:30-11:30 A.M. Mon.-Fri.

- **Guatemala:** Ed. Gabriela 3, 3rd Fl., República de El Salvador 733 at Portugal, tel. 2/245-9700, 9 A.M.-1 P.M. Mon.-Fri.

- **Ireland (consulate):** Yanacocha N72-64 at Juan Procel, tel. 2/357-0156, 10 A.M.-1 P.M. Mon.-Fri.

- **Israel:** Ed. Plaza 2000, 9th Fl., 12 de Octubre and Salazar, tel. 2/397-1500, 10 A.M.-1 P.M. Mon.-Fri.

- **Italy:** La Isla 111 at Albornoz, tel. 2/256-1077, 8:30 A.M.-12:30 P.M. Mon.-Fri.

- **Japan:** Ed. de Corporacion Financiera Nacional, Juan Mera N30 and Patria, tel. 2/256-1899, 9 A.M.-noon and 2-5 P.M. Mon.-Fri.

- **Mexico:** 6 de Diciembre 4843 at Naciones Unidas, tel. 2/292-3770, 9 A.M.-1 P.M. Mon.-Fri.

- **Netherlands:** 12 de Octubre 1942 at Cordero, tel. 2/222-9229, 8:30 A.M.-1 P.M. and 2-5 P.M. Mon.-Fri., by appointment only.

- **Paraguay:** Ed. Torre Sol Verde, 8th Fl., 12 de Octubre and Salazar, tel. 2/223-1990, 8:30 A.M.-2:30 P.M. Mon.-Fri.

- **Peru:** República de El Salvador 495 at Irlanda, tel. 2/246-8410, 9 A.M.-1 P.M. and 3-5 P.M. Mon.-Fri.

- **Spain** (consulate): La Pinta 455 at Amazonas, tel. 2/256-4373, 8:30 A.M.-noon Mon.-Fri.

- **United Kingdom:** Ed. Citiplaza, 14th Fl., Naciones Unidas and República de El Salvador, tel. 2/297-0800, http://ukinecuador.fco.gov.uk, 8:30 A.M.-12:30 P.M. and 1:30-5 P.M. Mon.-Thurs., 8:30 A.M.-1:30 P.M. Fri.

- **United States:** Avigiras and Guayacanes, tel. 2/398-5000, http://ecuador.usembassy.gov, 8 A.M.-12:30 P.M. and 1:30-5 P.M. Tues.-Fri.

- **Venezuela:** Ed. Cedatos, 8th Fl., Amazonas N30-240 at Eloy Alfaro, tel. 2/255-7209, 9 A.M.-12:30 P.M. and 2-4 P.M. Mon.-Fri.

POST OFFICES AND COURIERS

Quito's main **post office** is in New Town (Eloy Alfaro 354 at 9 de Octubre, tel. 2/256-1218, 8 A.M.–6 P.M. Mon.–Fri., 8 A.M.–noon Sat.). The Express Mail Service (EMS, tel. 2/256-1962) is at this office. There is also a branch post office one block east of the Plaza de la Independencia in Old Town (Espejo between Guayaquil and Venezuela, tel. 2/228-2175, 8 A.M.–6 P.M. Mon.–Fri.).

If you're sending something important, using an international courier service is preferable. There is a branch of **FedEx** (Amazonas 517 at Santa María, tel. 2/227-9180), and **DHL** has several offices throughout the city, including on Eloy Alfaro and Avenida de Los Juncos (tel. 2/397-5000), Colón 1333 at Foch (tel. 2/255-6118), at the Hilton Colón, and at the airport.

TELECOMMUNICATIONS
Telephone

You're never far from a *cabina* offering telephone service. The national companies **Andinatel** and **Pacifictel** no longer have a monopoly—together with Claro (Porta), Movistar, and Alegro, they both run competing offices. Movistar and Claro also have pay phones everywhere, and each type requires its own brand of prepaid card. The most convenient offices in Mariscal are at Juan León Mera 741 at Baquedano, and on Reina Victoria near Calama.

Internet Access

Internet access is even easier to find than a phone booth. Internet cafés are everywhere, particularly in Mariscal. Expect to pay $1 per hour and to have access at most cafés 8 A.M.–9 P.M. daily, possibly later on weekends. Although connection rates and computer quality vary widely, most cafés have fax service, scanners, printers, and Internet phone programs, allowing foreign visitors to call home for a fraction of the cost of a regular phone connection. The term *café* may be misleading, however, because many offer only water and snacks.

QUITO EMERGENCY TELEPHONE NUMBERS

Police	101
Fire Department	102
Red Cross	131
Emergency	911

Listing Internet cafés in Quito is an inherently futile gesture because they open and close so fast. In New Town, the block of Calama between Juan León Mera and Reina Victoria has a handful. The increasing number of hotels with free Internet access and Wi-Fi often makes a visit to a Internet café unnecessary.

MONEY
Banks and ATMs

ATMs for most international systems (Plus, Cirrus, Visa, and MasterCard) can be found at major banks along Amazonas and around the shopping centers. These tend to have limits on how much you can withdraw per day (usually $500), so if you need to, say, pay cash for a Galápagos trip, you'll have to go to a bank branch. It's best to take a taxi straight to the travel agency if you withdraw a large amount of money. **Banco del Pacífico** has its head office on Naciones Unidos at Los Shyris, and there is a branch at Amazonas and Washington. **Banco de Guayaquil** is on Reina Victoria at Colón, and on Amazonas at Veintimilla; **Banco de Pichincha** is on Amazonas at Pereira, and on 6 de Diciembre. **Banco Bolivariano** is at Naciones Unidas E6-99.

Exchange Houses

Since the introduction of the U.S. dollar, exchanging other currencies has become more difficult, and many exchange houses have closed. Try to bring U.S. dollars traveler's checks, as rates are poor for Canadian dollars, British pounds, and even the euro. Exchanging those currencies outside Quito, Guayaquil, and Cuenca is difficult if not impossible. If you really have to, try one of the large banks listed above.

Credit Card Offices

Visa (Los Shyris 3147, tel. 2/245-9303) has an office in Quito, as do **American Express** (Ed. Rocafuerte, 5th Fl., Amazonas 339 at Jorge Washington, tel. 2/256-0488) and **MasterCard** (Naciones Unidas and Shyris, tel. 2/226-2770).

Money Transfers

Western Union (8 A.M.–6 P.M. Mon.–Fri., 9 A.M.–5 P.M. Sat.–Sun.) has many locations around the city, including on Av. Del República and on Colón—check www.westernunion.com for a list of offices worldwide. The company charges $52 for a same-day transfer of $1,000, plus local taxes. It'll cost you $25 to transfer any amount to and from other places in the Americas, and $35 to and from Europe, at the **Banco del Pacífico** (Amazonas and Jorge Washington); you are also expected to cover the cost of contacting your home bank. If that much cash makes you itch, you can change it into American Express traveler's checks at the main branch of the Banco del Pacífico (República 433 at Almagro). This transaction costs $10 to change up to $1,000, and 1 percent of the total for additional amounts.

HEALTH
General Concerns

Unless you're traveling from an equally high city such as La Paz, you will certainly feel the effects of Quito's **elevation** within the first few hours of arriving. At best, you will feel a bit breathless and light-headed, but dizzy spells, headaches, and fatigue are also common. It is best not to overexert yourself, to minimize caffeine and alcohol intake, and

consume plenty of water and light food. After two or three days, you'll more or less be used to the elevation.

Don't let the cool climate at this elevation fool you into thinking that you don't need to bother with sunblock. The **sun** is far stronger up here, so slap it on. The **smog** from the traffic can leave you with a sore throat, particularly because Quito's location in a valley seems to trap all the pollution.

Like everywhere in Ecuador, you may suffer from stomach problems. Minimize the risks by avoiding salad, unpeeled fruit, ice, pork, and shellfish. Don't eat on the street or from bus vendors.

Hospitals and Clinics

The **Hospital Metropolitano** (Mariana de Jesús and Occidental, tel. 2/226-1520) is the best hospital in Quito and is priced accordingly. The American-run **Hospital Voz Andes** (Villalengua 267 at 10 de Agosto, tel. 2/226-2142) is cheaper and receives the most business from Quito's foreign residents. It's described as fast, competent, and inexpensive, with an emergency room and outpatient services. To get there, take the *trole* north along 10 de Agosto just past Naciones Unidas.

The 24-hour **Clínica Pichincha** (Veintimilla E3-30 at Páez, tel. 2/299-8700) has a laboratory that can perform analyses for intestinal parasites. Women's health problems should be referred to the 24-hour **Clínica de la Mujer** (Amazonas N39-216 at Gaspar de Villarroel, tel. 2/245-8000).

Private Doctors

Dr. John Rosenberg (Foch 476 at Almagro, tel. 2/252-1104, jrd@pi.pro.ec) is a highly recommended general practitioner who speaks English and German. He is the doctor for the U.S. Embassy and performs house calls. **Eduardo Larrea** (Centro Medico Metropolitano, 3rd Fl., Suite 311, tel. 2/226-7652 or 9/919-4665) also speaks English.

Carlos Ribadeneira (Mariana de Jesús and A St., tel. 9/448-9115) is a gynecologist who speaks English.

Renato León (Ascazubi and 10 Agosto, tel. 2/223-8342 or 2/255-2080) is a tropical disease specialist who speaks English and does parasite lab tests more quickly and cheaply than the hospitals.

Roberto Mena (Coruña and Isabel la Católica, tel. 2/256-9149) comes very highly recommended for quality dental work. He speaks English and German.

OTHER SERVICES
Laundry

Wash-and-dry places are common in New Town: There are several on Foch, Pinto, and Wilson between Reina Victoria and Amazonas. A few may even let you use the machines yourself. Laundry services are available in many hotels, and the receptionists in more expensive ones can point you toward a dry cleaner (*lavaseca*).

Getting There and Around

GETTING THERE AND AWAY
Air

The **Mariscal Sucre International Airport** (tel. 2/294-4900, www.quiport.com) is north of New Town beyond the intersection of 10 de Agosto, Amazonas, and De la Prensa. At the time of this writing, it remains Quito's main airport, but it will be replaced, most likely in 2012, by a new airport at El Quinche, 18 kilometers east of the city. This new facility, costing over $500 million, will host all national and international flights on a 1,500-hectare site and will accommodate over 5 million passengers per year.

Until the new airport opens, from Mariscal it's straightforward to get to and from the airport. Buses marked "Aeropuerto" head down 9 de Octubre, 12 de Octubre, and Juan León Mera. You can also take the trolley along 10 de Agosto and then transfer onto the Rumiñahui connecting bus (*alimentador*) from the Estación Norte, or onto the Metrobus on

INTERNATIONAL AIRLINES IN QUITO

- **Air France and KLM:** Ed. World Trade Center, Suite 401, 12 de Octubre N24-562 at Cordero, tel. 2/252-4201, shared offices

- **American:** Av. Patria and Amazonas, tel. 2/226-0900

- **Avianca:** Coruña 1311 at San Ignacio, tel. 2/223-2015

- **Continental:** Ed. World Trade Center, Suite 1108, 12 de Octubre and Cordero, tel. 2/255-7170

- **Copa:** República de El Salvador 361 and Moscu, tel. 2/227-3082

- **Delta:** Ed. Renazzo Plaza, 3rd Fl., Los Shyris and Suecia, tel. 2/333-1691 or 800/101-060

- **Iberia:** Ed. Finandes, Eloy Alfaro 939 at Amazonas, tel. 2/256-6009

- **Icelandair:** Diego de Almagro 1822 at Alpallana, tel. 2/256-1820

- **Japan Airlines:** Amazonas 3899 at Corea, tel. 2/298-6828

- **LAN:** Amazonas and Pasaje Guayas, tel. 2/255-1782

- **Lufthansa:** Ed. Harmonia, Amazonas N47-205 at Río Palora, tel. 2/226-7705

- **Taca:** República de El Salvador N34-67 at Suecia, tel. 2/225-4662

- **TAME:** Amazonas 13-54 at Colón, tel. 2/245-2657 or 800/500-800

- **United:** Ed. Almirante Colón, Av. Republica de El Salvador, tel. 2/225-4662

América, which stops at the airport. Be wary of pickpockets on these services, however. From the airport, take pretty much any bus heading south (left) to reach both New Town and Old Town.

A taxi ride from the airport during the day should cost about $3 to New Town and $5 to Old Town, but to get these prices you need to flag down a cab outside the terminal parking lot. Taking a taxi directly in front of the terminal costs a few dollars more.

Services at the airport include tourist information, a post office, late-night money exchange, duty-free shops, Andinatel phone service, and a few restaurants and cafés.

Once the new airport is built, it will be far more time-consuming to get to Quito. A taxi will take about 50 minutes, and a shuttle bus service will probably be offered, although that has not yet been confirmed.

TAME (Amazonas and Colón, tel. 2/396-6300) has flights from Quito to Baltra in the Galápagos ($350–400 round-trip) and to the following destinations for $50–80 one-way: Coca, Cuenca, Esmeraldas, Guayaquil, Lago Agrio, Loja, Machala, and Tulcán. **Icaro** (Palora 124 at Amazonas, tel. 2/245-0928) is sometimes marginally cheaper and has daily flights to Coca, Cuenca, Manta, and Guayaquil. **Aerogal** (Amazonas 7797 at Juan Holgún, tel. 2/225-7202) flies to Guayaquil and the Galápagos and also has daily flights to Cuenca. The newest line is **VIP** (Foch and 6 de Diciembre, tel. 2/396-0600), which has smaller planes to Coca, Lago Agrio, and seasonally to Salinas. **SAEREO** (Indanza 121 at Amazonas, tel. 2/330-1152) has a daily flight to Macas.

National Buses

Quito has replaced its dilapidated old bus station at Cumandá with two brand-new terminals. The biggest terminal, Quitumbe, in the far south of Quito, is a joy to visit; security and cleanliness are both excellent. This terminal serves all long-distance routes traveling west, east, and south as well as services to the north to Esmeraldas via Santo Domingo.

Those traveling to other destinations north and northwest need to head for either the new Carcelén terminal or La Ofelia terminal, both in the far north of Quito.

Trole, Ecovia, and Metrobus have extended their services to all three main bus terminals, running until midnight on weekdays and until 10 P.M. on weekends.

A few private bus companies have their own small departure terminals. **Panamericana Internacional** (Colón and Reina Victoria, tel. 2/255-1839) has service to Guayaquil (8 hours, $10), Machala and Huaquillas (13 hours, $11), Cuenca (10 hours, $10), Manta (9 hours, $10), Portoviejo (9 hours, $10), and Esmeraldas (6 hours, $9). **Flota Imbabura** (Larrea 1211 at Portoviejo, tel. 2/223-6940) has service to Cuenca, Guayaquil, and Manta. **Ecuatoriana** (Jorge Washington and Juan León Mera, tel. 2/222-5315) runs plush buses to Guayaquil. **Reina del Camino** serves Manabí from Pedernales to Puerto López, including Manta and Portoviejo, from its terminal (18 Septiembre and Larrea).

The new northern terminal at Ofelia, which is only for county buses, is where **Coop Pichincha** serves Guayllabamba and El Quinche; **San José de Minas** serves the northwest (Nanegal, Minas, Chontal, Cielo Verde); **Flor de Valle** goes to Cayambe, Pacto, and Mindo; **Transportes Otavalo** doesn't go to Otavalo—only Minas and Pacto; and **Malchingui** and **Cangahua** run buses to various locations. Ofelia is the end of the Metrovia city bus route, and dozens of connections spread out from here into the northern parishes. The terminal is clean, organized, and well signposted. The Mitad del Mundo buses come through here—use your existing bus ticket and pay just $0.15 extra for the transfer.

Rental Cars and Motorcycles

Renting a car may be a good way to get out of the city, but take into account the convenience and cheapness of buses as well as the many vagaries of driving in Ecuador. It's definitely not the way to see the city.

Small cars start at $50 per day. Several major car-rental companies operate in Quito:

- **Avis:** at the airport, tel. 2/601-6000, www.avis.com.ec
- **Bombuscaro:** at the airport, tel. 2/330-3304, www.bombuscarorentacar.com
- **Budget:** Colón 1140 at Amazonas, tel. 2/223-7026, www.budget-ec.com
- **Hertz:** at the airport, tel. 2/225-4257, www.hertz.com

Other options include **Safari Tours** (Foch E4-132 at Cordero, tel. 2/255-2505, fax 2/222-3381, tel./fax 2/222-0426, www.safari.com.ec), which has some 4WD vehicles and drivers available to head into the mountains, and it can arrange larger cars and buses for groups. **Ecuadorian Alpine Institute** (Ramírez Dávalos 136 at Amazonas, Suite 102, tel. 2/256-5465, fax 2/256-8949, eai@ecuadorexplorer.com, www.volcanoclimbing.com) has 4WD vehicles as well.

For motorcycles, try American-owned **Ecuador Freedom Bike Rental** (Juan León Mera N22-37 at Veintimilla, tel. 2/250-4339, www.freedombikerental.com), which has recently opened in Mariscal, offering a range of motorcycles as well as mountain bikes for rent. Guided tours or self-guided tours with a GPS unit are available. Always wear a helmet and be careful.

Trains

Quito's **Chimbacalle train station** (Sincholagua and Maldonado) is a few kilometers south of Old Town. The trolley is the easiest way to reach it, and the Chimbacalle stop is right at the station, which is a delightful step back in time.

At present there are services from Quito to Boliche, Machachi, and Latacunga (4 hours, $10). The route is being extended to Riobamba to link up with the Devil's Nose route and will continue all the way to Guayaquil by the end of 2013.

GETTING AROUND
Local Buses

If you traveling a relatively simple route, local

© BEN WESTWOOD

Quito's train service will soon run all the way to Guayaquil.

BUSES FROM QUITO TERMINALS

FROM QUITUMBE

Ambato	2.5 hours	$2.70
Atacames	7 hours	$8
Baños	3 hours	$3.70
Coca	9 hours	$10
Cuenca	9 hours	$12
Esmeraldas	6 hours	$7
Guaranda	5 hours	$4.50
Guayaquil	8 hours	$8
Lago Agrio	9 hours	$8
Latacunga	1.5 hours	$1.70
Macas	7 hours	$8
Puyo	5 hours	$5
Santo Domingo	3 hours	$3
Tena	5 hours	$6

FROM CARCELÉN

Atacames	7 hours	$8
Esmeraldas	6 hours	$7
Ibarra	2.5 hours	$2.50
Los Bancos (indirect to Mindo)	2 hours	$2.50
Otavalo	2 hours	$2.50
Tulcán	5 hours	$5

FROM OFELIA

Cayambe	1.5 hours	$1.50
Mindo (direct)	2 hours	$2.50
Mitad del Mundo (via the Metrobus line)	1.5 hours	$0.40

buses can be useful. The routes are rather complicated, so it's best to take short journeys along the major roads, especially Amazonas and 10 de Agosto. It's a good idea to ask a local at the bus stop which bus number goes to your destination. For more complex journeys, you're better off taking the trolley systems or a taxi.

Any of 10 de Agosto's major crossroads, including Patria, Orellana, and Naciones Unidas, are likely places to find a bus heading south to Old Town or north as far as the turn to Mitad del Mundo. "La Y," the meeting of 10 de Agosto with América and De la Prensa, is a major bus intersection, as is Parque Huayna Capac at 6 de Diciembre and El Inca. The flat fare is $0.25. Have it ready, and take care with your belongings on crowded buses.

Trolley Systems

Quito's network of three electric trolley buses is the best of its kind in Ecuador: It is cheap, clean, fast, and well-organized. The buses are separated from ordinary traffic to avoid delays. Flat fare for all services is $0.25, payable at kiosks or machines on entry. Cars pass every 5–10 minutes.

El Trole (5:30 A.M.–11:30 P.M. Mon.–Fri., 6 A.M.–10 P.M. Sat.–Sun.) runs north–south from Estación Norte north of New Town near La Y, south past stops at Mariscal and Colón, through Old Town past Chimbacalle train station, to the new southern bus terminal at Quitumbe. It takes about an hour to get to Quitumbe from New Town. The main *trole* thoroughfare, 10 de Agosto, reserves a pair of center lanes for the service, detouring down Guayaquil and Maldonado in Old Town, then continuing on Maldonado south of El Panecillo.

The **Ecovia** (6 A.M.–10 P.M. Mon.–Fri., 6 A.M.–9:30 P.M. Sat.–Sun.) is similar, but without the overhead wires. It also runs north–south from its northern Río Coca terminal along 6 de Diciembre past La Casa de la Cultura to La Marín near Old Town. Most trolleys turn around at La Marín, where there are interchanges with many country bus routes to the south and the valley; an extension continues past the exit of the old Cumandá bus terminal to Avenida Napo.

The third line, called **Metrobus** (5:30 A.M.– 10:30 P.M. Mon.–Fri., 6 A.M.–10 P.M. Sat.– Sun.), runs from La Marín in Old Town up Santa Prisca and along Avenida América, La Prensa, and north to both the Ofelia and Carcelén terminals, where there are connections to the northern highlands, cloud forest, and northern coast. It takes about 40 minutes to get to these terminals from New Town.

If you want to bypass Quito by traveling between Carcelén in the north and Quitumbe in the south, there is now a direct shuttle service.

It all seems too good to be true, and in one sense, it is: Unfortunately, all of the trolley lines are notorious for highly skilled **pickpockets,** and foreign visitors are easy targets. If you're going sightseeing with your camera, avoid crowded services and consider taking a taxi. Don't take valuables or large amounts of cash on the bus, and if possible, avoid traveling at peaks times in morning or late-afternoon rush hour.

For further information on the trolleybuses, visit www.trolebus.gov.ec.

Taxis

Digital meters are required in taxis by law. Many drivers will pretend that the meters are out of order (*"no funciona"*), in which case you should offer to find another cab. Saying this has a strange tendency to fix malfunctioning meters instantly, although many drivers will refuse to use them, even though that's illegal. Meters start at $0.35, with a $1 minimum charge, and run except when the cab is stopped. Rides within Old Town and New Town shouldn't be more than $2.50 during the day. Prices increase at night, but shouldn't be more than double. Drivers are particularly reluctant to use the meter for longer trips to the bus terminals. Rates tend to vary from $5 to Carcelén and Ofelia to $8 to Quitumbe.

Freelance yellow taxi cabs prowl the streets, and various small taxi stands exist all over the city, especially in front of expensive hotels. These have a set price list for destinations and are usually more expensive than a metered ride. Note that prebooking a taxi from your hotel is by far the best option because the hotelier will use a reliable company. Otherwise, never take an unmarked cab, and in the case of yellow taxis, check for the orange license plate as well as the company name and registration on the side of the cab and on the windshield. The driver should also have an ID. Don't be afraid to ask for this (*"identidad"*) before getting in. All these precautions will minimize the risk of being a victim of crime, which has become more common in Quito taxis in recent years.

Radio taxis can be called at a moment's notice or arranged the day before. Try the **Central de Radio Taxi** (tel. 2/250-0600 or 2/252-1112) or **Taxi Amigo** (tel. 2/222-2222 or 2/222-2220). Both are reliable and available at any hour. **Taxis Lagos de Ibarra** (Asunción 381 at Versalles, tel. 2/256-5992) sends five-passenger taxis to Ibarra for $8 pp, or to Otavalo for $7.50 pp. **Sudamericana Taxis** (tel. 2/275-2567) sends cabs to Santo Domingo or stops along the way, such as La Hesperia or Tinalandia, for $15 pp.

Vicinity of Quito

CALDERÓN

Just nine kilometers from Quito's northern suburbs, artisans in this tiny town craft figures out of a varnished bread dough called *masapan*. This technique, unique to Ecuador until Play-Doh came along, originated with the annual making of bread babies for Day of the Dead celebrations in November. Artisans in Calderón developed more elaborate and lasting figures, adding salt and carpenter's glue, and the villagers gradually created new techniques. With the introduction of aniline dyes, the *masa* became colored.

Today, Calderón is filled with artisan's shops and private houses that turn out the figurines by the hundreds. Tiny indigenous dolls called *cholas* stand in formation on tables and shelves next to brightly painted parrots, llamas, fish, and flowers. Each flour-paste figure is molded by hand or rolled and cut with a pasta maker and pastry cutter. They are then dried, painted, and varnished. The figures make unusual, inexpensive gifts and are popular as Christmas ornaments. Models of Nativity scenes, Santa Claus figures, and decorated trees are sold

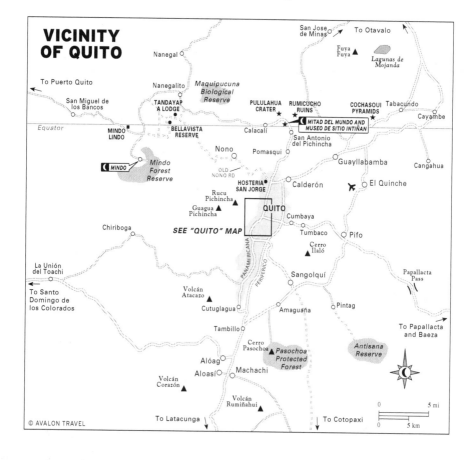

© AVALON TRAVEL

along the main street. Buses for Calderón leave regularly from the Ofelia terminal.

GUAYLLABAMBA AND VICINITY

Past Calderón, on the road to Cayambe and Otavalo, this small town on the river of the same name is home to the best zoo in the country.

Quito Zoo (tel. 2/236-8898, 8:30 A.M.–5 P.M. Tues.–Fri., 9 A.M.–4 P.M. Sat.–Sun., $4), which opened in 1997, is now considered one of the most spacious zoos in Latin America. The largest collection of native fauna in the country occupies the 12-hectare spread, including several animals rescued from the illegal fur trade. The focus is on mammals such as spectacled bears, wolves, monkeys, and pumas; this is also your best chance to see the elusive jaguar, so difficult to spot in the wild. Macaws, parrots, eagles, Andean condors, and toucans represent native birds, and a dozen Galápagos tortoises complete the collection. The zoo is three kilometers from the center of town—take a taxi ($1.25), or it's

a long 40-minute walk uphill. Tours are available for $5.

El Quinche

Six kilometers away, through the dry, eroded landscape south of Guayllabamba, is the village of El Quinche. The town's ornate church and sanctuary dedicated to the Virgin of Quinche draw crowds of pilgrims from Quito in search of the Virgin's blessing year-round, and especially at processions honoring the Virgin held on November 21. The shrine is thought to grant special protection to truck and taxi drivers. From here, you can follow the road south to Pifo, then west into Quito's valley suburbs and up into the city.

El Quinche will be on the tourist map from 2012, when Quito's new airport is expected to open just outside town. Visit www.quiport.com for further information.

◖ MITAD DEL MUNDO

You can't come to a country that's named after the Equator and not stand with a foot

Take a photo at Mitad del Mundo with a foot in each hemisphere.

QUITO

in each hemisphere; a visit to "The Middle of the World" complex is the most popular day trip near Quito. La Mitad del Mundo tourism complex (tel. 2/239-5637, 9 A.M.–6 P.M. Mon.–Fri., 9 A.M.–8 P.M. Sat.–Sun., www.mitaddelmundo.com, $3) lies just beyond the village of **Pomasqui,** 14 kilometers north of the city.

The centerpiece is a 30-meter-high monument topped by a huge brass globe; a bright red line bisecting it provides the backdrop for the obligatory photo. However, whisper it quietly—the real Equator is actually a few hundred meters away.

It costs an extra $3 to go inside the monument, but it's well worth it for the excellent **ethnographic museum.** Ascend to the top in an elevator for impressive views over the surrounding valley, and then descend the stairs through nine floors of colorful exhibitions on a dozen of Ecuador's diverse indigenous cultures, filled with clothing and artwork. Tours are available in English and Spanish.

The rest of the complex has an assortment of attractions, some more interesting than others. The **France building** is the best, with a well-presented exhibition on the expedition led by Charles Marie de La Condamine to plot the Equator in the mid-18th century. Another highlight is the intricate model of colonial Quito in the **Fundación Quito Colonial** ($1.50). The three-square-meter model took almost seven years to build and has labeled streets. Models of Cuenca, Guayaquil, and various old ships are also part of the display. There is also a **planetarium** with 40-minute presentations in Spanish ($1.50), artwork in the **Spain building,** and a small exhibition on insects in the **Ecuador room.** The **Heroes del Cenepa** monument near the entrance is dedicated to the soldiers killed in border clashes with Peru in 1995.

On the weekend, the square hosts colorful music and dance performances, and it's a very pleasant place to relax over lunch or a snack in the cluster of cafés.

Tourist agencies offer package tours to Pululahua and Rumicucho. **Calimatours** (tel.

2/239-4796 or 2/239-4797), with an office inside the Mitad del Mundo complex, has tours leaving 10 A.M.–1 P.M. for $8 pp.

To get here, take the Metrobus on Avenida América to the Ofelia terminal and catch the connecting Mitad del Mundo bus.

Museo de Sitio Intiñan

If you've come all this way to stand on the Equator, it's a bit of a shock to hear that the Mitad del Mundo complex was built in the wrong place by a few hundred meters. Understandably, this is kept rather quiet, and you could easily miss the excellent **Museo de Sitio Intiñan** (tel. 2/239-5122, www.museointinan.com.ec, 9:30 A.M.–5 P.M. daily, $3). Located about 300 meters east of the Mitad del Mundo complex, its name means "Museum of the Path of the Sun" in Kichwa, and the family that owns and operates it has done a great job with the collection, which includes displays on local plants and indigenous cultures. However, the real reason to come here

The Equator is actually at Museo de Sitio Intiñan.

are the experiments that you are invited to participate in to prove this really is the site of the Equator—flushing water in opposite directions on either side of the line, walking along the line and feeling the strong gravitational pull on either side, and the nearly impossible task of balancing an egg on the Equator (you get a certificate if you can do it).

Pululahua Crater and Geobotanical Reserve

About five kilometers north of Mitad del Mundo, the 3,200-hectare Pululahua Reserve ($5 pp) sits inside an extinct volcanic crater. Pululahua bubbled with lava thousands of years ago, but these days the main activity is that of farmers who reside in its flat, fertile bottom. The reserve was officially created in 1978 to protect the rich subtropical ecosystem within one of the largest inhabited craters in South America and possibly the world.

Regular buses and taxis take the road from the base of Mitad del Mundo's pedestrian avenue toward the village of Calacalí. Along the way, a dirt lane leaves the road to the right, after the gas station, and climbs to the lip of the crater at Moraspungo. You can also hike to Pululahua up a road between San Antonio de Pichincha and Calacalí, passing the Ventanilla viewpoint; this becomes a path that continues down into the crater.

El Crater (Pululahua, tel./fax 2/243-9254, from $91 s or d) is a hotel that perches on the edge of the crater. The panoramic view from the large windows justifies the prices of its restaurant (lunch and dinner daily, entrées $9–12). There's also a smaller café that sells drinks and snacks.

A few hours' hike will bring you to the bottom of the crater and left up the Calacalí road to a very basic **hikers refuge,** where you can spend the night; the stay is included with your admission to the reserve. Bring your own food, because there aren't any restaurants in the crater, and bring your own bedding. Hike over the rims to rejoin the paved road to Calacalí

© QUITO TURISMO

The dramatic descent into the Pululahua crater makes a great hike.

MEASURING THE EARTH

By 1735, most people agreed that the earth was round, but another question remained: *how* round was it? Some scientists theorized that the rotation of the earth caused it to bulge outward slightly in the middle, while others found that idea ridiculous. With explorers setting out daily to the far corners of the globe, it became more and more important to determine how much, if any, the earth bulged in the middle, since navigational charts off by a few degrees could send ships hundreds of kilometers in the wrong direction.

To answer the long-standing debate, the French Academy of Sciences organized two expeditions to determine the true shape of the earth. One team headed north to Lapland, as close to the Arctic as possible. The other left for Ecuador on the equator. Each team was tasked with measuring one degree of latitude, about 110 kilometers, in its respective region. If the length of the degree at the equator proved longer than the degree near the Arctic, then the earth bulged. If they were the same length, it didn't.

The Ecuadorian expedition was the first organized scientific expedition to South America. At the time, Ecuador was part of the Spanish territory of Upper Peru. It was chosen because of its accessibility – much easier to visit than alternate locations along the equator in the Amazon basin, Africa, and Southeast Asia. The Ecuadorian expedition was led by academy members Louis Godin, Pierre Bouguer, and Charles Marie de La Condamine.

With them came seven other Frenchmen, including a doctor-botanist, Godin's cousin, a surgeon, a naval engineer, and a draftsman.

Tensions hampered the expedition from the start, as Bouguer and La Condamine quickly learned they did not get along. Bouguer was stern, stoic, and accused of being paranoid about competitors, while La Condamine, a protégé of Voltaire, was comparatively easy-going. This personal rivalry sparked numerous quarrels as the extroverted, enthusiastic La Condamine effectively assumed leadership of the expedition.

The group arrived in Cartagena, Colombia, in 1735. There they were joined by two Spaniards, both naval captains under secret orders from the king of Spain to report back on the French expedition and conditions in the Spanish territories. In March 1736 the party sailed into Ecuador's Pacific port of Manta and soon traveled via Guayaquil to Quito. Quiteños received the earth measurers with delight, and dances and receptions filled the days following their arrival. As the festivities continued, Pedro Vicente Maldonado, an Ecuadorian mapmaker and mathematician, was chosen to join the historic expedition.

Eventually, the group got down to business. For the sake of accuracy, it was decided that the measurements would be made in the flat plains near Yaruquí, 19 kilometers northeast of Quito. As the work progressed, troubles mounted. The French and Spanish, unused to the elevation and the cold of the Sierra, began

---

(10–15 kilometers, 3–4 hours), where you can catch a bus back to the Mitad del Mundo. It's also possible to circle the crater rim on foot. **Horseback tours** of the crater are available through Astrid Müller's **Green Horse Ranch** (tel. 9/971-5933, ranch@accessinter.net, www. horseranch.de) in Quito.

Rumicucho Ruins

Often tacked onto the end of tours of the area, the modest pre-Inca Rumicucho Ruins (7:30 A.M.–5 P.M. daily, $1 pp) consist of a

series of rough stone walls and terraces on a small hilltop with a commanding view of the windswept surroundings. To get here, take 13 de Junio (the main drag) northeast from San Antonio de Pichincha, then turn right at the Rumicucho sign. It's quite hard to find, so ask around locally or take a taxi.

THE PICHINCHAS

The twin peaks that give the province its name tower over Quito, dominating the landscape as much as the city's history. It was on the flanks to fall ill. Soon the group suffered its first death: the nephew of the academy's treasurer, one of the youngest team members.

As the mourning scientists wandered the plains with their strange instruments, local residents grew suspicious. Rumors began circulating that they had come to dig up and steal buried treasure, maybe even Inca gold. The situation became so tense that La Condamine and a fellow member of the expedition were forced to travel to Lima to obtain the viceroy's support. They finally returned in July 1737 with official papers supporting their story. The measurements continued, and by 1739 the goal of determining the true shape of the earth was in sight. Then disastrous news arrived from the academy: The Lapland expedition had succeeded. The earth was flattened at the poles. The verdict was already in.

As La Condamine tried to keep the expedition from disintegrating, more bad luck struck. The party surgeon, Juan Seniergues, became involved in a dispute over a Cuencan woman and was beaten and stabbed to death at a bullfight in the Plaza de San Sebastián by an angry mob sympathetic to his local rival, the woman's former fiancé. The rest of the group sought refuge in a monastery. In the confusion, the team botanist, Joseph de Jussieu, lost his entire collection of plants – representing five years' work, this loss eventually cost him his sanity as well. The team draftsman was then killed in a fall from a church steeple near Riobamba. La Condamine had to fend off accu-sations from the Spanish crown that he had insulted Spain by omitting the names of the two Spanish officers from commemorative plaques he had already erected at Oyambaro.

Finally, in March 1743, the remaining scientists made the last measurements, confirming the Lapland expedition's findings and bringing the expedition to an end. Even though they had come in second, the group's efforts did lay the foundation for the entire modern metric system. Some members decided to stay on in Ecuador – two had already married local women – while others traveled to different South American countries. Most went back to Europe. La Condamine, accompanied by Maldonado, rode a raft down the Amazon for four months to the Atlantic Ocean. From there, the pair sailed to Paris, where they brought the first samples of rubber seen in Europe and were welcomed as heroes. Maldonado died of measles in 1748, while La Condamine enjoyed the high life in Paris until his death in 1774.

In 1936, on the 200th anniversary of the expedition's arrival in Ecuador, the Ecuadorian government built a stone pyramid on the equator at San Antonio de Pichincha in honor of the explorers and their work. This pyramid was eventually replaced by the 30-meter-tall monument that stands today at Mitad del Mundo. Busts along the path leading to the monument commemorate the 10 Frenchmen, two Spaniards, and one Ecuadorian who risked their lives – and sanity – for science.

of these volcanoes that Ecuador won its independence in 1822. Both are named Pichincha, which is thought to come from indigenous words meaning "the weeper of good water." **Rucu** (Elder) is actually shorter (4,700 meters) and nearer to the city, while **Guagua** (Baby) stands 4,794 meters high and has always been the more poorly behaved of the two.

Climbing Rucu is easier and more accessible, requiring no special equipment. Unfortunately, the trail to Rucu has been plagued by robberies in recent years. The opening of the *telefériqo* (cable car) has led to increased security, but it is wise to inquire locally about the current situation. Currently there are security patrols on the route from Cruz Loma on the weekend but not during the week.

Guagua sat quiet following an eruption in 1660 until October 1999, when it blew out a huge mushroom cloud of ash that blotted out the sun over Quito for a day and covered the capital in ash. Although things seem to have calmed down, you should still check for the latest update on Guagua, which is officially highly active.

Private transportation—preferably a 4WD vehicle—is almost essential to reach Guagua, the farther peak. The starting point is the pueblo of **Lloa,** southwest of Quito. A dirt road leaves the main plaza and heads up the valley between the Pichinchas, ending in a shelter maintained by the national civil defense directorate. Park here, pay the entry fee ($1), which goes toward the guardian's salary, and don't leave anything of value in the car. Sleeping space for 10 people costs $5 pp per night, including running water and cooking facilities.

Another hour's hike will bring you from the shelter to the summit. The west-facing crater is pocked by smoking fumaroles, active domes, and collapsed craters. A rocky protrusion called the Cresta del Gallo (Rooster's Crest) separates the old inactive side to the south from the newer active area to the north. Several climbing tour operators in Quito offer this trip.

HOSTERÍA SAN JORGE

Four kilometers up the road from Cotocollao to Nono in a 93-hectare mountain reserve is Hostería San Jorge (Vía Antigua a Nono Km. 4, tel. 2/224-7549, www.hostsanjorge.com. ec, $67 s, $73 d), run by the friendly and enthusiastic George Cruz. The traditional country house, once owned by former Ecuadorian president Eloy Alfaro, offers wonderful views of the Quito valley from 3,000 meters up the Pichincha foothills. Gardens, a lake, and a spring-fed swimming pool and hot tub surround the guest rooms warmed by fireplaces on chilly evenings. It is a good place to acclimate, and the owners offer a wealth of activities, including birding in the backyard and treks on pre-Inca trails to the coast. The Mindo and Nono areas are within mountain-biking distance. You can get here by taxi or call for pickup.

SANGOLQUÍ

Corn is king in this town southeast of Quito. A 10-meter statue of a cob, called "El Choclo," greets visitors in a traffic circle at the entrance. In late June, festivities mark the end of the harvest. During the fourth and final day, bullfights become venues for raging displays of machismo as alcohol-numbed locals try to get as close to the bull as possible without getting killed—unsurprisingly, someone usually gets injured. The central plaza area has been beautifully restored, and the town hosts an excellent indigenous market on Sundays and a smaller one on Thursdays. To get here, take a "Sangolquí" bus from the local terminal at Marin Bajo.

PASOCHOA PROTECTED FOREST

The densest, most unspoiled stretch of forest close to Quito is the Pasochoa Protected Forest (open daily, $5 pp), 30 kilometers southeast of the city. A long sloping valley preserves the original lush wooded state of the area surrounding Quito. The reserve ranges 2,700–4,200 meters in elevation, the highest point being Cerro Pasochoa, an extinct volcano. Primary and secondary forest topped by *páramo* supports 126 species of birds, including many hummingbirds and a family of condors.

Loop paths of varying lengths and difficulty lead higher and higher into the hills, ranging 2–8 hours in length. It's also possible to climb to the lip of Cerro Pasochoa's blasted volcanic crater in six hours. Campsites and a few dorm rooms with showers and cooking facilities are available near the bottom. Free guided tours are sometimes available.

To get here from Quito, take a bus marked "Playón" from the south end of the Plaza La Marín below Old Town to the village of Amaguaña (30–40 minutes, $0.60). Hire a pickup ($5–8) from the plaza in Amaguaña to the turnoff for the reserve, which is marked by a green sign facing south one kilometer toward Machachi on the Panamericana. From there, a dirt road leads seven kilometers up a rough, cobbled road to the reserve. Drivers may agree to come back for you, or you could catch a ride down with the reserve personnel in the evening. Take a phone card, and you can call from the cell phone at the entrance for a taxi to pick you up.

Some tour operators in Quito offer group day trips to Pasochoa.

QUITO

◖ MINDO

Set in a tranquil valley at an ideal elevation of 1,250 meters, surrounded by dense cloud forest teeming with birdlife, this small village has blossomed in recent years into Ecuador's best hub for bird-watchers. More than 400 bird species found in the surrounding forest include toucans, barbets, golden-headed quetzals, and hummingbirds galore, and there are also 250 species of butterflies and 80 species of orchids. Mindo isn't all about watching the trees, however; you can also fly through them on canopy zip-lines if you want a more action-packed trip.

Almost 21,000 hectares of forest, from tropical rainforest to *páramo,* fall within the **Mindo-Nambillo Protected Forest,** to the east and south of town. The rushing Mindo, Nambillo, and Cinto Rivers drain the area, and there are several waterfalls near Mindo. It's relatively easy to explore parts of the forest alone, but for a better-quality experience, particularly for bird-watchers, hiring a local guide is recommended.

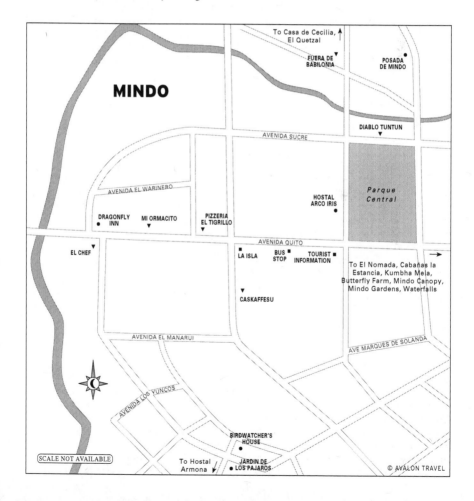

© AVALON TRAVEL

Mindo is still a relatively low-key place and retains a village atmosphere with few cars. However, more and more hotels are springing up in town and the surrounding area, and Mindo fills up on the weekend with day-trippers from Quito, so consider coming during the week for a quieter experience.

Recreation and Tours

Mindo is filled with knowledgeable **bird-watching guides** who can lead you through the forests at dawn to see toucans and quetzals and also up to leks where brilliant crimson-colored Andean cock-of-the-rock males compete for females. Most guides charge small groups $50 for half-day trips and $100 for a full day. Vinicio Pérez, owner of the **Birdwatchers House** (Colibries, tel. 2/217-0204 or 9/947-6867, vinicioperez@birdwatchershouse.com), is highly recommended. Other recommended guides include Marcelo Arias at **Ruby Birdwatcher's Place** (tel. 9/340-6321), Danny Jumbo (tel. 9/328-0796), and Julia Patiño (tel. 8/616-2816). For extended bird-watching tours in Mindo and elsewhere in Ecuador, contact **Andean Birding** (Salazar Gómez E-1482 at Eloy Alfaro, tel. 9/418-4592, www.andeanbirding.com) in Quito.

A German-Ecuadorian couple owns seven hectares of land uphill from Mindo called **Mindo Lindo** (tel. 9/291-5840, www.mindolindo.com), which offers easier access to the cloud forest than other properties in town. They charge $4 pp to use the trails and $20 pp for accommodations.

Southeast of town is the best access point into the **Bosque Protector Mindo-Nambillo** cloud forest. The road leads past several sets of accommodations before splitting. Take the left fork to reach the butterfly farm **Mariposas de Mindo** (www.mariposasdemindo.com, 9 A.M.–6:30 P.M. daily, $5), which breeds 25 species, including the brown owl eye and the Peleides blue morpho, the latter with a wingspan of 20 centimeters. The tour follows the life cycle from eggs to caterpillars to pupae to butterflies. Come in the early morning and you may see them hatch.

Where the road forks, walk up to the right to reach two sets of canopy-tour operators. The second company you come to, **Mindo Canopy Adventure** (tel. 8/542-8758, www.mindocanopy.com) was actually the first to bring their expert knowledge of zip-lines from Costa Rica in 2006. The company is fully accredited and has an excellent safety record. There are a total of 13 lines ranging up to 400 meters in length and 120 meters in height. You can spend 1.5 hours zipping across all 13 for $10 or do three lines for $5. Try out the "superman" or "butterfly" poses for extra fun. There is also a new "extreme Tarzan" swing, a 40-meter-long pendulum. The newer company, local-run **Mindo Ropes and Canopy** (tel. 9/172-5874, www.mindoropescanopy.com), offers 10 zip-lines for $10. A taxi from town costs $3.

If you haven't had your fill of adrenaline kicks, an unusual alternative to rafting is **tubing**—tumbling down the river rapids in an inflatable tube. This can be arranged with any of the agencies in Mindo ($8 pp).

About one kilometer up the hill from the canopy companies is a more relaxed way to travel across the treetops. The **La Tarabita** ($5 pp) cable car cruises 150 meters above a river basin, and on the far side there are trails leading to seven **waterfalls.** Although the paths are not well marked, you're unlikely to get lost because the route is circular. The entire circuit takes about two hours, and it gets muddy in places. Bring boots and waterproof clothing as there is regular rainfall. Access to the waterfall trails is included in the cost of the cable car. There is another waterfall on the opposite side, **Tambillo** ($3 pp), where you can swim or slide downstream. Walking up to La Tarabita and the waterfalls takes about an hour from town, so consider taking a taxi ($7).

A recommended tour operator that can organize all of these activities, including transportation, is **La Isla** (Av. Quito, tel. 2/217-0181, www.laislamindo.com), which has an office on Mindo's main street.

In Mindo, it's worth heading up to **El Quetzal,** a hotel north of town on 9 de Octubre, to see how chocolate is made. For

$3.50 you get an hour-long explanation of the process and a free brownie, hot chocolate, or ice cream. West of town, **Mindo Lago** organizes an evening walk to listen to frogs (tel. 9/709-3544, www.mindolago.com.ec, 6:30 P.M. daily, $3.50).

Accommodations
IN MINDO
In the center of Mindo, the cheapest option is the **Hostal Arco Iris** (9 de Octubre, tel. 2/390-0405, $9 pp) on the plaza. On the main Avenida Quito, as you arrive in town, **The Dragonfly Inn** (Quito and Sucre, tel. 2/217-0426, $27 s, $46 d), a new wooden cabin–style hotel, is a good mid-range choice, with balconies overlooking a garden patio along the river. For a more intimate setting, **(Caskaffesu** (Sixto Durán Ballén, tel. 2/217-0100, $16 s or d), run by an American-Ecuadorian couple, is a very good deal with cozy guest rooms, a leafy courtyard, and a good restaurant.

On the northern edge of town, **Casa de Cecilia** (north of 9 de Octubre, tel. 2/217-0243, $6.50–7.50 pp) is the best budget option, with guest rooms in two rustic cabins on the edge of a roaring river. Next door, **El Quetzal** (north of 9 de Octubre, tel. 2/217-0034, www.elquetzaldemindo.com, $17 pp, breakfast included) has three guest rooms and lots of chocolate made on the premises. **Posada de Mindo** (Vicente Aguirre, tel. 2/217-0199, $20 pp) has spotless new cabins with a good restaurant attached.

Walking southwest of the main street along Colibries are two great-value mid-range options. On the right, **Jardín de Los Pájaros** (Colibries, tel. 2/217-0159, $14 s, $26 d, breakfast included) has comfortable guest rooms, a balcony lounge, and a small heated pool. Across the street, **The Birdwatcher's House** (Colibries, tel. 2/217-0204, www.birdwatchershouse.com, $15 pp) has stunning photographs in the guest rooms, hummingbirds in the gardens, and an outdoor jetted tub. Farther down the street, another rustic place adjoining the soccer field is the friendly **Hostal Armonia** (Colibries, tel. 2/217-0131, $14 pp), which is

packed full of orchids and has private cabins with hot water. Nonguests can visit the impressive orchid garden ($2). The **Hostal Rubby** (tel. 2/217-0417 or 9/193-1853, $8–16 pp) has two classes of rooms and is in the process of moving to the edge of town.

VICINITY OF MINDO
Walking east of town toward the reserve, there are plenty of pleasant cabins set in the forest. The first is **Cabañas la Estancia** (tel. 9/878-3272, www.mindohosterialaestancia.com, $15 pp), with spacious cabins across a rickety bridge set in landscaped gardens with an outdoor restaurant, a swimming pool, and even a waterslide. Camping is available (from $3 pp). Deeper in the forest is **Kumbha Mela** (tel. 9/405-1675, dorm $16 pp, cabin $21 pp) with cabins and guest rooms nestled in extensive gardens. There's a good restaurant, a pool, and a private lagoon.

Past the Butterfly Farm is one of the best options in town, **(Mindo Gardens** (tel. 9/722-3260, www.mindogardens.com, $50–65 s or d, breakfast included), with comfy, brightly colored cabins on a 300-hectare private reserve of forest and waterfalls. There's a restaurant right on the Río Mindo, and the cabins have private baths with hot water.

Near the Mindo Gardens Lodge, **El Monte Sustainable Lodge** (tel. 2/217-0102, www.ecuadorcloudforest.com, $96 pp) is run by American Tom Quesenberry and his Ecuadorian wife, Mariela Tenorio. They offer three wooden cabins at the edge of the Río Mindo with hot water, private baths, and thatched roofs. Rates include all meals and birding guides for the hiking trails nearby. To reach the lodge, cross the river on a small cable car.

Food
Eating out in Mindo is far more varied than it used to be, and the main street, Avenida Quito, is lined with restaurants. The best of these is **El Chef** (Quito and Colibries, tel. 2/390-0478, 8 A.M.–8 P.M. daily, entrées $4–7), where the set lunch is great value at $2.50 and the specialty

is thick, juicy barbecued steak. Other options on Avenida Quito include **Mi Ormacito** (Av. Quito, no phone, lunch and dinner daily, entrées $4–5) for seafood, and the pizzeria **El Tigrillo** (Av. Quito, no phone, lunch and dinner daily, entrées $4–7) for Italian. Most of the best options are off the main street, however. For a more refined dining experience, try **Caskaffesu** (Sixto Durán Ballén and Quito, tel. 2/217-0100, 8 A.M.–10 P.M. daily, entrées $4–8) with steak, fish, and vegetarian dishes. East of the center is the best pizza in town, made in front of you in a wood-burning clay oven at **El Nómada** (Av. Quito, tel. 2/390-0460, noon–9 P.M. daily, entrées $6–9). North of town, **Fuera de Babilonia** (9 de Octubre, tel. 9/475-7768, 7:30 A.M.–9:30 P.M. daily, entrées $4–5) is great for seafood and local specialties like steamed trout. It is a funky little place with indigenous artifacts and misshapen tables, and it is a good place to hang out after dinner for a few drinks and listen to music. Nightlife in Mindo is limited, but on the weekend a few discos open in the center, including **Diablo Tuntun** (north end of Parque Central, no phone, 8 P.M.–2 A.M. Fri.–Sat., $1).

Information

There's a **Centro de Información** (8:30 A.M.–12:30 P.M. and 1:30–5 P.M. Wed.–Sun.) on Avenida Quito near the plaza. Ask for a list of members of the local naturalist guides association. Alternately, staff at **La Isla** (Av. Quito, tel. 2/217-0181, www.laislamindo.com) farther down the street are very helpful and knowledgeable.

Getting There

The road from Quito to Mindo runs west from Mitad del Mundo. It joins the old road just north of Mindo and continues west to Los Bancos and Puerto Quito. An eight-kilometer road connects Mindo to the main highway. Direct buses from Quito with the **Flor del Valle** cooperative leave at 8 A.M., 9 A.M., and 4 P.M. Monday–Friday; 7:40 A.M., 8:20 A.M., 9:20 A.M., and 4 P.M. Saturday; and 7:40 A.M., 8:20 A.M., 9:20 A.M., 2 P.M., and 5 P.M. Sunday. Daily buses return from Mindo to Quito at 6:30 A.M., 1:45 P.M., and 3 P.M. Monday–Friday; 6:30 A.M., 2 P.M., 3:30 P.M., and 5 P.M. Saturday, with extra buses at 3 P.M. and 4 P.M. Sunday.

If you miss the bus from Quito, take a taxi to Carcelén terminal and take the first bus to Los Bancos, which drops you on the main road at the top of the hill above Mindo, where you can catch a taxi (from $1). Leaving Mindo, take a taxi to the main road and flag down any Quito-bound bus.

THE ECUADORIAN ANDES

Quito is the best base to explore the Ecuadorian Andes, and there are many fascinating destinations that can be visited on day trips or longer if you have more time.

The northern highlands, which stretch from Quito to the Colombian border, contain spectacular mountain scenery and picturesque towns inhabited by thriving indigenous cultures. Otavalo's textile market, one of the most spectacular in South America, is the biggest draw in the region, and many of the smaller villages nearby specialize in particular crafts, so there are rich pickings on offer for those seeking handmade clothing, jewelry and ornaments. For nature-lovers, several spectacular lagoons are close by—notably Lagunas de Mojanda and the peak of Fuya Fuya, ideal for acclimation hikes.

South of Quito, the Central Highlands contain Ecuador's most dramatic Andean scenery. The Panamericana runs down between two parallel mountain chains along the famous "Avenue of the Volcanoes." There are so many peaks in this region that climbers are like children in a candy store, spoiled for choice on where to start. There's plenty for day hikers too, including Ecuador's most visited national park, Cotopaxi, and its most spectacular lake, the extinct Laguna Quilotoa, whose turquoise waters are a wonder to behold.

With the regeneration of the Quito–Guayaquil train line, exploring parts of the Central Sierra is easier than ever. The Avenue of the Volcanoes route between Quito and Latacunga is now open and the spectacular

© BEN WESTWOOD

THE ECUADORIAN ANDES

HIGHLIGHTS

◖ **Textile Market:** Otavalo's textile market, held every Saturday, is one of the best on the continent – patterned ponchos, sweaters, embroidered shirts, handmade jewelry, and felt hats are all on sale, so haggle away (page 67).

◖ **Lagunas de Mojanda and Fuya Fuya:** Explore these three beautiful lagoons high above the valley in the shadow of jagged mountains. Nearby Fuya Fuya is excellent practice for climbing more challenging peaks (page 76).

◖ **Cotopaxi National Park:** Ecuador's most popular mainland national park is home to llamas, wild horses, and the Andean condor, and it is dominated by the country's highest and most beautiful volcano (page 79).

◖ **Laguna Quilotoa:** The luminous turquoise water of this lake in an extinct volcano's caldera is one of Ecuador's most stunning sights, and the Quilotoa Loop around nearby indigenous villages is an unbeatable hike (page 90).

◖ **The Waterfall Route from Baños to Puyo:** Go cycling, hiking, rafting, and canyoneering to your heart's content in the Pastaza Valley before soaking in the thermal baths of this idyllic spa town nestled below Volcán Tungurahua (page 102).

◖ **Catedral Nueva:** Cuenca's historic center is dominated by the massive twin-towered facade and sky-blue domes of the new cathedral, a UNESCO World Heritage Site (page 105).

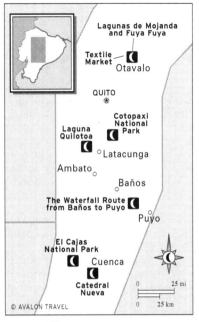

© AVALON TRAVEL

LOOK FOR ◖ TO FIND RECOMMENDED SIGHTS, ACTIVITIES, DINING, AND LODGING.

◖ **El Cajas National Park:** Only an hour from Cuenca, hike through rugged and chilly moorland, past jagged rocks and hundreds of lakes (page 118).

section descending La Nariz del Diablo, south of Riobamba, has reopened recently.

Away from the hustle and bustle is Ecuador's best spa town, Baños, a place so idyllic and relaxing that you may find it hard to leave.

Heading south, the towering mountains of the Central Highlands are replaced by undulating green hills. Everything is mellower down here—the climate warms up little by little as you move south and the people are well-known for their sweet temperaments and sing-song accents. Cuenca, Ecuador's

third city, is arguably its most beautiful with a stunning cathedral just one highlight of the UNESCO-protected historic center. The landscapes around Cuenca are equally appealing, particularly the rugged hills and lakes of national park of Cajas.

PLANNING YOUR TIME

The northern Sierra is the most compact Andean region. **Otavalo's textiles market** and other indigenous markets fill a day, while

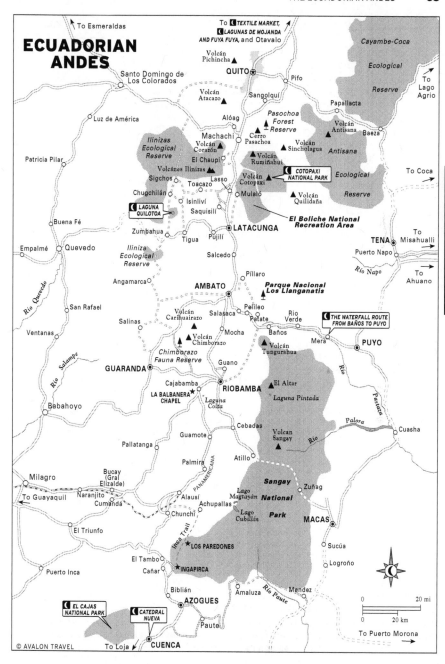

ECUADORIAN ANDES

To Esmeraldas

Santo Domingo de Los Colorados

Luz de América

Patricia Pilar

Buena Fé

Empalmé Quevedo

San Rafael

Ventanas

Babahoyo

Milagro

To Guayaquil Naranjito Bucay (Gral Elizalde)
Cumandá

El Triunfo

Puerto Inca

Volcán Pichincha

QUITO

Pifo

Volcán Atacazo

Sangolquí

Papallacta

Aláag

Machachi Cerro Pasachoa

Volcán Corazón

El Chaupi

Volcánes Ilinizas

Sigchos Lasso

Chugchilán Toacazo

Isinliví

LAGUNA QUILOTOA Saquisilí

Mulaló

Zumbahua Pujilí

Tigua

Salcedo

Angamarca

AMBATO

Píllaro

Salinas

Volcán Carihuairazo Salasaca Pelileo

Mocha Patate

Volcán Chimborazo

Guano

Guaranda

Cajabamba

LA BALBANERA CHAPEL

RIOBAMBA

Cebadas

Pallatanga

Guamote

Palmira

Alausí

Chunchi

El Tambo

Cañar

Biblián

EL CAJAS NATIONAL PARK

CATEDRAL NUEVA

To Loja **CUENCA**

Paute

AZOGUES

Amaluza

Mendez

MACAS

Sucúa

Logroño

To Textile Market, Lagunas de Mojanda and Fuya Fuya, and Otavalo

Cayambe-Coca

Ecological

Reserve

To Lago Agrio

Ilinizas Ecological Reserve

Pasochoa Forest Reserve

Volcán Sincholagua

Volcán Antisana

Baeza

Antisana

Volcán Rumiñahui

COTOPAXI NATIONAL PARK

Ecological

Reserve

To Coca

Volcán Cotopaxi

Volcán Quilidaña

El Boliche National Recreation Area

Iliniza Ecological Reserve

Parque Nacional Los Llanganatis

Río Verde

THE WATERFALL ROUTE FROM BAÑOS TO PUYO

Baños

Mera

PUYO

Volcán Tungurahua

TENA To Misahuallí

Puerto Napo

Río Napo

To Ahuano

Chimborazo Fauna Reserve

El Altar

Laguna Pintada

Laguna Colta

Volcán Sangay

Atillo

Lago Magtayán

Zuñag

Lago Cubillín

Sangay National Park

LOS PAREDONES

INGAPIRCA

Inca Trail

Achupallas

Cuasha

Palora

Río Paute

To Puerto Morona

0 20 mi

0 20 km

© AVALON TRAVEL

hikes to **Lagunas de Mojanda** take a day or two.

In the Central Sierra, by far the most popular destination is **Baños,** which doubles as both the adventure and spa capital of the region, with adrenaline and relaxation available in equal measure. It's best to spend a couple of days here, and don't be surprised if you stay longer than planned. **Cotopaxi,** Ecuador's picture-perfect volcano is also hugely popular, both as a day trip to the national park and as a climb (only if you are acclimated and prepared) over two or three days. The turquoise waters of **Laguna Quilotoa** are jaw-droppingly beautiful and can be visited on a day trip or overnight, but it's better to take your time and do at least a portion of the hike along the **Quilotoa Loop.**

The renovated train system is another highlight of this region. A new route has opened recently between Quito and Latacunga, which makes a pleasant day trip.

The southern Sierra is too far from Quito to do as a day trip unless you fly. **Cuenca,** with its historic center and museums, will take up a day or two. From there, add on another day to include a trip to the misty lakes and rugged, cold hills of **El Cajas National Park,** which offers excellent hiking; more serious hikers might consider staying overnight.

Otavalo and Vicinity

Despite its modest size, Otavalo (pop. 43,000) hosts the biggest textiles market in Ecuador and one of the most famous in South America. The market is a permanent fixture in the Plaza de Ponchos, but every Saturday the stalls spread out across the town, and thousands of locals and visitors mix it up in a festival of buying, selling, and haggling.

The unique local indigenous group, the Otavaleños, dominate the town, and much of the local population is dedicated to making and selling textiles, handicrafts, jewelry, and ceramics. Their textiles and indigenous music are carried around the world. There is so much to buy that shopaholics may consider leaving a trip to Otavalo until the end of their Ecuador visit to avoid dragging their purchases around the rest of the country.

Otavalo is not just about shopping, however, and there's plenty to keep you occupied in the vicinity. The setting of the town is very attractive, nestled at 2,530 meters in the verdant Valle del Amanecer (Valley of the Sunrise) between two dormant volcanoes: Cotacachi to the northwest and Imbabura to the east. Both peaks offer climbing opportunities, and there is great hiking around several stunning lakes close to town.

Otavalo is one of the oldest towns in Imbabura Province and was a market town long before the Incas arrived. After the Spanish conquest, exploitation of the local craftspeople pervaded, and they were forced to work in sweatshops in terrible conditions. Independence did little to improve matters with the equally oppressive *huasipungo* system, in which indigenous people labored in exchange for access to tiny farm plots. In the 19th century, mass production switched to factories, but handmade products remained popular. It wasn't until 1964 that the exploitation was outlawed by the Agrarian Reform Law and indigenous people were given land and control over their choice of work. Since then, textiles have become the product of choice, earning the Otavaleños global fame and quality of life that is worlds apart from most other indigenous groups in South America. It's easy to see that there is wealth here, with the younger generation driving shiny new 4WD vehicles blasting contemporary music in the streets in the early evening. The indigenous heritage is still dominant in Otavalo, however, and locals wear their distinctive hats, ponchos, embroidered shirts, and blouses with pride.

Sadly, the large number of visitors has led to occasional robberies, although far less frequently than in Quito. Never leave your hotel

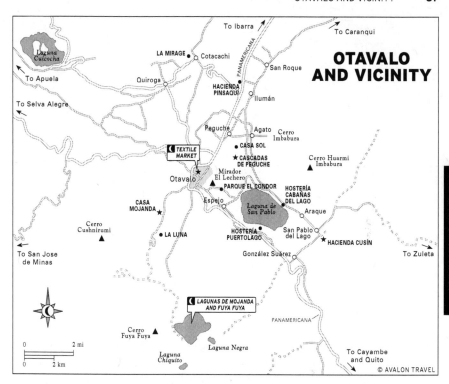

room unlocked, and be careful of bag-slashers and pickpockets in the crowded Saturday market. You should also be careful on the bus between Otavalo and Quito. When exploring the area's trails and more remote locations, it's better to travel in groups or on guide-led tours because lone hikers have occasionally been robbed. On the whole, however, the streets of Otavalo are safe at night.

SIGHTS
Textile Market

The town's biggest draw, and the reason you probably can't find a hotel room on Friday night, is the Saturday textile market. Vendors from town and surrounding villages set up shop well before dawn. By 8 A.M. the animal market is under way, and soon the Plaza de Ponchos is packed with a brightly colored, murmuring throng of vendors and visitors

haggling over every imaginable type of textile and craft. The market has become so successful that it is now open daily, and there's a wider choice of wares any day of the week than in other market towns. The Saturday market is still the biggest, though, and it's worth experiencing the hustle and bustle even if you don't intend to buy anything.

Anything made out of wool, cotton, or synthetic yarn can be found here in all shapes and sizes, including for infants. Clothing is the most popular buy: Thick wool and alpaca sweaters keep out the cold and come in interesting patterns; pajama-style thin cotton trousers come in every color imaginable; embroidered shirts, blouses, skirts, and wool mittens are popular; and rather less traditional is a huge range of T-shirts with Ecuadorian-themed designs. Carpets and blankets are often covered in llama designs, and wall hangings,

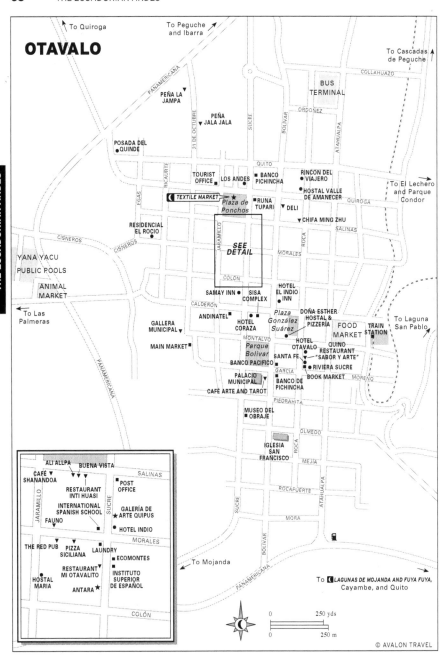

OTAVALO

To Quiroga

To Peguche and Ibarra

To Cascadas de Peguche

COLLAHUAZO

PANAMERICANA

PEÑA LA JAMPA

PEÑA JALA JALA

31 DE OCTUBRE

SUCRE

BOLIVAR

ATAHUALPA

BUS TERMINAL

ORDONEZ

POSADA DEL QUINDE

QUITO

RICAURTE

TOURIST OFFICE

LOS ANDES

BANCO PICHINCHA

RINCÓN DEL VIAJERO

HOSTAL VALLE DE AMANECER

To El Lechero and Parque Condor

TEXTILE MARKET

Plaza de Ponchos

RUNA TUPARI

QUIROGA

VEGAS

DELI

CHIFA MING ZHU

SALINAS

RESIDENCIAL EL ROCIO

JARAMILLO

CISNEROS

CISNEROS

SEE DETAIL

ROCA

MORALES

YANA YACU PUBLIC POOLS

ANIMAL MARKET

COLÓN

To Las Palmeras

CALDERÓN

SAMAY INN

SISA COMPLEX

HOTEL EL INDIO INN

ANDINATEL

HOTEL CORAZA

Plaza González Suárez

DOÑA ESTHER HOSTAL & PIZZERIA

FOOD MARKET

TRAIN STATION

To Laguna San Pablo

GALLERA MUNICIPAL

MONTALVO

Parque Bolivar

HOTEL OTAVALO

QUINO RESTAURANT "SABOR Y ARTE"

MAIN MARKET

PANAMERICANA

BANCO PACIFICO

SANTA FE

RIVIERA SUCRE

GARCIA

BOOK MARKET

MORENO

PALACIO MUNICIPAL

BANCO DE PICHINCHA

CAFÉ ARTE AND TAROT

PIEDRAHITA

MUSEO DEL OBRAJE

OLMEDO

ROCA

IGLESIA SAN FRANCISCO

MEJIA

To Mojanda

BOLIVAR

ATAHUALPA

ROCAFUERTE

MORA

PANAMERICANA

To LAGUNAS DE MOJANDA AND FUYA FUYA, Cayambe, and Quito

Detail

ALI ALLPA

BUENA VISTA

SALINAS

CAFÉ SHANANDOA

POST OFFICE

RESTAURANT INTI HUASI

SUCRE

JARAMILLO

INTERNATIONAL SPANISH SCHOOL

GALERÍA DE ARTE QUIPUS

FAUNO

HOTEL INDIO

MORALES

THE RED PUB

PIZZA SICILIANA

LAUNDRY

ECOMONTES

RESTAURANT MI OTAVALITO

HOSTAL MARIA

INSTITUTO SUPERIOR DE ESPAÑOL

ANTARA

COLÓN

0   250 yds

0   250 m

© AVALON TRAVEL

THE *INDÍGENAS* OF OTAVALO

Otavaleños are a special case among indigenous groups. Their unusual financial success and cultural stability allow them to travel and even educate their children abroad while still keeping a firm hold on their traditions at home.

Although many of Otavalo's residents are white or mestizo (mixed race), more than 40,000 Otavalo *indígenas* live in the town and the surrounding villages. Their typical outfits makes Otavaleños easily recognizable. "They walk, sit, and stand with exquisite grace," wrote Ludwig Bemelmans in the early 20th century. "The men have historic, decided faces, and the women look like the patronesses at a very elegant ball." Women traditionally wear elaborately embroidered white blouses over double-layered wool skirts, white underneath and black or dark blue on top. Shawls ward off the sun, provide warmth at night, or carry babies. Necklaces of gold metal or red beads (once coral, now usually colored glass or plastic) are worn around the neck, and their long, black hair is tied back in a single braid and wrapped in a woven *faja*.

Men also wear their long black hair braided in a *shimba,* often to the waist. (Their hair is such an important symbol of ethnic identity that *indígenas* of any ethnic group aren't required to cut it off when they enter the army). Blue wool ponchos are worn in all types of weather over white calf-length pants and rope sandals. A straight-brimmed felt fedora tops it off.

The history of the Otavaleños' famous weavings started before the arrival of the Incas, when the backstrap loom had already been in use for centuries. The Incas, appreciating the fine work, collected the weavings as tributes. Specially chosen women dedicated their lives to weaving fine textiles, some of which were burned in ritual offerings to the sun. On their arrival, the Spanish forced the Otavaleños to labor in workshops called *obrajes*. Despite the terrible conditions, the Otavalo *indígenas* became familiar with new weaving technology and learned how to produce textiles in mass quantities.

In the early 20th century, Otavalo's weavers caught the world's attention with a popular and inexpensive imitation of fine woven cloths from Asia called cashmere. The 1964 Agrarian Reform Law turned weaving into a profitable industry for the local people, who were now able to weave in their own homes. Today, the clack and rattle of electric looms turning out rolls of fabric can be heard in the smallest towns. Most private homes have an antique treadle-operated sewing machine along with a freestanding manual loom. Many weavers, though, still go through the entire process of hand-cutting, washing, carding, dying, and weaving wool over a period of days. Some backstrap looms are still in use; weaving a blanket on one can take over a week. Men traditionally operate the looms, either full-time or after finishing the day's work in the fields, while women perform the embroidery. Families start training children as young as age three to weave.

Most important, Otavaleño weavers have been able to hold onto their roots while keeping their business feet firmly in the present. Otavalo's *indígenas* own most of the businesses in town, as well as many stores throughout Ecuador and in other countries in South America. They travel extensively abroad in the Americas, Europe, and Asia to sell their products. The election of Otavalo's first indigenous mayor in 2000 shows how strong the native presence is in the Valley of Sunrise – organized indigenous strikes can bring the entire region to a standstill – and gives hope to other more downtrodden groups.

This success and visibility attracts both admiration and envy. Spend some time here and you'll see that Otavaleños have learned to straddle the fine line between making a profit and selling out their culture, and they seem to have come out ahead for their efforts.

woven with abstract patterns, are popular. The traditional hats made of felt or wool are another good buy as well as handbags and cloud-soft alpaca teddy bears. The best (and most expensive) ponchos, worn by the Otavaleños themselves, are made of thick wool dyed blue with indigo imported from abroad, and with a collar and gray or plaid fabric on the inside. Other ponchos are made of synthetic materials like Orlon, which is less expensive but brighter.

Long cloth strips called *fajas,* used by *indígenas* in the Sierra to tie back their hair, hang next to their wider cousins called *chumbis.* Many of these belts are woven in La Compañía, on the other side of Lago San Pablo. A single belt woven on a traditional backstrap loom (stretched between a post and the waist of the seated weaver) can take as long as four days to complete. Jewelry similar to that worn by indigenous women is spread out on tables: necklaces of black or red beads interspersed with earrings of turquoise and lapis lazuli. Other treasures include raw fleece, yarn, and dyes,

© CHRIS O'CONNELL

In Otavalo, clothing is made in the traditional way.

textiles from Peru and Bolivia, painted balsawood birds, and even novelty shrunken heads (fake, of course).

For the Saturday market, it's best to spend Friday night in town, but make a reservation because hotels fill up fast. Alternately, get up early Saturday morning to take the bus from Quito. Bargaining is expected, even in the many stores in town, and foreigners are naturally offered rather inflated prices, so haggle away, but don't be too pushy; if you get 30 percent off the starting price, you're doing well. Prices peak when the tour buses from Quito are in town, usually 9 A.M.–noon, so either shop very early or linger late for the best deals.

For a very different market experience, get up early and visit the **animal market,** held on Saturday morning starting at sunrise. Everything from cows, piglets, guinea pigs, puppies, and kittens (not for eating, thankfully) are for sale here. It's an animal rights campaigner's nightmare, and you're unlikely to make a purchase, but it's an interesting experience nevertheless. To get here, head west on Morales or Calderón and cross the bridge, passing the stadium. The market is straight ahead across the Panamericana.

Other Sights

Outside the market frenzy, the most attractive and historic part of Otavalo is at the south end of town. **Parque Bolívar** is dominated by the statue of brave Inca general Rumiñahui, who valiantly resisted the Spanish invaders and remains a symbol of indigenous pride. On the west side of the park is the main church, San Luis, and two blocks east on Calderón and Roca is a more attractive church, El Jordán. A block south is the **Museo del Obraje** (Sucre 6-08 at Olmedo, tel. 6/292-0261, 8 A.M.–12:30 P.M. and 3–5 P.M. Mon.–Sat., $2), which showcases the textiles that have made the area famous. It also offers courses in weaving and other handicrafts.

In the center of town, the **SISA** complex (Calderón 409 between Bolívar and Sucre, tel. 6/292-0154) has a handicrafts shop, a bookstore, an art gallery, a bar, and a restaurant on two floors. The name is an acronym for Sala de

Imágen, Sonido y Arte (Image, Sound, and Art Space), and it also means "flower" in Kichwa. Live music is performed on weekend nights.

Mirador El Lechero and Parque Condor

Otavalo is surrounded by great hiking opportunities. The walk to El Lechero and Parque Condor is the closest to town and is easily done independently. It's quite a steep climb, takes over an hour, and is poorly signposted, so ask for directions if you get lost; don't do the hike alone. Head southeast out of town on Piedrahita. The road quickly steepens into a series of switchbacks to Mirador El Lechero. This tree is renowned locally for the magical healing powers of the milky liquid contained in its leaves (hence its name, "the milkman"). From here you will have great views of Otavalo, Laguna de San Pablo, and Imbabura.

Parque Condor (tel. 6/292-4429, www.parquecondor.org, 9:30 A.M.–5 P.M. Tues.–Sun., $3 pp) is a short continuation of the Lechero hike and a rare opportunity to see condors, hawks, eagles, owls, and other birds of prey at close quarters. The birds are well cared for, and they fly freely for half an hour each morning at 11:30 A.M. and each afternoon at 4:30 P.M. It's quite a hike to do round-trip, so consider taking a taxi from Otavalo to the park ($4 one-way) and then walk back, which also reduces the risk of getting lost.

ENTERTAINMENT AND EVENTS
Nightlife

Nightlife is low-key in Otavalo most of the week but gets going on the weekend, particularly on Saturday when the locals celebrate a hard day's trading. You can catch live Andean music at several *peñas* in town, but locations change frequently, so ask around. Currently, the most popular places are **Peña Jala Jala** (31 de Octubre, tel. 6/292-4081, 7 P.M.–2 A.M. Fri.–Sat.) and **Peña La Jampa** (31 de Octubre, tel. 6/292-7791, www.lajampa.com, 7 P.M.–2 A.M. Fri.–Sat.), both northwest of

Plaza de Ponchos. Grab a high-octane pitcher of *canelazo* (hot cinnamon tea with *aguardiente*), sit back, and enjoy.

For a more international vibe with pitchers of beer and rock music, head to **The Red Pub** (Morales between Jaramillo and Sucre, tel. 6/292-7870, 4 P.M.–midnight Mon.–Thurs., 4 P.M.–2 A.M. Fri.–Sat.), a little slice of Britain in the Andes, or nearby **Fauno** (Morales between Jaramillo and Sucre, tel. 6/292-1611, 2 P.M.–midnight Mon.–Thurs. and 2 P.M.–2 A.M. Fri.–Sat.).

Festivals

Inti Raymi, the Inca festival of the northern solstice, has been absorbed into the Roman Catholic **Festival of San Juan** held in late June. Boats of every description dot Lago de San Pablo, and people cheer local favorites in bullfights.

Yamor, the region's best-known celebration, takes place close to the equinox, traditionally during the first weeks of September. In Otavalo, the Inca festival of Colla-Raymi, a harvest celebration of the earth's fertility, has been combined with the festival of San Luis Obispo, the patron saint of the harvest. Yamor is a two-week-long party with parades, marching bands, bullfights, cockfights, colorful costumes, and dances, all fueled by a special *chichi de yamor* made from seven different grains and drunk only during the festivities. Things can get very boisterous, so be careful late at night.

In *la entrada de ramos* (entrance of the branches), food and animals—from bread and fruit to live guinea pigs—are displayed, recreating a ritual presentation of food to the landowner dating to colonial times. A highlight is the appearance of the *coraza*, often played by a patron of the festivities. The only participant on horseback, the *coraza* wears an elaborate costume with a three-cornered hat and silver chains covering his face.

SHOPPING

In addition to the markets, throughout Otavalo are stores where you can browse in a less frantic atmosphere among huge selections of woven goods. **Antara** (Sucre near Colón) sells handmade Andean musical instruments. For more work by local artists, try the **Galería de Arte Quipus** (Sucre and Morales), which specializes in oil paintings and watercolors. You can buy, sell, or trade books at **The Book Market** (Hostal Riviera Sucre, Roca and García Moreno), which has a good selection of works in several languages. All day Saturday, the **produce market** overflows with food, household items, and clothes in and around the Plaza 24 de Mayo.

RECREATION AND TOURS

Although many of the areas around Otavalo can be explored independently, there are several agencies in town that organize tours to watch the production of crafts and textiles and see how the artisans live. Most agencies also offer hiking, driving, biking, and horseback trips of varying lengths and itineraries. All the agencies in town offer tours in English.

The agency that provides the most authentic indigenous experiences in the region is **Runa Tupari** (Plaza de los Ponchos, Sucre and Quiroga, tel. 6/292-2320 or 6/292-5985, www.runatupari.com). The company can set up homestays ($27 pp including meals and transportation) with 15 families in five small communities near Otavalo, where visitors live with and learn from traditional families, who benefit financially from the arrangement. Runa Tupari also sells products from various local community projects. Day tours ($27 pp) are to weaving villages as well as hikes to Cuicocha, Lagunas de Mojanda, and Fuya Fuya. Also offered are a shamanic medicine tour ($40 pp), horseback riding in Cotacachi-Cayapas National Park ($40 pp), and an excellent downhill bike ride into the Intag Valley ($65 pp). For climbers, there are ascents of Imbabura and Cotacachi (one day $70 pp, two days $150 pp). Multiday tours of the region are also available.

Another reputable agency in town is **Ecomontes Tour** (Sucre and Morales, tel. 6/292-6244, www.ecomontestour.com), which offers many of the activities and community

tours described above and can also arrange rainforest trips, Galápagos cruises, and climbing in other parts of Ecuador. They also have an office in Quito (J. Mera N24-91 at Mariscal Foch, tel. 2/290-3629).

ACCOMMODATIONS

Otavalo has a lot of accommodations, mainly budget and mid-range with some top-end haciendas outside town. During the week there is usually plenty of availability, but the best hotels fill up fast on Friday and Saturday nights, so consider booking ahead, or try to arrive before Friday if you're staying for a few days.

Under $10

The **Residencial El Rocio** (Morales between Ricaurte and Egas, tel. 6/292-0584 or 6/292-4606, $6 pp) offers some of the cheapest basic guest rooms in town, with more attractive cabins across the Panamericana ($12 pp) for those who want quiet and a parking space.

$10-25

The **❰ Hostal Valle del Amanecer** (Roca and Quiroga, tel. 6/292-0990, www.hostalvalledelamanecer.com, $10–12 pp) is the most pleasant budget place in town and has the feel of a backpacker hub with its cobbled, plant-filled courtyard, outdoor fireplace, hammocks, and friendly service. There is a restaurant and bikes for rent. This hostel is also your best bet for direct transportation to the community of Playa de Oro in Esmeraldas Province. On the same street, **Hostal Rincón del Viajero** (Roca 11-07, tel. 6/292-1741, $10–12 pp, breakfast included) is another hospitable option for budget travelers, with artwork on the walls, a TV lounge with a fireplace, a rooftop terrace with hammocks, a games room, and a restaurant.

If you want to stay near the Plaza de Ponchos, bear in mind it can get noisy. Right on the Plaza, **Hostal Los Andes** (Roca and Juan Montalvo, tel. 6/292-1057, $10 s, $15 d) is one of the cheapest options, with simple guest rooms overlooking the market. **Hotel Indio** (Sucre and Morales, tel. 6/292-0060, $15 pp), half a block up from the Plaza, is better, with colorful guest rooms and an open-air court-yard. The best value close to the market is probably the family-run **Samay Inn** (Sucre and Colón, tel. 6/292-2871, $10 pp), with firm beds, cable TV, and small balconies. The owner is opening a sister hotel on the eastern edge of town. Half a block south, guest rooms at the **Hotel Coraza** (Calderón and Sucre, tel./fax 6/292-1225, $17 pp, breakfast included) are very comfortable.

Many of the city's best mid-range hotels are situated south of the Plaza de Ponchos, along Roca one block southeast of Parque Bolívar. The colonial-style **(Hotel Otavalo** (Roca 504 at Juan Montalvo, tel. 6/292-0416, www.hotelotavalo.com.ec, $22 s, $44 d) offers great value, with a spacious peach-colored interior and immaculate guest rooms. **Hotel Santa Fe** (Roca and García Moreno, tel. 6/292-3640, $15 s, $30 d) also has excellent quality guest rooms furnished in pine and eucalyptus along with a good restaurant. On the corner, **Hotel Riviera Sucre** (Moreno 380 at Roca, tel./fax 6/292-0241, $15 s, $26 d) is another great option, with an open courtyard, a large garden, a lounge area, and spacious, colorful guest rooms.

$25-50

The renovated colonial **Doña Esther** (Montalvo 444 at Bolívar, tel. 6/292-0739, www.otavalohotel.com, $28 s, $40 d) is the best value in this range. Owned by a Dutch family, it has a verdant courtyard and a great restaurant with Mediterranean specialties. The **Hotel El Indio Inn** (Bolívar 904, tel. 6/292-2922 or 6/292-0325, $36 s, $53 d, breakfast included) has elegant guest rooms, cable TV, private parking, and a restaurant.

Otavalo's most distinctive hotel is the **(Posada del Quinde** (Quito and Miguel Egas, tel. 6/292-0750, www.posadaquinde.com, $44 s, $67 d, breakfast included), formerly known as Ali Shungu, at the northwest corner of town. The new owners continue to offer one of the best lodging options in town. The staff are very helpful, and the hotel is intricately decorated; each wall is lined with colorful masks, dolls, and weavings, and leafy plants fill all the corners. At the back are a gift shop and a patio overlooking the flower garden. The restaurant is very good (and open to nonguests), and there is live Andean music on the weekend.

FOOD

Otavalo has a sweet tooth: The freezers of most stores are stocked with freshly made sorbet (*helados de paila*), and you're never far from a bakery. One of the best is on the south side of the Plaza de Ponchos. **Café Shenandoah** (Salinas 5-15, no phone, 7:30 A.M.–9 P.M. daily, $1.50) has been serving homemade fruit pies for more than 30 years. Choose from 10 flavors that include lemon, passion fruit, and blueberry. Next door, **Alli Allpa** (Salinas 5-09 at Sucre, tel. 6/292-0289, 7:30 A.M.–9 P.M. daily, entrées $3–5) is an endearing little café offering meat and vegetarian options and a good-value set lunch ($3.50). Upstairs, **Buena Vista** (Salinas and Sucre, tel. 6/292-5166, 10 A.M.–10 P.M. Wed.–Mon., entrées $4–6) is a good place to watch the market from the balcony over a coffee and a chocolate brownie (the specialty) or feast on lasagna, trout, or steak from the wide-ranging menu. On the same street, for a more upscale meal, try **Inty Huasi** (Salinas tel. 6/292-2944, 8 A.M.–10 P.M. Tues.–Sat., 8 A.M.–5 P.M. Sun.–Mon., entrées $5–7) for well-presented meat and seafood dishes.

For Ecuadorian specialties, the best place in town is **(Mi Otavalito** (Sucre and Morales, tel. 6/292-0176, 8 A.M.–11 P.M. daily, entrées $5–7). A cozy cellar-like atmosphere, waitresses in traditional indigenous dress, artwork and artifacts on the walls, and an imaginative menu complete a very pleasant dining experience. Try the pork chops in orange sauce or the *trucha Otavalito* (trout in garlic sauce). Another good place for local specialties is **Quino Restaurant Sabor y Arte** (Roca near Montalvo, tel. 6/292-4094, 10 A.M.–11 P.M. daily, entrées $5–8), an intimate, colorful little restaurant with seafood specialties such as *ceviche* as well as mulled wine to warm the bones.

For international food, Otavalo has a good selection of high-quality establishments. For the best Mexican in town as well as delicious tomato soup, hot chocolate, crepes, and desserts, head to **❰ The Deli** (Quiroga and Bolívar, tel. 6/292-1558, www.delicaferestaurant.com, 9:30 A.M.–9 P.M. Sun.–Thurs., 9:30 A.M.–11 P.M. Fri.–Sat., entrées $4–8), a little gem of a café one block from the market.

For something more unusual, try the crepes at **❰ Café Arte and Tarot** (García Moreno and Bolívar, no phone, 8 A.M.–10 P.M. daily, entrées $3–5), an eclectically decorated place on the main square. The most popular seat in the house is a toilet seat in the café upstairs!

The best of the many *chifas* is the **Chifa Ming Zhu** (Roca and Salinas, tel. 9/771-0381, lunch and dinner daily, entrées $3–6), which is popular with locals for its generous portions of noodles, fried rice, sweet-and-sour dishes, and soups.

INFORMATION AND SERVICES

The **tourist office** (Quiroga and Jaramillo, tel. 6/292-7230, 8:30 A.M.–1 P.M. and 2:30–6 P.M. Mon.–Fri., 9 A.M.–2 P.M. Sat., 9 A.M.–noon Sun.) is at the corner of Plaza de Ponchos.

Banco Pichincha (Bolívar and García Moreno; Sucre and Quiroga) has ATMs. **Banco del Pacifico** (Sucre and García Moreno) on the Central Plaza will change traveler's checks. You can also try **Vaz Money Exchange** (Sucre and Colón), which handles many foreign currencies, traveler's checks, and Western Union money transfers. Some tour agencies change cash and traveler's checks as well. The **post office** (8 A.M.–7 P.M. Mon.–Fri., 8 A.M.–1 P.M. Sat.) is on the corner of Sucre and Salinas.

Most hotels do laundry, or you can try **Lavandería** (Morales and Sucre, no phone). Internet cafés have sprung up all over town, and there are several lining Sucre south of the Plaza de Ponchos, including **C@ffe Net** (tel. 6/292-0193). The local **hospital** (Sucre, tel. 6/292-0444) is northeast of town, and the

police station (tel. 101) is on Avenida Luis Ponce de León at the northeast end of town.

Spanish Lessons

Instituto Superior de Español (Sucre 11-10 at Morales, tel. 6/299-2424, www.instituto-superior.net) is recommended for Spanish classes. One-on-one instruction ($7 per hour) is offered for speakers of English, German, and French, and the school can arrange homestays and tours for students. Another option is the **Mundo Andino Spanish School** (Salinas 404 at Bolívar, tel./fax 6/292-1864, www.mundoandinospanishschool.com), which offers 4–7 hours of classes per day ($5 per hour) and homestays with local families.

GETTING THERE AND AROUND

Otavalo's **bus terminal** (Atahualpa and Ordoñez) is on the northeast corner of town, where you can catch buses to Quito (2 hours, $2.50) and Ibarra (40 minutes, $0.40) every 15 minutes, as well as to nearby villages such as Ilumán, Carabuela, Peguche, and Agato. You can also catch any bus heading north along the Panamericana and ask the driver to let you off at the appropriate intersection, then walk. Coming back is even easier—just flag down any bus heading south.

Taxis, which congregate at the bus terminal, plazas, and parks, charge about $1 for short journeys around town, $3 for attractions on the edge of town (Peguche waterfalls and El Lechero are two examples), and from $10 per hour for more out-of-the-way locations like Lagunas de Mojanda.

LAGUNA DE SAN PABLO

The nearest lake to Otavalo is the huge Laguna de San Pablo that you pass on the way from Quito. At the foot of **Volcán Imbabura,** surrounded by pastoral hamlets, it' a beautiful spot and popular on weekends with locals, who go sailing and waterskiing.

The road surrounding the lake is ideal for a day's bike ride or hike. The festivals of **Corazas** (Aug. 19) and **Los Pendoneros**

Volcán Imbabura dominates the valley around Otavalo.

THE ECUADORIAN ANDES

(Oct. 15) are celebrated in the tiny shoreline villages, which specialize in crafts such as woven reed mats. The walk from Otavalo south to the lake takes about an hour, or walk via El Lechero and Parque Condor. The bus from Otavalo marked "Araque" follows this road (catch it in front of the market on Atahualpa), or simply take any bus south toward Quito and get off when you pass the lake after about 10 minutes.

Accommodations and Food

A billboard along the Panamericana points down a dirt road to the **Hostería Puertolago** (tel. 6/292-0920, www.puertolago.com, $91 s, $103 d) on the southern shore of the lake. Meticulously mowed grounds surround a main building housing a nautical-motif bar, a restaurant, and an atrium with a wide window over the lake. Well-appointed guest rooms have fireplaces; rowboats and kayaks are available by the hour or the day, as are motorboats and paddleboats. Day or night lake

tours ($5.50 pp) are available. A taxi from Otavalo costs $3.

The comfortable **Hostería Cabañas del Lago** (Lago San Pablo, tel. 6/291-8108, www.cabanasdellago.com.ec, cabins $85 d), around on the eastern shore, caters to family groups and has two restaurants specializing in trout. Foot-powered paddleboats and motorboats are available for rent on the weekend. The two-person cabins have fireplaces and private baths.

HACIENDA CUSÍN

Outside the town of San Pablo del Lago is one of the most famous and luxurious country inns in South America. Built in 1602, the Hacienda Cusín (San Pablo del Lago, tel. 6/291-8013, fax 6/291-8003, www.haciendacusin.com, www.mythsandmountains.com, rooms $90 s, $120 d, cottages $120 s, $150 d, breakfast included) is one of the oldest in the country, named after a young local warrior who fought bravely against the Inca. Situated in a wide, scenic valley just south of Imbabura at 2,400 meters elevation, the hacienda is a relaxing, Old World type of place where llamas and sheep graze in the shadow of avocado trees. Old stone walls topped with moss encircle a hectare of gardens, which bloom continuously in the mild climate. Hummingbirds inhabit the forests of bougainvillea, belladonna, orchids, and foxglove.

Choose from 15 garden cottages or 25 guest rooms, all with private baths and garden views; some have bathtubs and fireplaces. This main colonial building is decorated with antiques and tapestries and houses the games room and a library graced by French windows. The restaurant seats 40 under a beamed ceiling, and food is served on carved wooden plates in front of a log fire. Horses are available to rent, and there are trails into the hills and fields.

◖ LAGUNAS DE MOJANDA AND FUYA FUYA

Half an hour south of Otavalo by car, a cobbled, winding road leads up to three stunningly beautiful lakes in the shadow of dark jagged mountains. Laguna Grande (also known as Caricocha), Laguna Negra (Huarmicocha), and Laguna Chiquita (Yanacocha) sit amid *páramo* at 3,700 meters elevation, some 1,200 meters above Otavalo. The peak of Fuya Fuya (4,263 meters) to the west is the highest point in the region and is a popular four-hour climb as acclimation practice for higher peaks. The first lake is by far the biggest, at two kilometers wide, and there is a hiking trail around it. A dirt road extends part of the way around the lake, and trails lead east and south to the other smaller lakes.

A taxi from Otavalo costs $10 one-way. Take a taxi driver's phone number or arrange a pickup time because this is a remote area. Be aware that there have been occasional robberies, so it's best to come here in a group or take a guided tour.

Casa Mojanda

The American- and Ecuadorian-run Casa Mojanda hotel (tel. 6/299-1010 or 9/973-1737, www.casamojanda.com, dorm $61 pp, $110 s, $183 d, breakfast and dinner included) is an ecologically and socially minded place with excellent views, five kilometers south of Otavalo at an elevation of 2,980 meters. On the road to the Lagunas de Mojanda, the hotel clings to the edge of a valley facing Cotacachi and the Cerro Cushnirumi, one of the few undisturbed tracts of Andean cloud forest in Ecuador. All the buildings were constructed using the *tapial* (rammed-earth) process in a simple, tasteful style with whitewashed walls, wood, terraces, and hammocks. Casa Mojanda prides itself on good environmental practice and has won ecotourism awards.

The airy main building houses the dining and living rooms, and there is a separate library building. There are eight guest cottages and two 10-bed dormitories. Outside is a small amphitheater that faces the valley, an outdoor hot tub with a great view, and an organic garden that supplies the restaurant. Nearby there are hiking trails, and you can go cycling, horseback riding, or kayaking. The owners also oversee the nonprofit Mojanda Foundation, working for environmental protection and the social welfare of surrounding communities.

La Luna

Farther up the road from Casa Mojanda to the Lagunas de Mojanda is the budget *hostería* La Luna (Vía a Lagos de Mojanda, tel. 9/315-6082, www.lalunaecuador.com, dorm $7 pp, $16–19 s, $24–32 d) with private guest rooms and campsites ($3.50 pp). The main building has a small restaurant and bar, and there is live Andean music on Saturdays. To get here, take the first left past the Casa Mojanda and head downhill a few hundred yards, then over the bridge. A taxi from Otavalo costs $4.

PEGUCHE

A small indigenous villages near Otavalo, Peguche (pop. 4,000) is renowned for its artisanal wares, particularly weavings and musical instruments. Various homes and workshops around town specialize in rugs, blankets, tapestries, and scarves. If you're looking for fine tapestries, stop by the home-workshop of **José Cotacachi** (tel. 6/269-0171, www.josecotacachi.com). From the Central Plaza of Peguche, take the sidewalk to the right of the church and turn right at the end of the street to reach the showroom. Or visit **Artesanía El Gran Condor** (Central Plaza, tel. 6/269-0161, www.artesaniaelgran-condor.com), another good textile workshop run by José Ruiz Perugachi.

On the musical side, **Ñanda Mañachi** (tel. 6/269-0076), just a couple of blocks north of the plaza, is an interesting place to visit—they give demonstrations of how several types of panpipes are made and played. A variety of in-struments, including *flautas* (reed flutes) and *rondadores* (Andean panpipes), are on sale.

Cascadas de Peguche

Perfect for cooling your feet after a day's hike, the small waterfall at forested Cascadas de Peguche park is just south of the town. Pass under two white arches to the signed park en-trance, where there is a small interpretive center (8:30 A.M.–5 P.M. daily). There is no entrance fee, but you are asked to make a small donation.

Follow the path through eucalyptus-scented forest; to the right there is a small bathing pool, and farther along are the falls. There is a bridge across the river and look-out points on each side. Past the right-side lookout, you can squeeze through a small cave to see another smaller waterfall. The waters from these falls plunge down the valley into Laguna San Pablo.

From Otavalo, the 45-minute walk to Cascadas de Peguche begins by following the railroad tracks north out of town. Follow the road when it leaves the tracks up and to the right, and look for the sign at the park en-trance. A taxi from Otavalo costs $3, or you can take a bus to Peguche and walk down. Note that robberies have occasionally been re-ported at the falls, so don't go alone or at night.

Accommodations

Peguche offers a few options for those who

© BEN WESTWOOD

THE ECUADORIAN ANDES

Cascadas de Peguche

want to stay outside Otavalo but remain nearby. Just up the hill from the entrance to the Cascada de Peguche is **❰ La Casa Sol** (Peguche, tel. 6/269-0500, Quito tel. 2/223-0798, www.lacasasol.com, $60 s, $72 d, breakfast included). With the same indige-nous owners as its namesake in Quito's New Town, the 10 guest rooms and two suites were built using traditional materials and meth-ods. Balconies and terraces offer great views over Peguche and the Otavalo Valley, staff are friendly, and the hotel is involved with local educational projects.

Peguche Tío Hostería (Peguche, tel./fax 6/269-0179, $10 pp) is housed in an unusual circular wooden building with a lookout tower. Inside you'll find a dance floor, a restaurant, and a library. The 12 guest rooms outside near the gardens all have hot water, fireplaces, and private baths. The hotel is frequently closed, so be sure to make reservations in advance.

Straddling the railroad tracks farther into

town is the **Hostal Aya Huma** (tel. 6/269-0333, www.ayahuma.com, $18 s, $29 d). It's well equipped with fireplaces, hammocks, a book exchange, Spanish classes, a vegetarian restaurant, live Andean music on Saturday nights, and a beautiful garden. Entrées in the restaurant, which serves all meals, are around $5. Follow the signs through town, or ask for directions.

AGATO, ILUMÁN, AND CARABUELA

About four kilometers northeast of Otavalo, just east of Peguche, is Agato, another village where artisans are known for their traditional-style weaving and fine embroidery. A great place to observe the process is the workshop of master weaver **Miguel Andrango** and his family (Agato, tel. 6/269-0282). You can watch the artists weaving wool on backstrap looms while others create intricate embroidery on the finished cloth. Miguel has woven fine ponchos and blankets for 60 years and continues to teach younger weavers who will carry on the traditions. Many of their high-quality textiles are for sale. Practically anyone in town can give you directions to the workshop, and many area tours stop by as well. Look for a sign to the right of the Panamericana, just past Peguche, or ask in Peguche for the road toward Agato. There are local buses to Agato from Otavalo's train station.

Ilumán, a small town noted for its felt hats and weavings, is a little farther up the Panamericana from Peguche, across from the entrance to Pinsaqui. Follow the cobbled road uphill straight toward Imbabura, and turn right when it levels out to reach the center of town and the plaza. South of the plaza on Bolívar is a sign for Carlos Conteron's **Artesanías Inti Chumbi** workshop (near Bolívar, tel. 6/294-6387). The couple at this workshop presents backstrap-loom weaving demonstrations and sells textiles and beautiful indigenous dolls. Throughout Ilumán there are workshops specializing in the colorful felt fedoras worn by the area's *indígenas*.

Ilumán is also famous for its *curanderos* (healers) and *brujos* (sorcerers). There are about 30 of them working in town, mixing indigenous and Christian rituals and herbal medicines to drive out evil spirits. Ask around in town to locate one, but be prepared for an intense experience and likely to get covered in spit, which is all part of the ritual. Buses from Otavalo go straight to the town center.

On the west side of the Panamericana, close to Ilumán, Carabuela is another weaving

ILUMÁN'S NATIVE HEALERS

Ilumán is known for its *curanderos* (native healers), who can be hired to cure or curse. Residents have passed down knowledge of natural remedies and spiritual cures here for centuries, treating everything from back problems to cancer. In 1988 there were 85 registered faith healers in Ilumán, eight of them women, but according to locals, only a small percentage were genuine. Dozens of Ecuadorians come to Ilumán daily to be cured or to pay for black magic, and even a few foreigners seek the wisdom of the healers every year.

Curing rituals are a blend of ancient wisdom, folklore, and modern faith. Invocations in Kichwa to Mama Cotacachi and Taita Imbabura, the old gods of the volcanoes, are sent up alongside prayers in Spanish to the Christian God and Jesus. *Curanderos* spit water and blow cigarette smoke on the patient, or rub the patient with special stones. A candle is passed over the patient's body, then lit to learn about the patient by studying the flickering flame. Cures can take the form of prayers or medicinal herbs like eucalyptus, poppies, and lemon, either rubbed on the patient's body or drunk as a tea.

Less public are the *brujos*, practitioners of the black arts. Traditionally working only at night, these wizards will cast malignant spells for jilted lovers or failing businesspeople – for the right price, of course. Rumor has it that their powers extend even to murder.

village. Local specialists include Don José Carlos de Torre, who spends months making each of his exquisite ponchos.

These villages can be visited independently, but for a better experience and to ensure weavers are expecting you and ready to give demonstrations, book a five-destination village tour with **Runa Tupari** (Plaza de Ponchos, Otavalo, tel. 6/292-2320 or 6/292-5985, www.runatupari.com).

HACIENDA PINSAQUÍ

An equestrian theme pervades this hacienda just north of Otavalo, on land that has been in the family of owner Pedro Freile for centuries. Hacienda Pinsaquí (tel. 6/294-6116, www. haciendapinsaqui.com, $105 s, $139 d) began in 1790 as a textile workshop that supported as many as 1,000 workers at one time. Simón Bolívar was a repeat guest on his way between Ecuador and Colombia during the struggles for independence.

The 30 guest rooms and suites feature thick walls, canopy beds, fireplaces, and tiled floors, and some suites contain hot tubs. Across the railing from the main hall and its fountain is a 120-seat restaurant and lounge with huge walk-in fireplaces reminiscent of Elizabethan houses in England. There are a variety of hiking and horseback day tours. Take a taxi from Otavalo ($4–5), or take a bus to Ibarra and get off just after the turnoff to Cotacachi.

Cotopaxi

◖ COTOPAXI NATIONAL PARK

Ecuador's top mainland national park is second only to the Galápagos in the annual number of visitors, and it's easy to see why. Less than two hours south of Quito, 33,400 stunning hectares enclose one of the most beautiful volcanoes in the Americas, along with two other peaks higher than 4,700 meters, and extensive verdant *páramo* where llamas graze and wild horses gallop. Tours of the park vary from gentle hikes and cycle rides to scaling the volcano itself, considered one of Ecuador's best climbs.

Flora and Fauna

The lower elevations on the edges of the park contain wet montane forests at about 3,600–3,800 meters, but the largest section is covered by sub-Andean *páramo* at 4,000–4,500 meters. This is where you'll find most of the park's animals: deer, rabbits, and the endemic marsupial mouse. More elusive are pumas and endangered spectacled bears. There are more than 90 species of birds, including carunculated caracaras, shrike-tyrants, ground-tyrants, great thrushes, rufous-naped brush-finches, Andean gulls, noble snipes, and brown-backed chat-tyrants (related to flycatchers). If you're lucky, you may spot an Andean condor soaring overhead.

Shrubby blueberries and lupines bloom next to Indian paintbrush and members of the daisy family, while the occasional terrestrial bromeliad is pollinated by hummingbirds. You might spot the *urcu rosa*, a small blue mountain rose, hidden among the tough *ugsha* grass. Above 4,500 meters to the snowline at 4,700 meters, plunging temperatures keep the mossy tussocks of the Andean tundra relatively empty.

Access

The two main entrances to the park are south of Machachi along the Panamericana. The first turnoff, 16 kilometers south of Machachi, is also the entrance to El Boliche National Recreation Area. It passes the CLIRSEN satellite tracking station before forking three ways. Take the right fork and follow the train tracks for 500 meters. From here, it's six kilometers downhill through a forest to a campsite with fireplaces and simple cabins.

The second entrance turnoff is nine kilometers farther south; this is the most popular access point, making it easier to hitch a ride into the park, especially on weekends (although the road washes out occasionally in the rainy season). It joins with the northern access road at the park boundary, where you pay the entrance fee ($10 pp) at the gate, which is open daily.

The road through the park curves in a semi-circle north around Volcán Cotopaxi. As it heads northeast, it passes the administrative center at **Campamiento Mariscal Sucre,** 10 kilometers from the gate. A small museum here has an exhibition on the geology, history, flora, and fauna of the park. Shortly beyond the museum, which is usually the first stop on a guided tour, there's a path leading to **Laguna Limpiopungo,** a shallow lake at 3,800 meters elevation whose reeds provide a habitat for several species of birds.

On a small hill 15 kilometers beyond the lake are the oval ruins of **El Salitre,** formerly an Inca *pucara* (fortress), abandoned soon after the arrival of the Spanish.

A trail leads around the lake to the northwest for access to Rumiñahui. Shortly beyond that trail, another jeep track heads nine kilometers south to the **Jose Rivas Refuge,** the best base for climbing expeditions. Note that the hike to the refuge is tougher than you may expect if you're not fully acclimated (which you won't be if you're coming from Quito).

Many of the day tours include mountain biking in the park, which is a great way to cover more distance. You are usually taken up to a refuge for a dramatic downhill ride, which gets the adrenaline pumping without tiring you out.

Climbing Volcán Cotopaxi

Cotopaxi may not be Ecuador's highest mountain but it's certainly the most photogenic. This perfectly symmetrical cone has been captivating climbers and photographers for years, and many of the local indigenous people, who named it "the neck of the moon" in Kichwa, still worship the volcano as god of the valley. However, Cotopaxi's beauty masks the beast that lies within. While it is probably not the world's highest active volcano (that title most likely belongs to Llullaillaco on the Chilean-Argentine border, which erupted in 1877),

there's no denying Cotopaxi's destructive ability.

Cotopaxi's first recorded eruption disrupted a battle between the Spanish and the Inca in 1534, and since then it has erupted on over 10 occasions, destroying Latacunga several times. Eruptions in 1742, 1768, and 1877 were the worst, killing hundreds of people. Cotopaxi registered minor eruptions in 1906 and as recently as the 1940s, but at present activity is limited to steam rising from the crater, only visible to climbers who reach the summit.

A German and Colombian climbing team first set foot on Cotopaxi's glacier-covered peak in 1872, followed 10 years later by Edward Whymper, who opened the northern route still in use today. The climb is not technically difficult, as the many climbers who scale the ice-covered slopes regularly will attest. Crevasses are usually large and obvious, making the climb mostly an uphill slog. However, less than half of those who attempt the summit actually reach it. You need to be in very

HOT LOVE

The Kichwa people of the Sierra have always revered the country's volcanoes, considering them to be people with human personalities and flaws. Long ago, according to legend, the handsome volcano Cotopaxi took a liking to the young, passionate Tungurahua. Tungurahua was no angel, however, and it wasn't long before the object of her affections turned to the taller Chimborazo. Their love child was Guagua Pichincha (*guagua* means "baby" in Kichwa), a badly behaved volcano that went north to live with his grandfather Rucu Pichincha. The last time that Guagua had a tantrum and erupted was in 1999, and soon afterward Tungurahua followed suit; locals believe that this was the mother answering the child. Luckily for climbers, Cotopaxi and Chimborazo have kept quiet about the whole geological drama.

good physical condition, be fully acclimated, and have an experienced guide and a certain amount of luck with the conditions. Technical equipment is necessary: ice axes, crampons, ropes, and marker wands.

Although Cotopaxi can be climbed year-round—it sees more clear days than almost any other peak in the Ecuadorian Andes—the best months are December–January. August–September are also good but windy. February–April can be clear and dry as well, while August–December are usually windy and cloudy.

As with any peak over 5,000 meters, acclimation is essential. If you've been staying in Quito at 2,800 meters, this is unlikely to be sufficient acclimation to scale Cotopaxi on a two-day excursion (although you may be lucky). Ideally you should trek and sleep at around 4,000 meters for a couple of days, or even better, do a practice climb of a smaller peak such as Iliniza Norte or Rumiñahui before attempting Cotopaxi.

The road to the refuge heads south from the main park road for nine kilometers to the parking area at 4,600 meters. A half-hour hike up a steep, sandy trail brings you to the José Ribas refuge (4,800 meters), which was built in 1971 by the San Gabriel Climbing Club. The two-story shelter is fully equipped with bunk beds ($20 pp), cooking facilities, running water, and snacks and water for sale as well as lockable storage space for gear. A night's stay is usually included in the price of a guided tour.

To reach the summit, catch a few hours of sleep before waking around midnight to start climbing. It takes 6–10 hours from the refuge, and the route contains smoking fumaroles reeking of sulfur. The views over the other volcanoes on the "avenue" are spectacular, and you should be able to see the lights of Quito in the distance. The descent takes 3–6 hours.

Climbing Volcán Rumiñahui

This peak, 13 kilometers northwest of Cotopaxi, was named after Atahualpa's bravest general, who famously hid the huge Inca ransom after Atahualpa's death and refused to give up its whereabouts when tortured by the Spanish. The history of its name is luckily the most violent aspect of Rumiñahui (4,712 meters), which is heavily eroded and officially dormant but most probably extinct. There are actually three peaks, and the volcano offers a relatively straightforward climb, combining an uphill hike with a bit of scrambling, but because the quality of rock can be poor, a rope and climbing protection are recommended for the more exposed stretches.

The east side of Rumiñahui is reached through Cotopaxi Park along tracks that skirt Laguna Limpiopungo to the north or south. A path toward the central peak is clearly visible along a well-defined ridge. From the lake to the base is about a two-hour hike, and camping along the way is possible. The south peak involves some moderate technical rock climbing (class 5.5). The IGM *Machachi* and *Sincholagua* 1:50,000 maps cover this area.

EL BOLICHE NATIONAL RECREATION AREA

Ecuador's smallest nationally protected area at 1,077 hectares, El Boliche National Recreation Area hugs the southwestern side of Cotopaxi National Park. Boliche is perfect for visitors who are more interested in weekend family picnics and mild hikes than mountaineering, with cabins, camping spots, sports fields, and self-guided trails. The habitat here at 3,500 meters is dominated by pine trees planted through reforestation programs in the 1960s and 1970s. The pines have actually disrupted the local ecosystem and caused problems for Quito's water supply, which draws heavily on this area. However, the thickly forested trails are very beautiful and make a refreshing change from the grasslands that dominate the rest of the region. Visitors may catch sight of deer, rabbits, and the occasional wolf. Llamas and *guarizos* (offspring of llamas and alpacas) have been released in the park and are reproducing well.

The entrance to El Boliche is the same as the northern turnoff for Cotopaxi off the Panamericana—16 kilometers south of Machachi. Admission ($10 pp) is combined with the entry to Cotopaxi. The train service from Quito to Latacunga passes through Thursday–Sunday.

ACCOMMODATIONS AND FOOD

There are no real towns in this area, just haciendas and hotels; the only venues that serve food are the hotels.

$10-25

Most of the accommodations in the area around Cotopaxi National Park are in the mid- to high-end category. The most economical option is **Cuello de Luna** (El Chasqui, Panamericana S. Km. 44, tel. 3/271-8068 or 9/970-0330, www.cuellodeluna.com, dorm $18 pp, $40 s, $50 d), just two kilometers from the main park entrance. There are spacious cabins or dorms in the loft.

About 25 kilometers south of the main entrance to the park is **Tambopaxi** (Quito office: Diego de Almagro and La Pinta, tel. 2/222-0241, www.tambopaxi.com, dorm $19 pp, $90 s, $110 d), which has comfortable dorms in the main lodge and more expensive private guest rooms in a separate lodge. There are great views of Cotopaxi. Camping costs $6 pp.

$25-50

Near the northern entrance of the park is **Hacienda El Porvenir** (Quito office: Lactea 250 at Chimborazo, tel. 2/204-1520, www.volcano-land.com, $43 s, $50 d), also known as Volcano Land. Straw mats on the walls and fireplaces in the dining room and living rooms supply a comfortable atmosphere, and there are views of Cotopaxi from the large patio. Tours are offered on foot, mountain bike, and horseback into the nearby hills. Camping is available for $4 pp.

A newer option is **Secret Garden Cotopaxi** (Cotopaxi National Park, tel. 9/357-2714, www.secretgardencotopaxi.com, dorm $38 pp, $65 s or d, meals included), sister hotel of the backpacker favorite in Quito. This eco-lodge is set in the foothills of Pasochoa, near the village

of Pedregal, overlooking the national park. The rates include three meals, snacks, drinks, and use of mountain bikes. Many guest rooms have their own fireplaces, and transfers are available from the Secret Garden in Quito (depending on the number of people).

$50-75

Located in Lasso about 10 minutes by car south of the main park entrance, **Hostería San Mateo** (Vía Latacunga Km. 55, Lasso, tel. 3/271-9015, fax 3/271-9471, www.hosteriasanmateo.com, $66 s, $72 d) has six beautiful guest rooms with private baths and a cabin for up to four people decorated in Ecuadorian country style. There's a swimming pool and a bar for relaxing after horseback riding and hiking. Owner Francisco Baca's family has a 400-year history in Ecuador, and he maintains interests in cattle and dairy ranching as well as organic vegetable farming.

One of Ecuador's oldest haciendas, dating from 1695, **Hacienda La Ciénega** (Quito office: Cordero, tel. 2/254-9126 or 3/271-9052, www.hosterialacienega.com, $63 s, $88 d, breakfast included) now operates as a hotel. The setting is straight out of the 17th century, when the estate belonged to the Marquis of Maenza and stretched from Quito to Ambato. La Condamine, Von Humboldt, Juan José Flores, and Velasco Ibarra all found shelter here over the centuries.

The square building surrounds a flower-filled courtyard with a fountain, where a set of ornately carved wooden doors open into the small private chapel. Horses graze near flower-filled greenhouses to the rear of the courtyard. A sign on the west side of the Panamericana one kilometer south of Lasso points down a paved lane, where the hacienda gate opens on the left after one kilometer.

Gabriel Espinosa and his friendly family run the comfortable **Hacienda La Alegria** (Alóag, Machachi, tel. 2/246-2319 or 9/980-2526, info@alegriafarm.com, www.hacienda-laalegria.com, from $65 pp, breakfast included) on the old railroad line in the shadow of Volcán Corazón. Horseback riding is the focus here, and they run 1–2-day trips into the hills in every direction. Old equestrian photos and equipment decorate the beautiful old building, which can accommodate 24 guests in newer extensions. Meals include produce from the hacienda's organic farm. Rates range from $65 pp for bed-and-breakfast to $180 pp for full board, including rides and hacienda visits. Transportation from Quito ($45) can be arranged.

$100-200

Immense pumice walls greet visitors at **Hato Verde** (Panamericana Km. 55, Mulalo, tel. 3/271-9348 or 3/271-9902, www.hacienda-hatoverde.com, $134 s, $183 d, breakfast included), with nine cozy guest rooms and a family atmosphere. The house has retained much of the 120-year-old building's character. At night, the fires are lit and the shutters closed; in the mornings, they are opened to display great views of Cotopaxi volcano and the farmlands. Fresh milk and cheese produced on the farm are a feature of the country breakfasts. Hato Verde is just a few hundred meters from the Panamericana, south of Cotopaxi.

Over $200

Opened in 1995, **Hacienda Yanahurco** (Cotopaxi National Park, tel. 2/244-5248, www.haciendayanahurco.com, $225 pp, all meals and tours included) is east of the volcano, and access is normally from the northern entrance road to Cotopaxi National Park. This retreat offers outdoor activities on the lands of an old family hacienda: guided hiking, fishing, bird-watching, and especially horseback-riding

excursions on 26,000 private hectares. Seven guest rooms in the ranch-style buildings have fireplaces and private baths. The fishing here is particularly good; brook, rainbow, and brown trout fill the streams. The annual roundup of wild horses in November is a very special three-day weekend event that should be reserved well in advance.

All-inclusive packages include activities, food, and accommodations in the expansive main hacienda, based on a minimum group size of four. Camping is available from $15 pp. The private, locked entrance road is reached by turning east from the main park entrance road at Laguna Limpiopungo.

Hacienda San Agustín de Callo (Lasso, Cotopaxi, tel./fax 3/271-9160, Quito office tel. 2/290-6157, www.incahacienda.com, $278 s, $424 d, three meals and excursions included) owes as much of its history to the Inca as to the Spanish. It was originally built as an Augustinian convent on the site of a ruined Inca outpost. The chapel and dining room both incorporate massive Inca stonework, and Inca remains have been unearthed during restorations. The nearby Cerro de Callo is a perfectly round hill thought to be an Inca burial mound. Trekking, fishing, and cycling excursions are included.

The hacienda sits along the road that parallels the Panamericana north of Mulaló. Take the southern turnoff to Cotopaxi National Park and turn right (south) toward Mulaló instead of continuing straight into the park. You'll pass the Hacienda Los Nevados before reaching the San Agustín turnoff to the west.

Latacunga and the Quilotoa Loop

Latacunga is the capital of Cotopaxi Province and the closest city to Volcán Cotopaxi, which towers over the valley just 30 kilometers northeast. Since Topa Inca Yupanqui left his regional chiefs to oversee this newly conquered region with the words *Llagtata-cunuai* ("I leave this land in your care"), the residents of Latacunga (pop. 75,000) seem to have remained content for their city's fate to be forever linked to the volcano.

As the land erupted into war between the Spanish and the Incas in 1534, Cotopaxi also began to spit fire, and the conquerors, who had never witnessed a volcanic eruption, fled in terror. The local indigenous people, however, worshipped Cotopaxi as god of the valley, and the regular eruptions didn't prevent the founding of Latacunga on the banks of the Río Cutuchi in the late 1500s. In the past three centuries Cotopaxi has destroyed the city several times in more than 10 eruptions: Those in 1698, 1742, and 1877 were the most destructive, and whether through human folly or dogged determination, the city was rebuilt each time in the exact same location. Cotopaxi continued to rumble away in minor eruptions in the early 1900s and as recently as the 1940s, and it is still considered active, with smoke visible to climbers who reach the crater. Needless to say, nobody bothers much about insurance around here.

Modern-day Latacunga is a charming, friendly city where people go about their business calmly in Cotopaxi's shadow. First impressions are not great on arrival at the bus station in the city's industrial outskirts, but persevere to the center and you'll find well-preserved colonial squares, churches, and cobbled streets. While it takes less than a day to take in Latacunga's sights, the city also makes a good base to explore Cotopaxi and the Quilotoa Loop, and hikes and climbs to both

Latacunga's cathedral and Parque Vicente León

© BEN WESTWOOD

THE ECUADORIAN ANDES

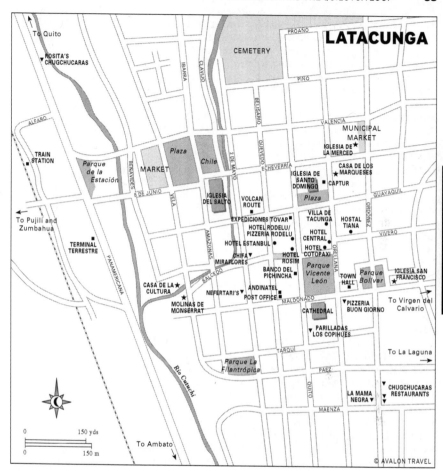

To Quito

ROSITA'S
CHUGCHUCARAS

CEMETERY

PROANO

LATACUNGA

PINO

ALFARO

IBARRA
GUAYAO
BELISARIO
VALENCIA

MUNICIPAL
MARKET

QUEVEDO

IGLESIA DE ★
LA MERCED

TRAIN
STATION

Parque
de la
Estación

BENAVIDES

Plaza

MARKET

2 DE MAYO

Chile

ECHEVERRIA

CASA DE LOS
MARQUESES

IGLESIA DE
SANTO
DOMINGO

■ CAPTUR

5 DE JUNIO

VELA

IGLESIA
DEL SALTO

VOLCAN
ROUTE

Plaza

GUAYAQUIL

To Pujili and
Zumbahua

EXPEDICIONES TOVAR ■

VILLA DE
TACUNGA

HOSTAL
TIANA
●

TERMINAL
TERRESTRE

AMAZONAS

HOTEL RODELU/
PIZZERIA RODELU

HOTEL ESTAMBUL ●

HOTEL
CENTRAL
●

VIVERO

CHIFA ▼
MIRAFLORES

HOTEL
ROSIM

HOTEL
COTOPAXI

ORELLANA

CASA DE LA ★
CULTURA

SALCEDO

BANCO DEL
PICHINCHA
■

NEFERTARI'S ▼

ANDINATEL

POST OFFICE ■

Parque
Vicente
León

MALDONADO

TOWN
HALL

Parque
Bolívar

IGLESIA SAN
FRANCISCO
★

To Virgen del
Calvario

PANAMERICANA

MOLINAS DE
MONSERRAT

CATHEDRAL

▼ PIZZERIA
BUON GIORNO

▼ PARILLADAS
LOS COPIHUES

To La Laguna
→

TARQUI

Parque La
Filantrópica

Río Cutuchi

PAEZ

QUITO

LA MAMA
NEGRA ▼

▼ CHUGCHUCARAS
RESTAURANTS

MAENZA

0   150 yds

0   150 m

To Ambato

© AVALON TRAVEL

THE ECUADORIAN ANDES

SIGHTS

Latacunga's pretty main square, **Parque Vicente León,** is flanked on the south side by an impressive whitewashed **cathedral** with carved wooden doors and the elegant **town hall** on the east side. One block to the east is **Parque Bolívar,** and a couple of blocks north is another impressive church, **Iglesia Santo Domingo,** overlooking Santo Domingo square, which hosts a small market. A few blocks

destinations can be organized by a few excellent local operators in town.

southwest, **Parque La Filantrópica** is guarded by the grand old **Hospital General,** a historic landmark to the south.

For the best views of the town and surrounding valley, head east of town to **Mirador de la Virgen del Calvario.** On clear days you can see Cotopaxi. To get here, go east on Maldonado, climb the steps, and walk to the left, up Oriente, to the statue.

Markets

Plaza Chile, northwest of the center, hosts Latacunga's market, which spills down almost to the river on the busiest days, Tuesday and Sunday. It's not aimed at visitors, but there is a small selection of textiles and hats as well as plenty of snacks and fruit. To the east, the less spectacular daily municipal market borders the Iglesia de la Merced between Valencia and Echeverría.

Museums

Built on the site of an old Jesuit flour mill along the river, the **Casa de la Cultura** (8 A.M.–noon and 2–6 P.M. Tues.–Fri., 8 A.M.–3 P.M. Sat., $0.50) contains part of the old water mill as well as an impressive ethnographic collection of ceramics, paintings, dolls in indigenous festival costumes, and colonial artifacts.

The flower-filled courtyard of the **Casa de los Marqueses** (8 A.M.–noon and 2–6 P.M. Mon.–Fri., free) has a small exhibition of archaeological artifacts and antique furniture.

ENTERTAINMENT AND EVENTS

Latacunga's **Fiesta de la Santissima Virgen de la Merced** (Sept. 22–24), known familiarly as **Fiesta de La Mama Negra,** is one of the more colorful and outstanding events in Ecuador. It centers on a small black icon of the Virgin carved by an indigenous artisan in the 17th century to protect the city against Volcán Cotopaxi. The streets fill with a colorful cast of characters, dancers, and revelers.

There are two separate festivals of the same name: the religious Mama Negra (Sept. 22–24) and the secular Mama Negra, on the Saturday before November 11, when Latacunga celebrates its **Independence Day.**

RECREATION AND TOURS

Latacunga has a small selection of climbing and hiking operators, including these recommendations: **Volcán Route** (2 de Mayo and Guayaquil, tel. 3/281-2452, www. volcanroute.com), **Expeditiones Tovar** (Guayaquil and Quito, tel. 3/281-1333, www.tovarexpeditions.com), **Tierra Zero** (Padre Salcedo and Quito, tel. 3/280-4327), and **Tributrek,** which operates out of Hostal Tiana (Vivero and Ordoñez, tel. 3/281-0147,

www.tributrek.com). All operators offer climbs of Cotopaxi (day trips from $45 pp, two-day climbs from $160 pp), and tours to Quilotoa (one day from $40 pp, three-day trek of the loop from $130 pp).

ACCOMMODATIONS

Latacunga has a decent selection of accommodations, both budget and mid-range.

Under $10

Latacunga's best hotels are within a block or two of Parque Vicente León. The quiet **Hotel Estambul** (Quevedo 6-44, between Salcado and Guayaquil, tel. 3/280-0354, $9–11 pp) is a perennial budget traveler's favorite, with decent guest rooms with shared or private baths. Run by a friendly Dutch-Ecuadorian couple, **Hostal Tiana** (Vivero and Ordoñez, tel. 3/281-0147, www.hostaltiana.com, dorm $9 pp, $11–25 pp) has recently changed location but still offers good-quality guest rooms with private or shared baths as well as dorms. The hotel's agency can organize tours.

$10-25

Hotel Cotopaxi (tel. 3/280-1310, $10 pp) and **Hotel Central** (tel. 3/280-2912, $10 pp) occupy the same building overlooking the main square, Parque Vicente León, and both offer comfortable guest rooms with private baths and cable TV. Slightly quieter and more elegant is **Hotel Rosim,** just off the square (Quito and Salcedo, tel. 3/280-2172, www.hotelrosim. com, $13 pp), with firm beds and cable TV.

$25-50

The **Hotel Rodelu** (Quito 1631 and Salcedo, tel. 3/280-0956, fax 3/281-2341, www.rodelu.com. ec, $27 s, $44 d) has swish guest rooms with private baths, TVs, and in-room telephones. The wood paneling, indigenous motifs, and an excellent restaurant make this a top-notch choice. A new mid-range option in town is **Villa de Tacunga** (Sánchez de Orellana and Guayaquil, tel. 3/281-2352, www.villadetacunga.com, $42 s, $61 d) with elegant guest rooms adjacent to a spacious courtyard restaurant.

LA MAMA NEGRA

Latacunga hosts one of the biggest festivals in the Ecuadorian highlands. It's worth making a beeline for the city to experience this most flamboyant of celebrations, which combines Roman Catholic, indigenous, and African traditions in a heady mix of religion and hedonism.

There are actually two festivals: the religious festival, known as **Santísima Tragedia,** held on September 24, and the more raucous secular **Fiesta de Mama Negra,** usually beginning on the Saturday prior to November 11, Latacunga's Independence Day.

The exact origin of the festival has various versions. The most likely origin of the religious festival is in the 18th century when local residents petitioned the Virgin Mary, patron saint of Cotopaxi, to protect them from the erupting volcano. Even though it didn't really work, because Latacunga was destroyed several times, the annual celebration in honor of *La Virgen de las Mercedes* persisted. The character of La Mama Negra, a blackened man dressed up as a gaudy woman that flies in the face of political correctness, probably originated from the local fascination with African slaves brought to Ecuador by the Spanish conquerors to work in the mines.

During La Mama Negra festivities, the streets are filled with a colorful cast of characters. Verse tellers – more or less public jesters – tell poems and recite comical *loas* (limericks) filled with nuggets of ironic truth. Whip-wielding, colorfully attired *camisonas* (transvestites) share the stage with *huacos* (witches) dressed in masks and white robes, who act out a ritual cleansing by blowing smoke and *aguardiente* on the spectators (including unsuspecting visitors). The celebration culminates in the arrival on horseback of La Mama Negra herself, dressed in an elaborate costume and bearing dolls to represent her children. She sprays the crowd with milk and water, and the drinking continues long into the night and beyond.

THE ECUADORIAN ANDES

FOOD

The best-known local specialty is *chugchucara*—a singular fried dish that includes chunks of pork, crispy skins, potatoes, plantains, and fresh and toasted corn—and *allullas* (ah-YU-zhahs), doughy cookies made with cheese and pork fat. If your arteries can take it, the best place to try them are restaurants along the stretch of Ordoñez southeast of the center. The grand pillars and stone decor of **La Mama Negra** (Ordoñez and Rumiñahui, tel. 3/280-5401, 10 A.M.–7 P.M. Tues.–Sun., $6–7) is one of the better establishments.

As in most towns in the Andes, you can always depend on the pizza in Latacunga. One of the best places to try a variety of toppings as well as pasta dishes is **Pizzeria Rodelu** (Quito 1631 and Salcedo, tel. 3/280-0956, 7:30 A.M.–10 P.M. Mon.–Sat., 7:30 A.M.–8 P.M. Sun., $6–9), which also does excellent meat and chicken. **Pizzeria Buon Giorno** (Orellana and Maldonado, tel. 3/280-4924, 1–11 P.M. Mon.–Sat., closed Sun., $4–6) on the main square is another good choice with great lasagna and a wide range of large salads.

For cheap set lunches ($2.50) and range of pricier barbecued chicken and meat specialties, try the cozy **El Copihue Rojo** (Quito and Tarqui, tel. 3/280-1725, noon–3 P.M. and 6–9 P.M. Mon.–Sat., $7–9) behind the cathedral.

For Chinese soups, noodles, fried rice, and sweet and sour dishes, head to **Chifa Miraflores** (Salcedo and 2 de Mayo, tel. 3/280-9079, 10 A.M.–10 P.M. daily, $3–5).

SERVICES

On the main square, Parque Vicente León, the **Banco Pichincha** has an ATM and handles some foreign currency, or try **Banco de Guayaquil** (Maldonado 7-20). The **post office** is at Quevedo and Maldonado. The **hospital** is on Hermanas Páez near 2 de Mayo.

CAPTUR (Sánchez de Orellana and Guayaquil, tel. 3/281-4968, 9 A.M.–6 P.M.

Mon.–Fri.) is the local tourist office; maps, brochures, and a little information in Spanish are available.

GETTING THERE AND AROUND

Latacunga's **bus terminal** is right on the Panamericana at the west end of town. Various companies run buses to Quito (1.5 hours, $1.50), Ambato (1 hour, $1), and Saquisilí (20 minutes, $0.50). Transportes Cotopaxi heads to Quevedo (5 hours, $5) via Zumbahua. Transportes Primavera buses go to Salcedo (20 minutes, $0.50), and Transportes Pujilí will take you to Pujilí (15 minutes, $0.25).

To get to Quilotoa and Chugchilán, there is only one direct bus per day (around noon). If you miss it, take the first bus to Zumbahua and take a taxi from there.

Taxis are available for day trips to Zumbahua or Quilotoa and Cotopaxi National Park ($40–50). Taxis around town cost from $1.

SAQUISILÍ

Saquisilí, a 20-minute bus ride northwest of Latacunga, is known for its bustling Thursday market. It's not really aimed at visitors, but it is gaining popularity as a more authentic experience of an indigenous market than Otavalo. On market day, eight plazas in the center of town flood with traders. There's a food market, an animal market, and a textile market to keep you busy as well as all manner of household goods for sale. You can buy Otavalo sweaters, Tigua paintings, herbal remedies, and squealing piglets (if you want to adopt one), and the smells of roasted pork and guinea pig are never far away. The animal market is particularly interesting, with chickens, llamas, alpacas, cows, sheep, and horses being traded.

Most people come just for the morning, but accommodations are available at the **San Carlos Hotel** (Bolívar and Sucre, tel. 3/227-1981, $7 s, $12 d), with private baths and hot water. **Gilocarmelo** (Calle Chimborazo, tel. 3/272-1630, www.hosteriagilocarmelo.com, $15–19 pp, breakfast included), a five-minute walk east of the main northern bus parking area near the cemetery, offers more comfortable guest rooms as well as a sauna, a steam bath, and a swimming pool; hiking and horseback tours are available.

Saquisilí is a few kilometers off the Panamericana, two hours south of Quito. Ask the bus driver to drop you off at the junction and take another bus, or a better option is to catch the regular buses from Latacunga's bus terminal (20 minutes, $0.50).

THE QUILOTOA LOOP

The road northwest of Latacunga loops through a series of remote indigenous villages. The spectacular scenery in this region—in particular the incredible beauty of Lake Quilotoa—makes this a very popular hiking destination. The lake itself can be reached on a day trip, or you can spend anything from a couple of days to the best part of a week hiking through the undulating landscapes.

Transportation around the entire loop is limited to two direct buses per day, and less than half of the 200 kilometers of road are paved, with the remainder made up of rough dirt tracks that are sometimes impassable in the rainy season. While this makes getting around a little complicated, it's also part of the reason why the loop remains refreshingly remote and unspoiled. In addition to the breathtaking scenery, the indigenous communities have held on to their traditions. Along with the villages around Otavalo, this is one of the best regions in the Andes to experience thriving Kichwa culture.

Getting There and Around

There's no escaping that getting around the Quilotoa Loop can be a challenge. There are only two buses daily, often jam-packed with locals and even the occasional animal. If you miss the bus, you can try your luck at hiring a pickup truck to take you to the next town.

Two regular Transportes Iliniza buses travel the entire loop daily, one in each direction. All times listed below are the official times. You must arrive on time or risk missing the bus (and most likely not getting a seat). Bear in mind that the bus is often late. The bus traveling on the most popular route leaves daily at noon from Latacunga's bus terminal, heading clockwise around the loop. It passes Zumbahua at 1:30 P.M. ($1.50), Quilotoa at 2 P.M. ($2), and arrives in Chugchilán at about 3:30 P.M. ($3). The other bus heads counterclockwise around the loop from Latacunga to Chugchilán, leaving from the Latacunga bus terminal at 11:30 A.M. It passes Saquisilí at 11:50 A.M. ($0.50), Sigchos at about 1:30 P.M. ($2), and Chugchilán around 3 P.M. ($3).

Both buses stay overnight in the plaza at Chugchilán, leaving before dawn the next morning as they head in opposite directions back to Latacunga. The counterclockwise bus leaves at the ungodly hour of 4 A.M., passing Quilotoa at 5 A.M., Zumbahua at 5:30 A.M., and reaching Latacunga at 7:30 A.M. In the other direction, the bus leaves Chugchilán even earlier at 3 A.M., passing Sigchos at 4 A.M., Saquisilí at 7 A.M., and arriving in Latacunga at 7:30 A.M.

If you miss the daily bus, all is not lost. Going clockwise from Latacunga, there are hourly buses to Zumbahua (2 hours, $1.50) bound for Quevedo near the coast. From Zumbahua, you can hire a pickup truck ($5 pp, $10 minimum per group) to Quilotoa. Hiring a truck to Chugchilán is more difficult because of the quality of the road, and it costs at least $25 from Quilotoa and $35 from Zumbahua.

Going counterclockwise, there are several buses hourly from Latacunga to Saquisilí (20 minutes, $0.50), and seven buses 9:30 A.M.–6 P.M. to Sigchos (2 hours, $2). Getting to Chugchilán from Sigchos is tricky, but you may be able to hire a pickup truck for about $25.

Pujilí

Some 12 kilometers west of Latacunga, this bustling little market town springs to life on Sundays and Wednesdays when Plaza Sucre, a couple of blocks from the main squares, fills with market stalls. It is not aimed at visitors, but it is pleasant to visit.

Of more interest are the multicolored steps just up from the bus terminal that lead up to the *mirador* (lookout) at **Cerro Sinchaguasín.** It's a steep 15-minute walk to the top, which commands spectacular views of the valley with Cotopaxi in the distance.

Tigua

West of Pujilí, the road climbs higher, offering stunning views over the valley below. After about 40 kilometers, you reach the village of Tigua (elevation 3,600 meters), a cluster of indigenous communities famed for their artwork. Hundreds of artists in town paint bright depictions of Andean life onto sheep hides. On the main road, one of the best galleries in town is **Galería Tigua-Chimbacucho** (no phone), run by Alfredo Toaquiza, whose father pioneered the art form.

There is not much else to do in Tigua, but if you want to stay, the best place is **La Posada de Tigua** (Hacienda Agricola-Ganadera Tigua-Chimbacucho, Vía Latacunga-Zumbahua Km. 49, tel. 3/281-3682 or 3/280-0454, $30 pp, breakfast and dinner included), a working 19th-century ranch with cozy guest rooms, fresh food, and horseback tours available.

Zumbahua

About 15 kilometers west of Tigua, the town of Zumbahua becomes the weekend hub of the region during its busy **Saturday market,** when indigenous people flock to town with livestock and various wares carried by llama. The town gets surprisingly noisy on Saturday nights, and most travelers just pass through, but you could be stuck if you miss the bus and can't find a pickup truck to take you to Quilotoa. Note that it can be hard to find a room on Friday night.

Of the basic hotels around the main plaza, **Hotel Quilotoa** (Plaza Central, tel. 8/614-0686, $6–7 pp) is a dependable, friendly place with private baths and a rooftop terrace. Tigua painters have a gallery next to the new community **Samana Huasi** (Vía Latacunga-Zumbahua, tel. 3/282-4868, $6), on the main road toward Pujilí.

THE ECUADORIAN ANDES

🄲 Laguna Quilotoa

The luminous turquoise water of this lake in an extinct volcano is perhaps the most breathtaking sight in Ecuador. On a clear day, the spectacle of the sky reflected in the mineral-rich waters 400 meters below the rim, with the snow-capped peaks of Ilinizas and Cotopaxi in the distance, is jaw-droppingly beautiful. Laguna Quilotoa was formed about 800 years ago after a massive eruption led to the collapse of the volcano. Locals believe that the lake is bottomless, and geologists estimate its depth at 250 meters.

Now part of the Iliniza Ecological Reserve, the entrance fee is a mere $1 pp to enter the village of Quilotoa (elevation 3,900 meters) and access the lake. Note that the lake is sometimes shrouded in mist (most commonly in the afternoon), so it's best to plan an overnight stop here to avoid disappointment.

The hike around the rim (4–5 hours) is the best way to appreciate the stunning views. The walk down to the lake (under 2 hours round-trip) is also spectacular. Donkeys ($5) are sometimes available to carry you back up, and canoes ($5 pp) can be rented on the lake.

Accommodations can be found along the turnoff from the main road, where a few Tigua artists run humble hostels with fireplaces, wool blankets, and simple home-cooked food. It gets very cold at night here, so bring plenty of warm clothes. Local artist Humberto Latacunga's **Hostal Cabañas Quilotoa** (Vía Quilotoa, tel. 3/281-4625 or 9/212-5962, $8–10 pp, breakfast and dinner included) has simple guest rooms with fireplaces and hot-water showers. Humberto's beautiful paintings and carved wooden masks are for sale in the restaurant. Another option farther up the hill is **Princesa Toa** (tel. 9/455-6944, $8–10 pp, breakfast and dinner included), which offers cheap set lunches ($2.50).

The only mid-range lodging in town is the **Quilotoa Crater Lake Lodge** (tel. 2/252-7835 or 9/794-2123, $40 s or d, breakfast included), which overlooks the lake and boasts panoramic views. Guest rooms are warm and comfortable, and the restaurant is the best in the village.

© UDY BRILL

Laguna Quilotoa, in an extinct volcano, is one of Ecuador's most spectacular sights.

Chugchilán

One of the most popular trails on the Quilotoa Loop is the five-hour hike to Chugchilán (elevation 3,180 meters), 22 kilometers to the north. The dramatic route skirts cliff edges, passes through the village of Guayama (the only place for refreshments), and descends into the precipitous Río Toachi canyon at Sihui before making the final uphill push to Chugchilán. Maps are available at the Black Sheep Inn in Chugchilán and at Cabañas Quilotoa. It's not advisable to do this hike alone, and it is best to leave no later than 1 P.M. It's possible to do the return trip between Chugchilán and Laguna Quilotoa in one long day, but you would have to start very early. Doing it in the opposite direction, from Chugchilán, involves more uphill hiking, but the advantage is that you can time your trip to catch a bus back from Quilotoa at 2 P.M.

The hike west to Isinliví or Guantualó, which has a traditional Monday market, starts on the road about three kilometers north of Chugchilán. Take the path opposite the road to the cheese factory or the turnoff at Chinaló to reach Itualó, and cross the bridge over the Toachi River.

Chugchilán itself is a poor, remote mountain village, home to about 25 families. There's a women's **knitting cooperative** selling clothing and a small **cheese factory** outside town on the road to Sigchos. There is a small **Sunday market** and a few small shops in the center, good for stocking up on provisions for hiking. The phone service in town is quite unreliable, and your best bet is the **Andinatel** office on the main plaza.

The best budget accommodations in town are found at the homey **Hostal Mama Hilda** (tel. 3/270-8075 or 3/270-8005, $17–21 pp, breakfast and dinner included). Run by the friendly owner, Mama Hilda, the building dates from the 1850s and used to be the town's schoolhouse. There are simple but comfortable guest rooms with shared or private baths, and some have woodstoves to keep warm.

The nearby **Hostal Cloud Forest** (tel. 3/270-8016 or 8/270-8181, www.hostalcloudforest.com, $12–15 pp, breakfast and dinner included) has expanded recently and now has 80 guest rooms. It's another good budget option with guest rooms that have shared or private baths, a popular restaurant, and a living room kept warm by a fireplace. Volunteer placements to teach in the local school are available.

Both hostels offer horseback riding (4–5 hours, $15 pp), and guides to hike from Laguna Quilotoa to Chugchilán cost $15 per group. Transportation can be hired on local trucks to or from Laguna Quilotoa, Zumbahua, or Sigchos ($25–30).

The town's most famous accommodations used to be found at the award-winning **Black Sheep Inn** (tel. 3/270-8077, www.blacksheepinn.com). In 2011, however, the inn, run by founders Michelle Kirby and Andres Hammerman, was converted into a retreat center specializing in hosting group events and is no longer open to visitors. The inn has been a model of ecological sustainability and self-sufficiency for many years, with composting toilets, organic gardens, a greenhouse, and a full recycling program. There's a gym, a yoga studio, a steam room, and a hot tub as well as a solar-powered waterslide and a 100-meter-long zip-line between two eucalyptus trees. Llamas, ducks, dogs, chickens, and, of course, the odd black sheep wander the grounds, which spill down the hillside above the town. For further information on organizing group events, which must be booked well in advance, consult the website.

Sigchos

About 24 kilometers north of Chugchilán, the road undulates down to the little town of Sigchos, which fills up for its Sunday market but is otherwise unremarkable. If you're hiking from Chugchilán, you could opt to stay here at **La Posada** (Galo Atiaga and Las Ilinizas, tel. 3/271-4224, $6 pp), which has small but clean guest rooms and a good restaurant (7 A.M.–9 P.M. daily) downstairs offering set meals ($2) and chicken, meat, and fish entrées ($3–4).

Isinliví

A worthwhile detour from the traditional

Quilotoa Loop is 12 kilometers southeast of Sigchos to the village of Isinliví, which boasts a beautiful setting and is home to an Italian-run cooperative of artisans specializing in wood-carving. There are many excellent hiking and mountain-biking routes in the area, including trails to Quilotoa (7 hours' hike), Chugchilán (4 hours), and the colorful Monday market in Guantualó (1 hour).

A good place to stay is **Llullu Llama Hostal** (tel. 3/281-4790, www.llullullama.com, $18–21 pp), run by the same Dutch-Ecuadorian couple that runs Hostal Tiana in Latacunga. The name means "new flame" in Kichwa. Set in a renovated old country house are five private guest rooms, four loft rooms, and a dormitory. Breakfast and dinner are available, along with box lunches on request. You can rent horses with local guides and obtain clear hiking maps with instructions.

Baños and Vicinity

Locals proudly call Baños (pop. 18,000) *pedacito de cielo* (a little piece of heaven), and this is no exaggeration. Don't be surprised if you end up staying longer than planned. In fact, you may find it very hard to leave. Foreigners and locals alike flock to this tranquil town at an ideal elevation of 1,820 meters in the verdant Andean lowlands to enjoy its springlike climate, abundant spas, and adventure sports. Here you can be as active or as downright lazy and self-indulgent as you like. Hike, cycle, raft, and bungee-jump to your heart's content in the stunning hills of the Pastaza Valley, and then have your muscles pummeled into sweet submission at one of the many spas. Then, of course, there are the relaxing soaks in the volcanic baths that give the town its name. Baños also has an excellent range of accommodations, experienced tour operators, some of the best international restaurants in Ecuador, and busy nightlife on weekends.

Perched between the base of the Tungurahua volcano and the Río Pastaza gorge, Baños enjoys a mild subtropical climate year-round. The Cascada Cabellera de la Virgen (Virgin's Hair Waterfall), visible from anywhere in town, tumbles down the steep hillside and is the site of the town's most popular hot springs. The town is well-known to Ecuadorians and foreign backpackers, but while many of Ecuador's other relaxation spots on the beach have boomed to the point of being spoiled, Banños is only marginally busier than it was a decade ago, which only adds to its charm. This may have something to do with the fact that the town is literally paradise at the gates of hell in the form of the enormous active volcano Tungurahua. After many years of uneasy sleep, Tungurahua, which fittingly means "throat of fire" in Kichwa, erupted suddenly in 1999. The volcano's crater is just 20 kilometers from Baños, but luckily it lies on the opposite side of the mountain to the town; Baños was covered in ash but otherwise remained unscathed. The government took the precaution of ordering a complete evacuation. Residents protested but were forcibly removed by the army. Four months later, about half the city's inhabitants returned, finding Baños still in one piece but many of their homes and businesses emptied by looters. Tungurahua has erupted regularly, in 2006, 2008, and 2010, but Baños continues to escape damage and the tourism industry remains robust, although landslides have affected areas on the edge of town. Tungurahua remains highly active at the time of writing. It is often wreathed in clouds and only visible from the hills above town.

It's not surprising in a devoutly Catholic country that the locals believe that the town's continued survival in the face of volcanic destruction is the work of the Virgin Mary, who, according to legend, appeared on the hill when Tungurahua erupted in 1773 and diverted the lava flow away from the town. Locals also believe that the Virgin blessed the town with holy water containing healing properties, hence the construction of public baths, and the town's

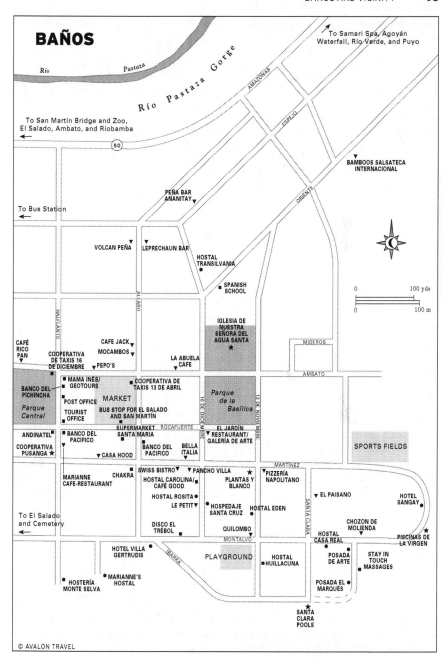

BAÑOS

Río   Pastaza

Río Pastaza Gorge

To Samari Spa, Agoyán
Waterfall, Río Verde, and Puyo

To San Martín Bridge and Zoo,
El Salado, Ambato, and Riobamba

50

AMAZONAS

ESPEJO

BAMBOOS SALSATECA
INTERNACIONAL

To Bus Station

ORIENTE

PEÑA BAR
ANANITAY

VOLCAN PEÑA

LEPRECHAUN BAR

HOSTAL
TRANSILVANIA

SPANISH
SCHOOL

ALFARO

0   100 yds
0   100 m

IGLESIA DE
NUESTRA
SEÑORA DEL
AGUA SANTA
★

MIDEROS

CAFÉ
RICO
PAN

HALFLANTS

CAFE JACK

MOCAMBOS

PEPO'S

LA ABUELA
CAFE

AMBATO

COOPERATIVA
DE TAXIS 16
DE DICIEMBRE

BANCO DEL
PICHINCHA

MAMA INÉS/
GEOTOURS

POST OFFICE

TOURIST
OFFICE

MARKET

COOPERATIVA DE
TAXIS 13 DE ABRIL

BUS STOP FOR EL SALADO
AND SAN MARTÍN

16 DE DICIEMBRE

Parque
de la
Basílica

12 DE NOVIEMBRE

Parque
Central

ANDINATEL

COOPERATIVA
PUSANGA ★

BANCO DEL
PACIFICO

CASA HOOD

SUPERMARKET
SANTA MARIA

ROCAFUERTE

BANCO DEL
PACIFICO

BELLA
ITALIA

EL JARDÍN
RESTAURANT/
GALERÍA DE ARTE

SPORTS FIELDS

MARIANNE
CAFE-RESTAURANT

CHAKRA

SWISS BISTRO

HOSTAL CAROLINA/
CAFÉ GOOD

HOSTAL ROSITA

LE PETIT

PANCHO VILLA   ★

PLANTAS Y
BLANCO

HOSPEDAJE
SANTA CRUZ

HOSTAL EDEN

MARTÍNEZ

PIZZERÍA
NAPOLITANO

EL PAISANO

SANTA CLARA

HOTEL
SANGAY

To El Salado
and Cemetery

DISCO EL
TRÉBOL

QUILOMBO

MONTALVO

CHOZON DE
MOLIENDA

HOSTAL
CASA REAL

PISCINAS DE
LA VIRGEN ★

HOTEL VILLA
GERTRUDIS

IBARRA

PLAYGROUND

HOSTAL
HUILLACUNA

POSADA
DE ARTE

STAY IN
TOUCH
MASSAGES

HOSTERÍA
MONTE SELVA

MARIANNE'S
HOSTAL

POSADA EL
MARQUÉS

SANTA
CLARA
POOLS ★

© AVALON TRAVEL

full name: Baños de Agua Santa (Holy-water Baths).

SIGHTS
Iglesia de Nuestra Señora de Agua Santa

The center of town is dominated by the enormous church, La Basílica de Nuestra Señora de Agua Santa, erected in the Virgin Mary's honor. The black rock walls of the Dominican church are accented with red trim and twin white-topped towers. Inside, 10 huge paintings around the perimeter of the nave record incidents when the Virgin saved the faithful from various disasters, including Tungurahua's eruptions, car wrecks, and plunges into the river Pastaza.

The statue of the Virgin sits near a holy-water spring to the left of the main body of the church. Upstairs, a **museum** (8 A.M.–4 P.M. daily, $0.50) houses the Virgin's processional clothing, religious relics, and a slightly odd collection of stuffed animals.

Thermal Baths

The thermal springs from which Baños takes its name are recommended for the curative properties of their dissolved minerals. There are a total of four sets of public baths around town, but only two are warm. Many of the better hotels in town also have their own baths, but they don't draw on volcanic waters. The public baths get very busy on weekends and even on weekdays in the afternoons and early evenings. Many locals use the springs as actual baths, so it's best not to submerge your head, and the earlier you get here, the cleaner they are. The brownish-yellow waters don't immediately look appealing, but there's no denying the therapeutic effects of an hour or so soaking in them.

Piscinas de la Virgen (5 A.M.–5 P.M. and 6–10 P.M. daily, $2 pp daytime, $3 pp evening) are the most popular baths in town, with three pools ranging from very cold (18°C) to warm (37°C) and hot (45°C). The location is spectacular, at the foot of the Virgin's Hair waterfall, with views over the town and valley. Cold spouts make for a bracing but refreshing break

from the hot baths, and at the center of the complex you can see where the scalding waters gush from the rocks. Stow your belongings in the locker room. Although thefts are rare, it's best to avoid bringing valuables.

There are two other sets of baths in town, but the waters are cold and they are mainly used by local families as swimming pools. **Santa Clara Pools** (9 A.M.–5 P.M. Sat.–Sun., $1 pp) features a large cold pool, waterslides, a sauna, and a steam room.

On the eastern edge of town, on the far side of the Bascún Creek canyon, **Piscina El Salado** (5 A.M.–5 P.M. daily, $3 pp) is the best alternative to Piscinas de la Virgen, with five pools ranging from lukewarm (16°C) to hot (42°C). Note that the complex has recently been rebuilt after being destroyed by a landslide in 2008. It's still officially in a high-risk area, so it is best avoided when the volcano is active or after heavy rains. Look for a paved road just across the bridge east of Baños on the way to Ambato and Riobamba. Buses

the thermal baths at Piscinas de la Virgen in Baños

from the center of town run to the springs every half hour throughout the day, or else it's a 40-minute walk or 10-minute taxi ride ($1.50). Another route from town is reached by walking west on Martínez.

Volcán Tungurahua

The fate of Baños is inextricably linked to the 5,016-meter volcano that lies just eight kilometers south of town. The fact that the crater lies on the opposite side to the town has saved Baños from destruction, and the volcano supplies the thermal waters that have made it famous. This comparatively young volcano is one of Ecuador's more temperamental, having erupted violently in 1773, 1877, and 1916 before its most recent awakening in 1999. The current level of activity shows no signs of abating, with regular eruptions in the last decade, including an eruption in 2010 when a 10-kilometer-high ash cloud covered this author's backyard in Guayaquil, about 300 kilometers away.

Tungurahua's activity has made climbing it complicated. Two Germans first scaled the peak in 1873, but subsequent eruptions changed the mountain's appearance and summit completely. The crater has expanded to more than 400 meters in diameter—five times wider than it was when it began to erupt. Tungurahua used to be considered the easiest snow climb in Ecuador—one of the few in the country where you started out amid tropical vegetation and finished in snow and ice. Until the risk of eruption lessens, however, climbing is highly discouraged. Check with the **South American Explorers** (SAE, Quito clubhouse: Jorge Washington 311 at Plaza, tel./fax 2/222-5228, quitoclub@saexplorers.org, www.saexplorers.org, 9:30 A.M.–5 P.M. Mon.–Fri., 9:30 A.M.–8 P.M. Thurs., 9:30 A.M.–noon Sat.) or locally for the latest volcano update. The best source is the **Ecuadorian Geophysical Institute** (www.igepn.edu.ec), which frequently updates its website.

If you want to get close enough to the volcano to see some plumes of steam or fire, most operators in Baños organize tours to go up, but bear in mind that on most nights you will see very little action.

ENTERTAINMENT AND EVENTS
Nightlife

Baños has very good nightlife for such a small town. The constant stream of backpackers is joined on weekends by a flood of locals who head for the stretch of Eloy Alfaro north of Ambato, the main street. **Mocambo** (Alfaro, tel. 3/274-0923, 4 P.M.–midnight Sun.–Thurs., 4 P.M.–2 A.M. Fri.–Sat.) has three floors with darts, pool, and music videos and is popular with gringos. Farther up is a long-established rock bar, **Jack Rock Café** (Alfaro, tel. 3/274-1329, 4 P.M.–midnight Sun.–Thurs., 4 P.M.–2 A.M. Fri.–Sat.), which mixes in Latin music on the weekend. Toward the end of the street are the more raucous options. The **Leprechaun Bar** (Alfaro and Oriente, tel. 3/274-1537, 7 P.M.–midnight Sun.–Thurs., 7 P.M.–2 A.M. Fri.–Sat.) has the best of both worlds, with a bar in the back garden with a roaring fire and a dance floor that gets packed later on. Opposite, **Volcán Peña Bar** (Alfaro and Oriente, tel. 3/274-2379, 7 P.M.–midnight Sun.–Thurs., 7 P.M.–2 A.M. Fri.–Sat.) attracts a more local crowd onto its dance floor.

The **Peña Bar Amanitay** (16 de Diciembre and Espejo, tel. 3/274-2396, 9 P.M.–midnight daily) has folkloric music from 9:30 P.M. on weekends. Away from the main drag at the south end of town, **Trebol** (Montalvo and 16 de Diciembre, tel. 3/274-1501, 9 P.M.–2 A.M. Thurs.–Sat., $2) is another very popular disco.

Festivals

Baños's **Canonization Festival** is celebrated December 15–16 with bands and processions, and the festival of **Nuestra Señor del Agua Santa** brings in crowds of pilgrims in October.

SHOPPING

Baños certainly has a sweet tooth, and the traditional local candy makes a popular gift. The best are *membrillo* (a red gelatinous block of

THE ECUADORIAN ANDES

FOOL'S GOLD: THE INCA'S LOST RANSOM

One of the most famous mysteries – and treasure hunts – in the Americas began in 1532 when Inca leader Atahualpa was captured by the Spanish at Cajamarca in Peru. Conquistador Francisco Pizarro threatened to execute him unless he bought his freedom, and with customary confidence, Atahualpa placed his hand on the wall to indicate how he could fill the room with gold and silver to save his own life. Atahualpa's subjects, who revered him as a god, set about collecting the largest ransom ever assembled from all corners of his conquered empire.

Pizarro became fearful of Atahualpa's power, however, and went back on his word, staging a mock trial and sentencing him to death. Just before his execution, Atahualpa converted to Christianity in return for leniency, believing that being burned at the stake would prevent his body reaching the afterlife. He was strangled in July 1533. When this news reached Atahualpa's general, Rumiñahui, he quickly hid the largest part of the ransom, which was being transported from Ecuador. The fortune was estimated at 15,000 kilograms of gold and silver, including an 82-kilogram throne of solid gold. The entire ransom was spirited away almost overnight on the shoulders of porters who were ordered to commit suicide to avoid interrogation. The Spanish began a frantic campaign of torture and killing but failed to find any answers. Even as they were burned alive, Inca nobles taunted the invaders, saying that the treasure would never be found.

Over the years, accounts of the treasure's size, location, and very existence have drifted like clouds over the Andes. The wild, inhospitable Llanganati Mountains soon emerged as the most probable location of the lost riches. Part of the Eastern Cordillera, the range stretches across the Central Sierra from the Río Patate Valley north almost to Volcán Quilindaña, with the highest point at Cerro Hermoso (4,571 meters). Rumiñahui could hardly have found a more forbidding spot in the entire Inca empire, where wind, rain, and fog make it all too easy to get lost. Rumors about the treasure's exact whereabouts included deep caves and the bottom of an icy lake.

Enter a poor Spanish soldier under Pizarro named Valverde, who married an indigenous woman in Latacunga. As unlikely as it seems, he claimed that his wife's father, the chief of Píllaro, the closest town to the Llanganatis, told him where the ransom was hidden. On his deathbed, Valverde dictated a map named the *Derrotero* ("Path") that contained detailed directions through the Llanganati Mountains to

guava) and *milcocha,* chewy sugarcane bars that you can watch being made, swung over wooden pegs.

For indigenous clothing, take your pick from scores of stores on and near the main street, Ambato. Haggling is obligatory. On the **Pasaje Artesanal,** which leads along the side of the market between Ambato and Rocafuerte, there are many stalls selling jewelry and *tagua* carvings.

The **Galería de Arte Huillacuna** (12 de Noviembre and Montalvo, tel. 3/274-0909, 8:30 A.M.–7:30 P.M. daily) displays sculptures, paintings, and drawings by local artists and offers accommodations upstairs.

For handmade guitars, visit **Guitarras Guevara** (Halflants, tel. 3/274-0941), which has instruments ranging $75–300 in price.

RECREATION AND TOURS
Hiking Around Baños

The steep hillside west of town can be scaled by two routes. The most common is to head south on Maldonado and take a path that climbs up to **Bellavista,** where a white cross stands. At night, when the hills fade from view, this illuminated cross seems to float in the middle of the sky above town. The views are spectacular over Baños and the Pastaza Valley stretching down toward the Oriente. The path continues steeply up to the village of Runtún (elevation 2,600 meters), two hours a lake where the treasure lay, although it also contained some vague, confusing passages. The king of Spain sent the map to the authorities in Latacunga, where various expeditions were organized, but no treasure was found, and many explorers never returned, fueling the rumor that both the area and the treasure it contained were cursed.

The trail went cold until British botanist Richard Spruce came across a copy of the map in the 1850s. He also uncovered a map drawn by Anastasio Guzman, a Spanish botanist and farmer who had lived in Píllaro. Building on the knowledge of many trips into the Llanganatis, Guzman's 1800 map roughly corresponded with Valverde's guide. Seven years later, Guzman walked off a cliff in his sleep. The account of the treasure, along with a copy of the *Derrotero*, appeared as the final chapter in Spruce's *Notes of a Botanist on the Amazon and Andes*, published in 1908.

Spruce's writings inspired Nova Scotian explorer Barth Blake to travel to Ecuador. According to letters written to a friend, Blake did indeed strike gold after an expedition into Llanganati. In one letter he wrote: "There are thousands of gold and silver pieces of Inca and pre-Inca handicraft, the most beautiful goldsmith works you are not able to imagine." He

took as much gold as he could, but claimed, "I could not remove it alone, nor could thousands of men." Blake's best friend, who accompanied him on the expedition, died in the mountains, and Blake reportedly journeyed to North America to organize an expedition to remove the rest of the gold, but mysteriously disappeared on the way.

Many treasure hunters in the early 20th century followed Blake and shared similarly mysterious fates, including Scotsman Erskine Loch, who shot himself after a failed expedition, and American Colonel Brooks, who ended up in a mental institution after his wife died of pneumonia in the mountains.

British author Mark Honigsbaum is the most recent writer to investigate the story in his 2004 book *Valverde's Gold*. He concluded:

My own feeling is that this gold was probably taken out centuries ago. If not, and it's still there, I think it's lost forever, because those mountains are so vast and inaccessible that you're looking for a needle in a haystack.

It remains to be seen whether his words will dampen the gold lust of future treasure hunters.

away and with good views of Tungurahua. You can then loop around and head back down to Baños past the statue of **La Virgen del Agua Santa.**

Alternately, head south on Mera, and then head to the right past the cemetery to reach the Virgin statue. The walk up takes about half an hour and provides good views of Tungurahua around the corner. The path continues above the statue all the way to the top of the hillside and Runtún, or a downhill branch can be taken back down to Mera.

More good hikes follow the Pastaza: cross the main road near the bus station and continue over the road bridge at **Puente San Francisco.** A network of trails crisscrosses the

hillside facing Baños. The village of **Illuchi,** about a two-hour hike from the river, is a good turning-around point, with views of Baños, Tungurahua, and the river.

The **Puente San Martín** crosses the Pastaza just to the west of town. To reach it, cross the bridge out of Baños, pass the turnoff to Piscina El Salado, and turn right. Near the bridge is the **Cascada Inés María,** a small waterfall, and the **San Martín Zoo** (8 A.M.–5 P.M. daily, $1.50) opened in 1994 as a refuge for sick and injured animals from the Amazon. The zoo has an impressive range of birds and mammals, including monkeys, pumas, and a jaguar, although some of the enclosures are rather small. There is a small

aquarium (8 A.M.–5 P.M. daily, $1) opposite the zoo that has tropical fish as well as reptiles and birds.

Mountain Biking

A faster and more exhilarating way to enjoy the stunning scenery around Baños is on two wheels. By far the most popular excursion is the downhill route to Puyo. The old road passes along the gorge of the Río Pastaza, offering spectacular views and dropping nearly 1,000 meters through rapidly changing terrain that becomes more and more tropical as you reach Puyo, 61 kilometers to the east. Most people don't make it that far but are content to visit the series of waterfalls, including **Manto de la Novia** and **Pailón del Diablo**, in the first half of the route, and then either cycling or catching a bus back (you can usually stow the bike on the roof). Bikes can be rented at most agencies in Baños for $8 per day including a helmet, a repair kit, and a map, or take a full-day guided tour ($40 pp) to visit the waterfalls, ending in Machay.

Horseback Riding

Horses are another popular way to get into the hills, costing around $16 pp for two hours including a guide, or $60 per day. The most popular route is Nahuazo, at the foot of Tungurahua. Keep in mind that reports of ill or mistreated horses have been on the rise in the last few years. Look for healthy, well-treated animals, and try out the saddle for fit before you head out on your ride. Don't accept blankets instead of saddles.

Rafting and Kayaking

Although it's not as renowned as Tena, the white-water rafting near Baños is good. The most popular routes are along Río Patate, which has sections of Class 3 rapids and short sections of Class 4. A half-day trip costs $30 pp.

Kayaking is also available, but you need to take a course ($60 pp per day) if you're not experienced.

Adventure Sports

There are various other activities to get your adrenaline flowing. Canyoneering in Río Blanco is great fun. Full-day trips cost $30 pp, usually including four waterfalls. Swing jumping (not bungee) is available off the 100-meter-high Puente San Francisco ($20 pp), and tandem paragliding can be done in Pelileo. Renting all-terrain vehicles is another popular craze around Baños, but be careful, particularly on hilly terrain, as accidents have been reported.

Climbing to the summit of Tungurahua is obviously not allowed (and highly dangerous), but there are excursions to the refuge at 3,830 meters. You can do it in one day for $60 pp or overnight for $120 pp.

A range of rainforest trips can be arranged from Baños, and after Quito it's probably the best place to book one. The most common and economical tours go into communities near Puyo, but bear in mind that this is secondary rainforest. For primary rainforest, you need to book a trip that goes through Coca or Lago Agrio, although there are pockets of primary rainforest east of Tena and Misahualli.

Tour Operators

Baños has an enormous number of tour agencies, and it's tough to keep the trustworthy separate from the fly-by-night rip-off artists. The following agencies have been repeatedly recommended, but it's a good idea to check with the **South American Explorers** (SAE, Quito clubhouse: Jorge Washington 311 at Plaza, tel./fax 2/222-5228, quitoclub@saexplorers.org, www.saexplorers.org, 9:30 A.M.–5 P.M. Mon.–Fri., 9:30 A.M.–8 P.M. Thurs., 9:30 A.M.–noon Sat.) for a current list. Almost all agencies offer hiking, cycling, rafting, kayaking, canyoneering, swing-jumping, climbing tours, and rainforest expeditions.

Geotours (Ambato and Halflants, tel./fax 3/274-1344, geotoursbanios@yahoo.es, www.geotoursbanios.com) was the first adventure operator to open in town nearly 20 years ago and is still one of the best. **Córdova Tours**

(Maldonado and Espejo, tel. 3/274-0923, ojosvolcan@hotmail.com, www.cordovatours. banios.com) is also dependable for a wide range of tours and rents 4WD vehicles. **Jose and Two Dogs** (Maldonado and Martínez, tel./ fax 3/274-0746) is more professional than its name suggests and is recommended for horseback riding and hiking.

Many agencies specialize in tours of the Amazon. **Sebastián Moya Expediciones** (Oriente and Halflants, tel. 3/248-4287, wulopez@hotmail.com) is owned by Shuar guide Sebastián Moya and run under the auspices of the Yawa Jee Shuar Indigenous Foundation, a private nonprofit dedicated to sustainable, low-impact tourism to benefit Shuar communities. **Expediciones Amazonicas** (Oriente between Alfaro and Halflants, tel. 3/274-0506, www. baniosxtreme.com/amazonicas) has received positive reports for its wide range of rainforest trips via Puyo and Lago Agrio as well as adventure tours, rafting, and climbing.

Most feedback on **Rainforestur** (Ambato and Maldonado, tel./fax 3/274-0743, www.rainforestur.com.ec) has been positive. Guides speak English, French, and German and offer tours of the surrounding area and Cuyabeno. **Vasco Tours** (Alfaro and Martínez, tel. 3/274-1017) is run by Flor Vasco and Juan Medina in Quito and has received positive feedback for their tours to Huaorani indigenous communities.

Massage and Spa Therapies

No spa town would be complete without massages, and Baños has plenty of places offering a wide range of spa therapies to soothe those aches and pains. Many of the hotels have an on-site masseuse, but quality is variable. One of the best in town is **Chakra** (Alfaro and Luis Martínez, tel. 3/274-2027, www.chakramassages.com), run by a local, Carmen Sánchez, who specializes in Swedish massage as well as reflexology and beauty treatments. Also recommended are the American-Ecuadorian husband-and-wife team Geoffrey and Edith at **Stay in Touch** (Av. Montalvo, tel. 3/274-0973). A one-hour full-body massage costs $27; spinal manipulations are also available.

ACCOMMODATIONS

Baños has more than 130 hotels, and competition keeps prices down. Most are budget and mid-range hotels and will negotiate their rates for midweek stays. However, be warned that prices usually double on national holidays, and locals are happy to pay these rates, so you'll be hard-pressed to find a room without a reservation. The best hotels are at the south end of town.

Under $10

There are plenty of cheap hotels in town, but avoid the ones toward the northern end, which tend to be run-down. The backpacker institution **Hostal Plantas y Blanco** (Martínez and 12 de Noviembre, tel. 3/274-0044, dorm $5.50–7.50 pp, rooms $8.50–11 pp) continues to offer a great deal and is a good meeting spot for kindred spirits. There's a rooftop terrace, sun loungers, kitchen, Turkish baths ($2.75 pp), free Internet access, and compact but clean guest rooms. The hotel's fresh fruit and pancakes are one of the best breakfasts in town. **C Hostal Transilvania** (16 de Diciembre and Oriente, tel. 3/274-2281, www.hostal-transilvania.com, $7.50 pp, breakfast included) is far more welcoming than its name suggests. This Israeli-owned place is an incredibly good deal with well-maintained guest rooms and a colorful café where big breakfasts are served on petrified-wood tables. It fills up fast.

Hospedaje Santa Cruz (16 de Diciembre and Martínez, tel. 3/274-0648, $9.50 pp) is another good budget option, with two ground-floor patios with fireplaces, games, magazines, a self-service bar, free Internet access, and simple but colorful guest rooms. **Hostal Carolina** (16 de Diciembre, tel. 3/274-0592, $7 pp) is another safe bet, with friendly service and simple, well-maintained guest rooms above a vegetarian café. **Hostal Rosita** (16 de Diciembre near Martínez, tel. 3/274-0396, $7 pp) is another good-value budget option with free Internet access and two larger apartments for longer stays.

$10-25

For a few extra dollars, Baños has an excellent

selection of mid-range hotels. **Hostal Eden** (12 de Noviembre, tel. 3/274-0616, $10 pp) is a cut above the budget options with decent guest rooms with cable TV facing a pleasant garden courtyard and a cheap restaurant attached. **Hostal Casa Real** (Montalvo y Pasaje Ibarra, tel. 3/274-0215, $12 pp) is a great-value choice close to the waterfall. Guest rooms have murals of wildlife, and the massages in the spa upstairs are very good. For a more artistic experience, stay at **Huillacuna** (12 de Noviembre and Montalvo, tel. 3/274-2909, $15 pp, breakfast included), a beautifully laid-out hotel with guest rooms set around a gallery offering both a feast of art on the walls and a culinary feast at breakfast.

One of the best options in this range is the French-run **(Hostal Jardín Marianne** (Montalvo and Halflants, tel. 3/274-1947, $15 pp). These comfortable new guest rooms with balconies in tranquil surroundings are perfect for a relaxing break.

Off Montalvo near the waterfall is the **Posada El Marqués** (tel. 3/274-0053, $23 s, $35 d), a homey, family-run place with newly upgraded guest rooms in the large main house. Guest rooms are spacious, clean, and quiet, with private baths and hot water.

$25-50

(Hostal Posada del Arte (Pasaje Ibarra and Montalvo, tel. 3/274-0083, www.posadadelarte.com, $28–30 s, $52–56 d) is a special place with walls adorned with South American art and plushly decorated guest rooms with chimneys to keep you warm. The restaurant is excellent, with home-brewed ales and a range of international specialties.

The best place to stay in Baños itself is **(Hostería Monte Selva** (tel. 3/274-0566, www.monteselvaecuador.com, $38 s, $63 d, $99 suites). These cabins and guest rooms snuggled at the foot of the hillside at the south end of Halflants are set in beautiful gardens with excellent facilities that include a large pool, a sauna, a steam room, and jetted tubs. A range of spa therapies are on offer, and the hotel has an "eco-park" near Puyo where it

runs excursions—although you may find it hard to leave the comfort of the hotel.

With a more businesslike atmosphere, the big peach-colored building at the base of the waterfall is **Hotel Sangay** (tel. 3/274-0490, fax 3/274-0056, $24–56 s, $40–70 d). Choose between guest rooms in the main hotel, cabins out back, and executive suites beyond that. Guests can work up a sweat with tennis or squash before crossing the street to the baths. The hotel's spa therapies are highly recommended.

$100-200

On the crest of the hill overlooking Baños sits Swiss-Ecuadorian **Luna Runtún** (tel. 3/274-0882, fax 3/274-0376, www.lunaruntun.com, $154 s or d, breakfast and dinner included). The guest rooms are rustic but underwhelming for the cost; the surroundings, however, are what make this a special place. The hacienda feel is enhanced by flower gardens, fountains, and tiled roofs. Enjoy massage, Reiki, and beauty treatments in the garden spa, which uses plants from the garden and ashes and stones from the nearby volcano. The highlight is the spectacular view over Baños and the Pastaza Valley from the hot pools and adjacent Café del Cielo. Tungurahua also peeks through the clouds to the south. A taxi to the hotel from Baños costs about $7, and a private shuttle is available.

Samari Spa (tel. 3/274-1855, fax 3/274-1859, www.samarispa.com, $186 s or d, breakfast included) is on the road to the rainforest just one kilometer out of town, so it's quiet and relaxing. The opulent facilities include 37 guest rooms, suites, a covered pool, a sauna, a steam-hydro massage, and spa-therapy and massage rooms. The original volcanic-rock building has been tastefully restored and sits in beautifully landscaped gardens. The acclaimed restaurant offers all meals and caters to conventions or small groups.

FOOD

Like its hotel offerings, Baños has an amazing range of food options for such a small town, with restaurants that rival those in Quito and Cuenca. The best food tends to be international, with plenty of standard Ecuadorian fare also on offer. If you really want to go local, sink your teeth into one of the *cuyes* (guinea pigs) that are roasted in front of the market on Ambato. For those with a sweet tooth, sip sugarcane juice at the stalls near the bus terminal and munch on candy such as *membrillo* (a red gelatinous block of guava) and *milcocha* (chewy sugarcane bars), available from dozens of stalls all over town.

Ecuadorian

La Abuela Café (Ambato and 16 de Diciembre, tel. 3/274-2962, 8 A.M.–11 P.M. daily, entrées $6) is popular for local specialties such as *churrasco* and *llapingacho*. **Café Rico Pan** (Ambato, tel. 3/274-0387, 7 A.M.–8 P.M. Mon.–Thurs., 7 A.M.–noon Sun., entrées $2–4) is one of the best bakeries in town and a good place for breakfast and snacks.

International

One of the best restaurants in town is **Casa Hood** (Martínez and Halflants, tel. 3/274-2668, 4–10 P.M. Wed.–Mon., entrées $4–5), run by American expat and longtime resident Ray Hood. His restaurant is renowned for its healthy, eclectic menu with Asian, Mexican, and Italian entrées plus a wide range of juices, smoothies, teas, and cakes. The funky art and books will keep you busy until your tasty food arrives.

For delicious French cuisine, try the **Marianne Café-Restaurant** (Halflants between Martínez and Rocafuerte, tel. 3/274-1947, noon–11 P.M. daily, entrées $6–9), a quaint little restaurant snuggled in an interior courtyard. Specialties include beef fondue, steak milanesa, fresh trout, French onion soup, and crepes galore. **Le Petit Restaurant** (16 de Diciembre and Montalvo, tel. 3/274-0936, noon–10 P.M. Tues.–Sun., entrées $6–9), part of Le Petit Alberge hotel, is another good choice for French food. For the best cheese and meat fondues in town, as well as a range of European specialties, head to the friendly **Swiss Bistro** (Martínez and Alfaro,

tel. 3/274-2262, noon–11 P.M. daily, entrées $6–10).

For Italian pasta and pizza in all its variations, stop by **La Bella Italia** (Martínez and Alfaro, tel. 3/271-0121, 7 A.M.–9 P.M. daily, entrées $4–8). **Pizzeria Napolitano** (12 de Noviembre and Martínez, tel. 3/274-2341, noon–10 P.M. daily, entrées $4–8) cooks up 11 different kinds of pizza along with meat and seafood dishes.

Pancho Villa (Martínez and 16 de Diciembre, tel. 3/274-2138, 12:30–10 P.M. Mon.–Sat., closed Sun., entrées $6–7) does the best Mexican tacos, fajitas, and enchiladas in town.

The restaurant at **Hostal Posada del Arte** (Pasaje Ibarra and Montalvo, tel. 3/274-0083, www.posadadelarte.com, 8 A.M.–10 P.M. daily, entrées $5–8) is excellent, with home-brewed ales and a range of international specialties that include Swedish meatballs and beef stroganoff.

For the best grilled meats, try the eccentric, creative surroundings of **Quilombo** (Montalvo and 16 de Diciembre, tel. 3/274-2880, noon–3 P.M. and 6 P.M.–9:30 P.M. daily, entrées $6–10), a friendly Argentine-run place where the menu is written on dice. Barbecued meat, imaginative dishes such as steak in ginger sauce, and oven-baked pizzas are served under a thatched roof in a spacious garden at **Chozón de Molienda** (Montalvo and Pasaje Ibarra, tel. 3/274-1816, 6:30–11:30 P.M. daily, entrées $5–8).

For vegetarian food, the building housing **El Paisano** (Santa Clara 288 at Martínez, tel. 9/261-0037, 7 A.M.–10 P.M. daily, entrées $3–6) doesn't look very inviting, but the vegetarian fare is cheap and excellent, making good use of fresh ingredients. For more vegetarian options, **El Jardín Restaurant/Galería de Arte** (Rocafuerte and 16 de Diciembre, tel. 3/274-0875, 1–11 P.M. daily, entrées $6–9) has a good selection as well as specialties such as Thai shrimp and steak with pepper and cream, served in a garden overlooking the cathedral. **Café Good** (16 de Diciembre, tel. 3/274-0592, 8 A.M.–10 P.M. daily, entrées $4–7) is another vegetarian option with a mix of local, European, and Asian fare.

INFORMATION AND SERVICES

Head to the **Departamento de Turismo del Municipio** (Halflants and Rocafuerte, tel. 3/274-0483, www.baniosadn.ec, 8 A.M.–12:30 P.M. and 2–5:30 P.M. daily) on the Parque Central for brochures, maps, and directories on Baños's long list of places to stay, places to eat, and things to do.

The **Banco del Pacífico** (Halflants and Rocafuerte) and **Banco del Pichincha** (Ambato and Halflants) both have ATMs and change traveler's checks.

There are dozens of Internet cafés, and many hotels have free Internet access, but **Direct Connect** (Martínez) also provides Internet access. For international phone calls, head to **Andinatel** (Rocafuerte and Halflants).

The **police station** is on Thomas Halflants near Ambato (tel. 3/274-0122), the **hospital** is on Montalvo near Pastaza (tel. 3/274-0443), and the **post office** is on Halflants near Ambato (tel. 3/274-0901).

Spanish Lessons

Outside of Quito and Cuenca, Baños is probably the most popular place in Ecuador to stay and study Spanish. Most schools offer individual and group instruction, starting at $5 per hour. Recommended is **Baños Spanish Center** (Oriente and Cañar, tel./fax 3/274-0632, tel. 8/704-5072, baniosspanishcenter@hotmail.com, www.spanishcenterschool.com) was the first school to open in Baños and is run by Elizabeth Barrionuevo, who speaks Spanish, English, and German. She has been recommended as an excellent teacher and also offers dancing and cooking lessons.

Other recommended schools include **Ciudad de Baños Languages School** (Ambato and Alfaro, tel. 3/274-0317, www.escueladeidiomas.banios.com), **Mayra's Spanish School** (Efren Reyes and Martínez, tel. 3/274-2850, www.mayraspanishschool.com), and **Raices Spanish School** (16 de Diciembre and Suárez, tel./fax 3/274-1921, www.spanishlessons.org).

GETTING THERE AND AROUND

The central **bus station** is bordered by Reyes and Maldonado, along the main road at the north end of Baños. Buses run to most cities in the Sierra as well as the Oriente, including buses to Quito (3.5 hours, $3.50), Ambato (1 hour, $1), Puyo (2 hours, $2), and Riobamba (2.5 hours, $2.50), which will be cheaper and take only 1.5 hours if the direct road reopens. Local buses to **El Salado** and **San Martín** leave regularly from the bus stop at Alfaro and Martínez, beside the Santa María supermarket.

There are lots of taxis at the bus station and around the main square. Journeys within town cost $1, and to the outskirts $1.50. If you want to reserve a taxi ahead of time, stop by **Cooperativa de Taxis** (Ambato and Halflants) or **Cooperativa de Taxis 13 de Abril** (Rocafuerte and Alfaro).

◖ THE WATERFALL ROUTE FROM BAÑOS TO PUYO

This spectacular 61-kilometer road drops nearly 1,000 meters in elevation along the Pastaza Valley to the edge of the Oriente. There are nearly a dozen waterfalls along the newly christened Ruta de las Cascadas, which has developed into a major tourist attraction with several *tarabitas* (cable-cars) across the valley as well as a range of adventure sports. There are three ways to see this route: You can hop on a Baños–Puyo bus and stop off at the waterfalls, take a guided tour, or the best option is to hire a bicycle and take in the scenery at your leisure and see how far you get toward Puyo. If you feel too tired to cycle back uphill, you can always take a bus back and stow your bike on top.

The new Baños–Puyo road goes through half a dozen tunnels, only the first of which is open to cyclists. Along the rest of the route cyclists bypass the tunnels and take the old road, enjoying wonderful canyon views along the cliff face.

Leaving Baños, cross the Agoyán hydroelectric dam and the first set of cable car rides to small waterfalls, including the Agoyán. After

© BEN WESTWOOD

There are now two waterfalls at Manto de la Novia following a landslide in 2010.

40 minutes, you pass one of the most impressive waterfalls on the route, **Manto de la Novia** (Bride's Veil). For a small tip, the *tarabita* staff will watch your bike. Take the hair-raising *tarabita* ($1) 500 meters across the gorge from where you can take a short walk down to a viewing platform or a longer hike (20 minutes) down to the bottom of the gorge to stand at the foot of the waterfall. It's an awe-inspiring sight, but also sobering. In February 2010 a huge landslide here killed five residents and swept away houses, and there are now two waterfalls where for centuries there was only one. You can cross the rickety bridge back across the gorge and walk back up to the main road.

After Manto de Novia, it's 40 minutes farther to Río Verde, 18 kilometers from Baños, an emerging town with several hotels, small restaurants, and shops selling local crafts. More importantly, this is the access point to **El Pailón del Diablo** (Devil's Cauldron), a

dramatic waterfall tumbling between vertical walls into a deep depression. Follow the signs to the path leading down into a forested gorge, which offers welcome shade. There is a tiny suspension bridge (maximum capacity: 5 people), and it costs $1 to walk down to a set of three platforms to view the waterfall up close. There is also a path cut into the rocks called Grieta al Cielo (Crevice to Heaven) that you can walk along, crouching, to go inside a cave behind the waterfall.

Most people visit Río Verde for an hour or so, but the stunning setting has led to some good accommodations options. **Miramelindo** (Vía Baños–Puyo Km. 18, tel. 3/249-3004, www.miramelindo.banios.com, $25 pp, breakfast included) has rustic guest rooms beside the river, with an orchid garden, a jetted tub, a sauna, steam baths, and free guided tours to the waterfall. A couple of kilometers farther east on the Baños–Puyo road is **Pequeño Paraíso** (tel. 9/981-9776, www.hostel-banos-pequenoparaiso.com, $17–20 pp, breakfast and dinner included), where comfortable cabins and dorms sit on grounds full of fruit trees with great views over the canyon.

About 2.5 kilometers east of Río Verde is the village of **Machay,** where trails lead up into the hills to a series of small waterfalls. The most impressive, **Manantial del Dorado,** is at the end of the trail, but this is quite a hike—over four hours there and back—and better done on a guided tour.

Most people turn back at this point, but if you keep going along the road, you'll reach **Río Negro,** after which the scenery opens out to reveal views of the widening valley, and the scenery becomes noticeably more tropical. The town of **Mera** is next, after 17 kilometers, and then there's a **police checkpoint** where you will probably be required to show your passport. About seven kilometers farther is the small airport of **Shell,** which runs small charter services to visit remote indigenous communities in the rainforest. About 10 kilometers farther on is **Puyo.**

THE ECUADORIAN ANDES

Cuenca and Vicinity

Ecuador's third city is arguably its most beautiful, and with only 331,000 inhabitants, it's far smaller than Quito and Guayaquil, retaining a more intimate atmosphere. The city is comparatively safe, the climate pleasantly cool, and the locals with their singsong accents are very welcoming. There are plenty of kindred spirits too because Cuenca has become very popular both with travelers and retired folk looking for a quiet, scenic city to study or simply relax.

Cuenca (elevation 2,530 meters), capital of Azuay Province, is known as the "Athens of Ecuador" because of its architectural beauty. The center was declared a UNESCO World Heritage site in 1996, and walking around the stately squares, churches, and colonial houses is a delightful experience. Devout Catholicism dominates the city, both architecturally and culturally; consider the city's municipal motto: *Primero Díos, Después Vos* (First God, Then You). The city is not without its Bohemian streak, however: There are seven universities here with a large student population, and Cuenca was also the first regular meeting place for poets in Latin America.

Cuenca also has a proud sporting tradition. The city is home to Jefferson Pérez, who became Ecuador's first and only Olympic medalist in 1996 by taking the gold in speed walking. At age 22, he was also the youngest-ever Olympic walking champion. A devout Catholic, he chose not to bask in his fame but celebrated his Olympic win by embarking on a 450-kilometer pilgrimage from Quito to Cuenca. He went on to become a three-time world champion, set the world record for the 20-kilometer walk, and retired after winning the silver medal in Beijing in 2008. Cuencanos—and all Ecuadorians—are fiercely proud of Jefferson Pérez, and locals will often be seen practicing speed walking in the city's parks. Luis Chocho, Pérez's first trainer, has a city academy that has trained generations of champion speed-walkers. Cycling and jogging are also very popular in Cuenca; on a

recent visit, I met a diminutive, middle-aged taxi driver who was enthusing about beating a "Dutch giant" half his age in a half-marathon.

HISTORY

Cuenca began as a Cañari settlement called Guapondelig, meaning "valley of flowers." The Incas arrived in the 15th century and overcame fierce resistance from the Cañari before transforming the site into the palatial city Tomebamba. It was a favorite residence of Huayna Capac, the ruling hub of the northern reaches of the Inca Empire, and its grounds and buildings, suitably fit for a king, were said to rival Cuzco itself.

In the civil war that followed the sudden death of the ruling Inca, his son Atahualpa was briefly imprisoned by his half brother with the help of the local Cañari *indígenas.* After a narrow escape, Atahualpa defeated his brother and razed the city in revenge, putting its entire population to death.

After Atahualpa's death and the completion of the Spanish conquest, lieutenant Gil Ramírez Dávalos refounded the city of Santa Ana de los Cuatro Ríos de Cuenca (*cuenca* means "river basin") in 1557 on the ruins of Tomebamba, using much of the original Inca stonework to construct churches. Alongside Quito and Guayaquil, it served as a capital of one of the three provinces that made up the territory of Ecuador. Growth over the following centuries was slow because of Cuenca's isolation from the northern Sierra. The 1739 French expedition to measure the size of the earth at the Equator provided the most excitement in years, before a local economic boom in the 19th century, as Cuenca became a major exporter of Panama hats, quinine, and other goods.

It wasn't until the mid-20th century that decent roads connecting Cuenca to the rest of the country were completed, transforming it from a sleepy market center into a modern city. The economic crisis in 2000 hit Cuenca

© BEN WESTWOOD

Cuenca's Catedral Nueva is one of the most spectacular cathedrals in South America.

hard, however, and thousands of residents emigrated. Some have returned, using their savings from the United States and Spain to build dream homes, while many others remain abroad. Ironically, as many locals have left, North American and European seniors have arrived, drawn to Cuenca as a retirement destination. However, the city is large enough not to become dominated by the burgeoning expat community, and Cuenca retains its colonial character, preserved further by its status as a UNESCO World Heritage Site.

ORIENTATION

Four rivers feed the fertile Tomebamba Valley that cradles Cuenca. The Ríos Tomebamba and Yanuncay flow down from El Cajas National Park to the west, joining with the Ríos Tarqui and Machángara to form the Río Cuenca on their way east to the rainforest. The Tomebamba divides the city center into two sections: to the north, the historical center has changed little since colonial times, whereas gleaming glass buildings and modern

suburbs, less frequented by visitors, are found to the south.

Central Cuenca is relatively safe to walk around until 10 P.M. or so, although it's wise to be careful in the market areas, particularly Mercado 9 de Octubre. Later on, it's advisable to take a taxi.

SIGHTS

Cuenca's wealth of religious architecture makes it easy to believe the local saying that the city has a church for every Sunday of the year (the tourist office claims that there are indeed 52). The churches of San Sebastián to the west and San Blas to the east once marked the city's boundaries. Note that many museums and attractions (as well as most restaurants) are closed on Sunday, the best day to take a day trip outside the city.

(Catedral Nueva and Parque Calderon

Palm and pine trees fill charming Parque Calderón, Cuenca's central park. On its west

THE ECUADORIAN ANDES

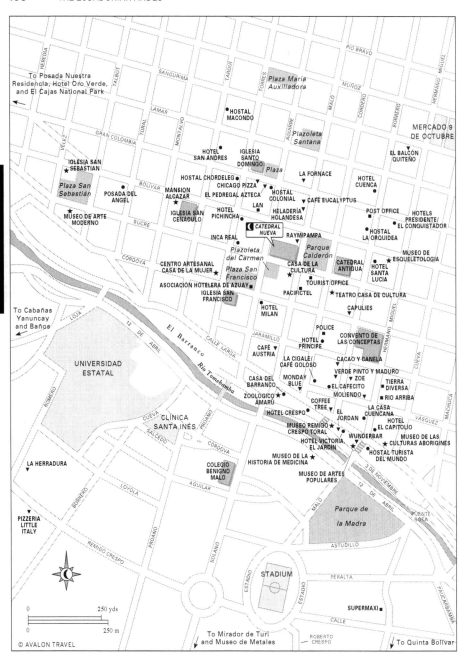

PIO BRAVO

HEREDIA

To Posada Nuestra
Residencia, Hotel Oro Verde,
and El Cajas National Park

SANGURIMA

TALBOT

TARQUI

TORRES

MALO

MUÑOZ

CORDERO

BORRERO

HERMANO

MIGUEL

Plaza Maria
Auxiliadora

LAMAR

MONTALVO

AGUIRRE

MERCADO 9
DE OCTUBRE

GRAN COLOMBIA

TORAL

HOSTAL
MACONDO

Plazoleta
Santana

EL BALCÓN
QUITEÑO

VELEZ

HOTEL
SAN ANDRES

IGLESIA
SANTO
DOMINGO

Plaza

IGLESIA SAN
SEBASTIAN

HOSTAL CHORDELEG

LA FORNACE

HOTEL
CUENCA

Plaza San
Sebastián

POSADA DEL
ANGEL

BOLIVAR

MANSION
ALCAZAR

CHICAGO PIZZA
EL PEDREGAL AZTECA

HOSTAL
COLONIAL

CAFÉ EUCALYPTUS

POST OFFICE

HOTELS
PRESIDENTE/
EL CONQUISTADOR

MUSEO DE ARTE
MODERNO

SUCRE

IGLESIA SAN
CENACULO

HOTEL
PICHINCHA

LAN

HELADERÍA
HOLANDESA

INCA REAL

CATEDRAL
NUEVA

RAYMIPAMPA

HOSTAL
LA ORQUIDEA

MUSEO DE
ESQUELETOLOGIA

CORDOVA

Plazoleta
del Carmen

Parque
Calderón

CATEDRAL
ANTIGUA

HOTEL
SANTA
LUCIA

CENTRO ARTESANAL
CASA DE LA MUJER

Plaza San
Francisco

CASA DE LA
CULTURA

ASOCIACIÓN HOTELERA DE AZUAY

IGLESIA SAN
FRANCISCO

TOURIST OFFICE

PACIFICTEL

TEATRO CASA DE CULTURA

To Cabañas
Yanuncay
and Baños

LOJA

12
DE
ABRIL

El Barranco

CALLE LARGA

HOTEL
MILAN

JARAMILLO

CAPULIES

POLICE

Río Tomebamba

CAFÉ
AUSTRIA

HOTEL
PRINCIPE

CONVENTO DE
LAS CONCEPTAS

HERMANO MIGUEL

CUEVA

UNIVERSIDAD
ESTATAL

ROMERO

LA CIGALE/
CAFÉ GOLOSO

CACAO Y CANELA

VERDE PINTO Y MADURO
ZOE

CASA DEL
BARRANCO

MONDAY
BLUE

EL CAFECITO

TIERRA
DIVERSA

PRIANO

ZOOLÓGICO
AMARU

MOLIENDO

RIO ARRIBA

VÁSQUEZ

MACHUCA

CUEVA

CLÍNICA
SANTA INÉS

CORDOVA

COFFEE
TREE

EL
JORDAN

LA CASA
CUENCANA

HOTEL CRESPO

SALCEDO

MUSEO REMIGIO
CRESPO TORAL

HOTEL
EL CAPITOLIO

WUNDERBAR

MUSEO DE LAS
CULTURAS ABORIGINES

HOTEL VICTORIA,
EL JARDIN

LA HERRADURA

COLEGIO
BENIGNO
MALO

MUSEO DE LA
HISTORIA DE MEDICINA

HOSTAL TURISTA
DEL MUNDO

BORRERO

PRIANO

AGUILAR

MUSEO DE ARTES
POPULARES

3 DE NOVIEMBRE

12
DE
ABRIL

LOYOLA

PIZZERIA
LITTLE
ITALY

REMIGIO CRESPO

SOLANO

MALO

Parque de
la Madre

ASTUDILLO

PUENTE
ROTO

0   250 yds

0   250 m

ESTADIO

ESTADIO

STADIUM

PERALTA

PASCARRAMBA

© AVALON TRAVEL

To Mirador de Turi
and Museo de Metales

ROBERTO
CRESPO

CALLE

SUPERMAXI

To Quinta Bolívar

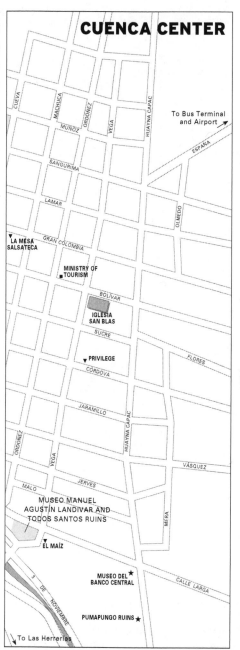

CUENCA CENTER

To Bus Terminal
and Airport

CUEVA
MACHUCA
ORDÓÑEZ
VEGA
HUAYNA CAPAC
MUÑOZ
ESPAÑA
SANGURIMA
LAMAR
OLMEDO
LA MESA
SALSATECA
GRAN COLOMBIA
MINISTRY OF
TOURISM
BOLÍVAR
IGLESIA
SAN BLAS
SUCRE
PRIVILEGE
FLORES
CÓRDOVA
JARAMILLO
HUAYNA CAPAC
ORDÓÑEZ
VEGA
VÁSQUEZ
MALO
JERVES
MUSEO MANUEL
AGUSTÍN LANDÍVAR AND
TODOS SANTOS RUINS
MERA
EL MAÍZ
MUSEO DEL
BANCO CENTRAL
CALLE LARGA
3
DE
NOVIEMBRE
PUMAPUNGO RUINS
To Las Herrerías

side is the immense twin-towered facade of one of Ecuador's architectural wonders—the Catedral de la Inmaculada Concepción, usually called simply the Catedral Nueva (New Cathedral). Begun in 1880 by an ambitious local bishop who decided the old cathedral wasn't big enough, it was originally planned as South America's largest church, with room for 10,000 worshippers. Work stopped in 1908 because of "architectural miscalculations," leaving the square twin towers unfinished. Quite how it would have looked if the bishop's ambitions had been realized defies imagination, but the pink travertine facade is still a stunning sight. For an even better view, walk around to the north side of the park to see the twin blue domes, covered with tiles imported from central Europe.

Inside, the Catedral Nueva is even more awe-inspiring, with a stunning gold-leaf altar, pink marble pillars, and stained glass windows from Belgium and Germany. Services fill the nave with voices chanting prayers in Latin and Spanish. Even if you're feeling burned-out on churches, this one is not to be missed.

On the opposite side of the park, the Catedral El Sagrario, better known as **Catedral Antigua** (Old Cathedral), is the city's oldest building, begun in 1557 with stones from the ruins of the Inca palace of Pumapungo. The steeple was used by La Condamine's group as one of the fixed points in measurements of the shape of the earth, inspiring a Spanish scientist visiting in 1804 to comment that this spire was more famous than the Egyptian pyramids. In a recent renovation, original 16th-century frescoes were discovered on the walls. Religious services were held here until the construction of the Catedral Nueva. Today it is often used for concerts.

Plazoleta del Carmen, Plaza San Francisco, and Iglesia Santo Domingo

West of Parque Calderon, next to the Cathedral, flower vendors in new kiosks fill this tiny square plaza, also called the Plaza de las Flores, with colors and scents every day. The twin spires of the **Iglesia El Carmen de**

la Asunción, founded in 1682, rise behind a small fountain with stones carved in Spanish baroque style framing the main entrance. A handful of nuns inhabit the **Monasterio del Carmen.** A painted refectory includes colonial masterworks by Caspicara (Manuel Chili) and Miguel de Santiago.

One block to the south is a clothes market on Plaza San Francisco, overlooked by the peach-and-white church of the same name, reconstructed in the early 20th century. It contains a lavish baroque altarpiece, which is intricately carved and covered with gold leaf.

Three blocks to the north, on Gran Colombia and Padre Aguirre, the Virgen del Rosario is the most precious icon in the **Iglesia Santo Domingo** (Colombia between Torres and Aguirre). Gold and jewels donated by Cuenca's wealthiest women encrust the Virgin's crown.

Plaza San Sebastián and Museo de Arte Moderno

At the western edge of the colonial center, the 17th-century **Iglesia San Sebastián** occupies the north side of this park. Facing it is the Museo de Arte Moderno (Sucre 15-27 at Coronel Talbot, tel. 7/283-1027, 8:30 A.M.–1 P.M. and 3–6:30 P.M. Mon.–Fri., 9 A.M.–1 P.M. Sat.–Sun., free), which has an interesting history. The building began as a *Casa de Temperancia* (House of Temperance). In the late 19th century, the story goes, a local bishop returning home one night came across a drunken man laid out in the street. When he turned out to be a priest, the bishop decided that Cuenca's drunks needed a place to sleep it off, and he began the Casa de Temperancia in 1876. Cells used to house the inebriated were later used for criminals when the building became a jail. After passing through various incarnations as a home for beggars, children, and the insane, the stately old structure was barely saved from destruction by the famous Ecuadorian painter Luis Crespo Ordóñez and was inaugurated as a museum in 1981. The setup is excellent, with lots of white space (notice the thick colonial walls) and long,

flower-filled courtyards setting off intricate modern sculptures and paintings.

Museo and Convento de las Conceptas

Cuenca's richest religious art collection is housed in the museum of the Convento de las Conceptas (Hermano Miguel 6-33 at Jaramillo, tel. 7/283-0625, 9 A.M.–5:30 P.M. Mon.–Fri., 10 A.M.–1 P.M. Sat.–Sun., $2.50), which occupies the block bounded by Córdova, Jaramillo, Borrero, and Hermano Miguel; the entrance is on Miguel. In the late 17th century, one Doña Ordóñez dedicated one of the finest houses in the city to serve as the convent on the condition that her three daughters would be accepted. The doors were shut in 1682, leaving a holiday on December 8 as one of the few times the Conceptor nuns are allowed to glimpse the outside world. Twenty-two rooms of sculpture and painting include many treasures from the Sangurima school of colonial art, along with crucifixes dating back to the 17th century.

Along Calle Large and Río Tomebamba

A stroll along Calle Larga takes visitors past five museums as well as hotels housed in restored colonial buildings, restaurants, and many new nightspots. Beginning at the west end is the **Museo del Sombrero** (Larga 10-41 at Torres, tel. 7/283-1569, 9 A.M.–6 P.M. Mon.–Fri., 9:30 A.M.–5 P.M. Sat., 9:30 A.M.–1:30 P.M. Sun., free), where the process of making and finishing Panama hats is explained. Huge old machines used to form the hats are on display, as well as good descriptions of the different stages of production. It's a good place to shop, although more expensive than in the surrounding villages such as Chordeleg and Sígsig. Standard hats cost $15, *finos* cost from $50, and *superfinos* from $200.

One block to the west is the **Zoologico Amarú** (Benigno Malo 4-64 at Larga, tel. 7/282-6337, 9 A.M.–1 P.M. and 3–6 P.M. Mon.–Fri., 10 A.M.–5 P.M. Sat.–Sun., $2). Ogle at Ecuador's multitudinous snakes, including the feared fer-de-lance, as well as other reptiles, amphibians, and fish, including piranha.

Two blocks farther down is the restored home of a 19th-century intellectual, **Museo Remigio Crespo Toral** (Larga 7-27 at Borrero, tel. 7/283-3208, 9 A.M.–1 P.M. and 3–6 P.M. Mon.–Fri., 9 A.M.–1 P.M. Sat.–Sun., free). This wooden building overlooking the Río Tomebamba contains a sparse but high-quality collection of religious sculptures, paintings, archaeological relics, and *artesanías*.

Most impressive of all the museums along Calle Larga is the extraordinary private collection of a local historian, Dr. Juan Cordero, on display at the **Museo de las Culturas Aborígenes** (Larga 5-24 at Cueva, tel. 7/283-9181, 8:30 A.M.–6:30 P.M. Mon.–Fri., 9 A.M.–1 P.M. Sat., $2). Some 5,000 pre-Columbian pieces, second only to the collection in Museo Banco Central in Quito, span every Ecuadorian culture from 13,000 B.C. up to the Spanish conquest. Highlights include La

© BEN WESTWOOD

This La Tolita statue is just one of 5,000 archaeological pieces at Museo de las Culturas Aborígenes.

Tolita statues of breastfeeding women, coca-chewing Guangalo figurines complete with bulging cheeks, Panzaleo pots made with tubes that act as built-in straws, and a macabre gold-toothed skull. Optional guides speak English, Spanish, and French and are recommended as they provide detail on the intricacies of this fascinating collection.

Walking east, you'll pass the **Puente Roto,** the broken remains of a bridge that once crossed the river, used as a viewpoint. A little farther is the **Museo Manuel Agustín Landívar** (Larga and Vega, tel. 7/282-1177, 8 A.M.–1 P.M. and 3–6 P.M. Mon.–Fri., $1). In 1970, workers clearing a small park between Calle Larga and Avenida Todos Santos unearthed a confusing jumble of rocks. Careful digging revealed layers of cultures: large, crude blocks of Cañari origin, finer Inca stonework with characteristic trapezoidal niches, and a Spanish watermill using both of the previous styles as a foundation. The entrance to the ruins is through the museum. Guides are available in English, Spanish, and Mandarin.

At the bottom of the La Escalinata stairway (a continuation of Hermano Miguel) along the river is the **Museo de Artes Populares** (Hermano Miguel 3-23 at Larga, tel. 7/282-9451, 9:30 A.M.–1 P.M. and 2–6 P.M. Mon.–Fri., 10 A.M.–1 P.M. Sat., free), with a collection of folk art and clothing that includes colorful masks and a crafts shop run by the Interamerican Center for the Development of Popular Arts (CIDAP).

Cross the river and walk across 12 de Abril to the right to the macabre **Museo de la Historia de la Medicina** (12 de Abril, no phone, 9 A.M.–5:30 P.M. Mon.–Fri., $1). This old military hospital houses a bizarre collection of medical history, from ledger books and bedpans to an X-ray machine that would make Dr. Frankenstein proud. Most unsettling are the saws and harnesses used for amputations and corpses in glass cases.

Museo del Banco Central

A 15-minute walk east of the center is the city's top museum and one of the best in Ecuador.

The glass edifice of the Banco Central doesn't look like much from the outside, but spread over three floors it houses the best archaeological collection in the southern Sierra, the **Museo del Banco Central** (Larga and Huayna Capac, tel. 7/283-1255, ext. 502, 9 A.M.–6 P.M. Mon.–Fri., 9 A.M.–1 P.M. Sat., $3 adults, $1.50 children). As well as pre-Columbian pottery, the museum also includes a large collection of colonial art and an excellent ethnographic exhibition of Ecuador's indigenous cultures, with animated dioramas, recreated dwellings, and a display of five *tsantsas* (shrunken heads).

The entrance fee includes access to the **Pumapungo ruins** at the back. Pumapungo was once Huayna Capac's palace-away-from-home and reputed to be one of the grandest in the Inca empire. It soon fell into ruin after the Spanish conquest, and many Pumapungo stones found their way into the foundations and walls of buildings in Cuenca's colonial center. German archaeologist Max Uhle rediscovered the ruins in 1922. Along with a temple to Viracocha, the Inca creator-god, Uhle uncovered the skeleton of a man in a specially widened section of wall, evidence of the pre-Columbian custom of burying a man alive in the foundation of a new wall to give it strength. Shattered jars, widespread scorching, and rooms filled with ash gave silent witness to Pumapungo's violent end.

Nowadays, the ruins on view to visitors are little more than row upon row of walls and foundations, but it's still an interesting site, and the hillside setting overlooking the river is impressive. Below the ruins are landscaped gardens and a bird rescue center with parrots, hawks, and a black-chested eagle.

Architecture and Green Space

The round portico of the **Banco del Azuay** (Bolívar and Borrero) features Doric columns supporting a cupola of rose-colored travertine, which forms the elegant entrance to another space for visiting art exhibits. The same material decorates the imposing three-story facade of the **Palacio de Justicia** on the southeast

corner of Parque Calderón, originally built for use as the University of Cuenca.

The district of Las Herrerías, with its ancient houses, is across the bridge at the southern end of Huayna Capac, below the Pumapungo ruins. Cuencanos come here to buy the traditional ornate crosses that adorn the roofs of finished homes; the wrought iron–working shops make a great variety of other useful items too. Nearby is an exuberant sculpture of the god Vulcan breaking free of the ground.

The grassy slopes of the Río Tomebamba, known as **El Barranco,** make an afternoon meander down 3 de Noviembre one of the more enjoyable urban walks in the country. Colonial houses and modern apartments spill down from Larga almost to the riverbank, where generations of indigenous women have laid out their washing to dry.

West of the city at La Quinta Balzay on the grounds of University of Cuenca, you can find the excellent *Orquidario* (tel. 7/284-2893, 8 A.M.–noon and 2 P.M.–6 P.M. Mon.–Fri., $1 pp), a beautiful orchid garden of some 400 species that's well worth a taxi ride (about $2–3).

Mirador de Turi

For the best views of Cuenca, head four kilometers south of the center along Avenida Solano up to the Mirador de Turi, a lookout with spectacular views over the city and the peaks of El Cajas in the distance. Look closely and you can pick out the blue domes of Cuenca's new cathedral. Processions from Cuenca on Good Friday lead to the small white Iglesia de Turi. Buses leave from 12 de Abril and Solano ($0.25), or a taxi costs about $3. Climb the stairs farther up to **Reina del Cisne** (tel. 7/403-8973), which sells a wide range of artisanal wares.

ENTERTAINMENT AND EVENTS
Nightlife

Nightlife is not nearly as raucous in Cuenca as in Quito or Guayaquil, which is not a bad thing. During the week many places close early, and it's very quiet after dark. On

Friday–Saturday evenings, though, the bars and discos along Calle Larga get quite busy with a predominantly young crowd.

Cuenca's local papers, *Tiempo* and *El Mercurio*, list what's showing at Cuenca's movie theaters—at least those still surviving since the opening of the six-screen **Multicines** in the Millenium Plaza (Peralta and Merchán), and another set at Mall del Rio beside the Rio Tarqui. The **Teatro Casa de la Cultura** (Cordero 7–42 at Córdova, tel. 7/282-2446), not to be confused with the Casa de la Cultura on Sucre and Aguirre, occasionally hosts movies and houses the popular Cinema Café.

Along Calle Larga, there are plenty of bars; it's a case of wandering down and seeing which one looks appealing. Look out for **Monday Blue** (Calle Larga and Cordero, tel. 7/282-3182, 4:30 P.M.–midnight Mon.–Sat., entrées $3–5). This funky little bar has walls covered in art and eclectic beer memorabilia, and serves cheap Mexican and Italian food. Farther down, the **Coffee Tree** (Larga 7-92 at Borrero, tel. 8/722-5225, http://coffeetree.com.ec) is a good place to sit outside and watch the evening get going. Head down the steps of La Escalinata (south from Miguel) to reach **Wunderbar** (Hermano Miguel 3-43 at Larga, tel. 7/283-1274, 8 A.M.–1 A.M. Mon.–Sat.), a small, cave-like place with German beers and occasional live music.

One block up, **El Cafecito** (Honorato Vásquez 7-36 at Borrero, tel. 7/283-2337, www.cafecito.net, 7 A.M.–midnight daily) is a good spot for a quiet drink. It's popular with backpackers and features music on the weekends. Just along the road, **Café Goloso** (Honorato Vásquez and Cordero, tel. 7/283-5308, 7 A.M.–midnight daily) has a wide range of cheap drinks during happy hour (5–8 P.M. daily).

For salsa dancing, head to the small *salsateca* **La Mesa** (Gran Colombia 3-55 at Ordóñez, tel. 7/283-3300, 9 P.M.–2 A.M. Wed.–Sat.). It's particularly good on Wednesday evenings. **Zoe's** (Borrero and Jaramillo, tel. 7/284-1005, 5 P.M.–midnight Mon.–Thurs., 5 P.M.–2 A.M. Fri.–Sat.) is a bar-restaurant with a busy dance floor on weekends pumping out electronica.

Across the street, the well-named **Verde, Pintón and Maduro** (Borrero and Honorato Vásquez, tel. 7/282-4871, 5 P.M.–midnight Mon.–Thurs., 5 P.M.–2 A.M. Fri.–Sat.) has a wider range of music.

For great food and drink and a friendly atmosphere, head to the American-run (**Café Eucalyptus** (Gran Colombia 9-41 at Malo, tel. 7/284-9157, www.cafeeucalyptus.com, 5 P.M.–midnight Mon.–Thurs., 5 P.M.–2 A.M. Fri.–Sat.). This Cuenca institution draws a more mature crowd that soaks up a Bohemian vibe, drinks from a wide-ranging international menu, and enjoys live music on weekends.

Festivals

Cuenca's main festivals include **Corpus Christi** (usually in June), nine weeks after Easter, which often coincides with an indigenous celebration, Inti Raymi. There are regular fireworks displays in Parque Calderón, paper balloons rise into the air, and the park resembles an open-air candy festival. The **Foundation of Cuenca,** April 10–13, is another big event, and celebrations for Cuenca's **Independence** on November 3 are combined with All Saints' Day (Nov. 1) and All Souls' Day (Nov. 2) for a three-day festival of theater, art, and dancing.

Cuenca's **Christmas festival** is one of the most famous in the country. The Pase del Niño Viajero—said to be the best holiday parade in Ecuador—begins on the morning of Christmas Eve. *Indígenas* from surrounding villages throng the streets. Symbols of prosperity, including strings of banknotes, poultry, and bottles of alcohol, are both carried and worn in the hope of arranging for even more of the same over the next year. The procession winds from the Iglesia San Sebastián to the cathedral, and the festivities don't stop until the next day.

Epiphany (Jan. 6) is also celebrated with parades and revelry.

SHOPPING

Cuenca and its surrounding villages offer great shopping opportunities—everything from

© BEN WESTWOOD

The Panama hat is one of Cuenca's prime exports.

finely wrought jewelry to handmade ceramics, indigenous textiles, antiques, and religious icons.

The most famous product made locally is the Panama hat. Even though these hats originate from Montecristi on the coast, Cuenca is Ecuador's production and export center. Some of Ecuador's finer hats are made in the southern Sierra by families who have woven the *toquilla* straw for generations. **Homero Ortega Padre e Hijos** (Dávalos 3–86, tel. 7/280-9000, www.homeroortega.com) exports sombreros around the world from a shop behind the *terminal terrestre*. Nearby on the same street, the German-Ecuadorian K. Dorfzaun (Dávalos, no phone, www.kdorfzaun.com) is another renowned manufacturer. In town, the most convenient place is **Rafael Paredes and Hijos** (Larga 10-41, tel. 7/283-1569) at the Museo del Sombrero, although prices tend to be higher. One of the oldest and most renowned hatmakers in Cuenca is octogenarian Alberto Pulla, who also has a shop (Tarqui and Córdova, tel. 7/282-9399).

For ceramics, **Eduardo Vega** has a private workshop and gallery (Vía a Turi 201, tel. 7/288-1407, www.eduardovega.com) in the gardens of his house 60 meters below the Turi lookout. In town, visit **Artesa** (Gran Colombia and Cordero, tel. 7/284-2647, www.artesa.com.ec), one of Ecuador's top ceramics manufacturers.

For jewelry, it's better to go to Chordeleg, but there are several *joyerías* (jewelry shops) in Cuenca, concentrated on Cordero near Colombia, along Colombia between Aguirre and Cordero, and in the Plazoleta Santana at the corner of Mariscal Lamar and Malo.

Many antiques stores surround Las Conceptas along Córdova. The **Centro Artesanal Casa de la Mujer** (General Torres, across from the Plaza San Francisco Market) is a mall with more than 100 vendors selling just about every type of *artesanía* imaginable, from baskets and balsa sculptures to Panama hats and paintings. Here you will find **Mama Kinoa,** the indigenous organization that runs a restaurant with traditional foods, and

Cushihuari, part of an organization promoting community tourism and cultural exchange programs.

Markets

Cuenca's main market day is Thursday, with smaller markets on Saturday and minimal vending the rest of the week. The **Mercado 9 de Octubre** sees the most goods changing hands, including crafts, clothes, and *cuyes* (guinea pigs), but be careful when shopping here. The flower and plant market in the **Plazoleta del Carmen** is one of the most photogenic in the southern Sierra.

Otavalo textiles and everyday goods are sold in the **Plaza de San Francisco** and the **Plaza Rotary,** and a local market fills the small plaza fronting **Las Conceptas.** Panama hat weavers sell directly to wholesalers in the **Plaza María Auxiliadora.**

On Sunday, head out of Cuenca to the surrounding villages of Gualaceo, Chordeleg, and Sígsig for the best bargains.

RECREATION AND TOURS

Cuenca does not have nearly as many tour operators as Quito, partly because many of the surrounding attractions can easily be visited independently. The local hiking and climbing specialists are the not-for-profit **Club de**

Andinismo Sangay (Gran Colombia 7-39 at Cordero, tel./fax 7/282-9958, www.clubsangay.com). They have information on climbing courses and hikes into El Cajas National Park and organize very cheap group hikes (under $10 pp), usually on Sunday.

Expediciones Apullacta (Gran Colombia 11-02 at General Torres, Suite 111, tel. 7/283-7815, www.apullacta.com) runs day trips to El Cajas ($40 pp), Ingapirca ($45 pp), and surrounding artisanal villages ($45 pp) that include English- or Spanish-speaking guides and lunch.

Terra Diversa (Hermano Miguel 5-42 at Vásquez, tel. 7/282-3782) is run by two experienced guides, Juan Heredia and José Saltos, and offers a wide selection of tours from Cuenca. The staff speaks English, and their information center is open daily.

Hualambari Tours (Borrero 9-67 at Colombia, tel./fax 7/283-0371) has day trips to El Cajas, Ingapirca, and nearby villages. Guides speak English, Spanish, German, French, and Italian.

Cuenca is very easy to explore independently, but if you want a whistle-stop bus tour (2 hours, $5 pp), they are run by **Vanservice** (tel. 7/281-6409, www.vanservice.com.ec, 9 A.M.–3 P.M. Tues.–Sat.) from Plaza San Sebastián.

THE ECUADORIAN ANDES

ANDEAN GENETIC ADAPTATIONS

Ever wondered why you're left breathless by the high altitude while locals in Ecuador seem to take it in stride? It's not all about acclimation, according to research from the University of British Columbia. Studies in Peru have shown that indigenous people living at high elevations have larger lungs and hearts – up to one-fifth bigger than normal. Their hearts are therefore able to pump two quarts more blood through their bodies than lowlanders.

The research also showed that highland people's muscles operate differently. When you and I push our muscles to the point of anaerobic metabolism (relying on stored-up energy, rather than oxygen from the outside air), they produce lactic acid that eventually builds up and causes cramps. Tests on local indigenous people have proved that muscles accumulate *less* lactate byproducts. It is not clear exactly why, but scientists theorize that it may be due to the highlanders' preference for carbohydrates (grains, potatoes, and rice) rather than fats as body fuel. Their muscles act the same, however, when they're brought down to sea level, suggesting an actual genetic adaptation.

Researchers hope to use this information to help people survive the temporary lack of oxygen caused by strokes and heart attacks.

ACCOMMODATIONS

Cuenca has a vast range of accommodations, mostly of a high standard. While budget accommodations are more limited, in the mid-range and high end there are dozens of appealing options in restored colonial buildings with courtyards or gardens for $20 pp upward, most including breakfast.

Under $10

Cuenca has relatively few hotels catering to travelers on a tight budget, and many of the cheapest venues in the center double as seedy motels, so avoid these. The best area for decent budget hotels is around Calle Larga and Hermano Miguel. One of the cheapest deals in town can be found at **Hostal Turista del Mundo** (tel. 7/282-9125, $6–10 pp), where the guest rooms have shared or private baths. There's also a TV room, a shared kitchen, and great views of the river. Nearby, **La Casa Cuencana** (Hermano Miguel 4-36, tel. 7/282-6009, $7–8 pp) has great-value guest rooms with terra-cotta walls adorned with artwork, a friendly family atmosphere, and a rooftop terrace. Opposite, **Hotel El Capitolio** (Hermano Miguel 4-19, tel. 7/282-4446, $8 pp) is an equally good budget option offering basic guest rooms with shared baths in a quiet setting.

A block in from Calle Larga, **El Cafécito** (Vásquez 7-36 at Cordero, tel. 7/283-2337, www.cafecito.net, dorm $7 pp, $15 s, $25 d) is a friendly little café with a twin in Quito. Choose from dorm beds or simple guest rooms with private baths. Just down the road, a new hotel of comparable quality and prices has opened: **Hostal La Cigale** (Vásquez and Cordero, tel. 7/283-5308, dorm $8 pp, $15 s, $22 d) has simple guest rooms, and the attached **The Café Goloso** is a popular place for drinks in the early evening.

North of the center, **Hotel Pichincha** (Torres 8-82 at Bolívar, tel. 7/282-3868, $6.50–7.50 pp) is a well-run hotel popular with budget travelers for its cheap guest rooms with shared baths and a shared kitchen.

$10-25

Most of the hotels along the river are quite pricey, but **Casa del Barranco** (Larga 8-41 at Cordero, tel. 7/283-9763, www.casadelbarranco.com, $20 s, $31 d) bucks the trend. This historic house has paintings by local artists and breakfast served in the café overlooking the river. Guest rooms have private baths and TVs.

The colonial **Hostal Macondo** (Tarqui 11-64 at Mariscal Lamar, tel. 7/284-0697, www.hostalmacondo.com, $19–25 s, $28–35 d, breakfast included) has a comfortable lounge area, kitchen facilities, and good guest rooms around a pretty garden. The hostel has the same owners as Expediciones Apullacta, where you can book a wide range of tours.

The warm guest rooms at the **Hostal La Orquidea** (Borrero 9-31 at Bolívar, tel. 7/282-4511, fax 7/283-5844, $15 s, $24 d) are great value. Each has a TV and a phone, and there's a good restaurant.

For a more historic ambience, the endearingly weathered 18th-century **Hostal Colonial** (Gran Colombia 10-13 at Aguirre, tel. 7/284-1644, $18 s, $34 d) has cozy guest rooms around a pleasant courtyard restaurant. Farther up the street, the colonial **Hostal Chordeleg** (Colombia and Torres, tel. 7/282-4611, fax 7/282-2536, $25 s, $40 d) is a little smarter with correspondingly higher rates.

$25-50

Hotel Principe (Jaramillo and Cordero, tel. 7/284-7287, www.hotelprincipecuenca.com, $31 s, $46 d) is actually a replica colonial house, but it certainly is convincing. Comfortable guest rooms are set around a compact courtyard, and the restaurant is adorned with local artwork. **Hotel Cuenca** (Borrero and Gran Colombia, tel. 7/283-3711, $30 s, $46 d) has 30 good-quality guest rooms and a restaurant, El Carbon, specializing in barbecue. **Hotel San Andres** (Gran Colombia 11-66, tel. 7/284-1497, www.hotelsansanandres.net, $42 s, $63 d) is another attractive colonial building with well-appointed guest rooms, a courtyard, and a small garden at the back. Orange and blue is an unusual choice of colors, but **Posada**

del Angel (Bolívar 14-11 at Estevez de Toral, tel. 7/284-0695, $40 s, $57 d) still manages to look elegant, with charming guest rooms around an enclosed courtyard.

$50-75

Hotel Inca Real (General Torres and Sucre, tel. 7/282-3636, www.hotelincareal.com.ec, $51 s, $67 d, buffet breakfast included) has smallish rooms in a restored 19th-century house. **Casa de Aguila** (Sucre and Montalvo, tel. 7/283-6498, www.hotelcasadelaguila. com, $67 s, $79 d, breakfast included), which means "eagle house," is a beautifully restored colonial building dating from 1802 with warm peach-colored walls and elegantly furnished guest rooms.

Beautiful guest rooms with wall-to-wall windows overlooking the Río Tomebamba are available at one of the top hotels in town, **Hotel Victoria** (Larga 6-93 at Borrero, tel. 7/282-7401, santaana@etapaonline.net.ec, $71 s, $91 d). Most of the spacious, elegantly furnished guest rooms have views of the extensive gardens and river. This renovated building also houses gourmet restaurant El Jardín downstairs.

$75-100

Farther along to the west, **Hotel Crespo** (Larga 7-93 at Cordero, tel. 7/284-2571, $89 s, $113 d, breakfast included) is a good choice, with guest rooms that have views over the river.

$100-200

A pair of recently renovated colonial mansions have been converted into two of the best city hotels in the country. The **Hotel Santa Lucía** (Borrero 8-44 at Sucre, tel. 7/282-8000, www. santaluciahotel.com, $108 s, $133 d) was built by Azuay's first provincial governor in 1859, and it also houses an attractive café in the front and an Italian restaurant on the central patio. The **Hotel Oro Verde** (Lasso, tel. 7/409-0000, www.oroverdehotels.com, $110 s, $134 d, airport transfers included) is three kilometers west of the city center on the way to El Cajas along the Río Tomebamba. Along with a Swiss restaurant considered one of the best in the city,

there's a bar, a deli, an outdoor pool, a gym, and a sauna.

The **Ⓒ Mansion Alcazar** (Bolívar 12-55 at Tarqui, tel. 7/282-3918, $122 s, $202 d) is one of the most stylish hotels in Ecuador, with a 19th-century ambience glittering with crystal chandeliers and locally crafted art and furniture. The hotel features 14 uniquely decorated guest rooms and suites, a gourmet restaurant called Casa de Alonso, a bar, a library, and extensive gardens.

FOOD

Cuenca has a great selection of restaurants, the best in Ecuador outside Quito, with many excellent local and international eateries. The city also has a sweet tooth, and it's worth browsing the stores for local specialties such as *membrillo* (a red block of gelatinous fruit) to munch on as you're wandering around.

Cafés and Sweets

El Cafecito (Vásquez 7-36 at Cordero, tel: 7/283-2337, www.cafecito.net, entrées $3) is very popular, partly because the hamburgers, pasta, and Mexican entrées are so cheap. Another very popular place is **Ⓒ Cacao and Canela** (Jaramillo and Borrero, tel. 7/282-0945, 4 P.M.–midnight Mon.–Sat., $2–3). This snug café serves a huge selection of chocolate drinks with flavors ranging from almond and mozzarella to rum. The cakes and pastries are a perfect accompaniment.

Local

The best place in the center to enjoy Ecuadorian food is **Raymipampa** (Benigno Malo 859, tel. 7/283-4159, 8:30 A.M.–11 P.M. daily, entrées $4–6) under the colonnaded arches of the New Cathedral on the west side of Parque Calderón. It gets very busy with visitors and locals alike wolfing down seafood, meat and chicken specialties as well as sweet and savory crepes. Along Calle Larga, another authentic place with a quieter atmosphere is a yellow house called **El Maiz** (Larga 1-279 at Vega, tel. 7/284-0224, 11 A.M.–9 P.M. Mon.–Sat., entrées $5–6), serving goat stew, trout, and a variety of creative dishes using quinoa. Another good local restaurant doing all the meat, chicken, and fish staples well is **Los Capulies** (Córdoba and Borrero, tel. 7/284-5887, 9 A.M.–4 P.M. and 6–11 P.M. Mon.–Sat., entrées $4–6), in a pleasant courtyard setting.

International

El Jardín (Larga 693 at Borrero, tel. 7/282-7401, lunch and dinner daily, entrées $8–20), in the Hotel Victoria, is one of the best restaurants in town. There are wonderful views over the river along with international cuisine prepared from scratch—everything from *ceviche* and langoustine to beef bourguignonne—which means the service is accordingly very slow.

El Pedregal Azteca (Colombia 10-33, tel. 7/282-3652, lunch and dinner Mon.–Sat., entrées $5–10) is one of the best Mexican restaurants this side of Yucatán. Try specialties such as *mole poblano* (chicken with chocolate, chilies, and almonds).

Now German-run, **Café Austria** (Malo and Jaramillo, tel. 7/284-0899, 9 A.M.–11 P.M. daily, entrées $6–8) offers specialties like roulade and goulash plus great coffee and cakes. Note that this is one of the best options on Sunday, when most places are closed.

For Middle Eastern, head to **El Jordan** (Larga 6-111 at Borrero, tel. 7/285-0517, lunch and dinner Mon.–Sat., entrées $6–9), which serves well-presented moussaka, falafels, and the like in a beautiful setting overlooking the river with Moorish and French decor.

For the best curry in town, head to new favorite **Taj Mahal** (Larga and Benigno Malo, no phone, lunch and dinner daily, entrées $3–5). Run by a cheerful Pakistani, this brightly colored place serves great *jalfrezi* and *biryani* as well as traditional yogurt, and it doubles as a kebab restaurant. There are often highly entertaining Bollywood movies on the big screen.

For tasty Colombian *arepas* and filling lunches, head to **Moliendo** (Honorato Vásquez 6–24, tel. 7/282-8710, 9 A.M.–9 P.M. Mon.–Sat., entrées $2–4).

New York Pizza (Tarqui and Mariscal Lamar, tel. 7/284-2792, 11 A.M.–10 P.M. daily, entrées $2–10) is one of the best options for Italian slices (from $2.50) and family-size pizzas ($10–15). Everything else on the menu, from ravioli to *churrasco,* is under $6.

Supermarkets

To stock up for yourself, there's a **Supermaxi** (De las Américas) just north of Ordóñez Lazo, west of the center. You can also go to the new malls, Millenium Plaza or Mall del Río.

INFORMATION AND SERVICES
Visitor Information

There's a well-staffed **Itur office** (Sucre between Cordero and Malo, tel. 7/285-0521, 8 A.M.–8 P.M. Mon.–Fri., 8:30 A.M.–1:30 P.M. Sat.) on Parque Calderón in the municipal offices, where you can also pick up a free copy of the useful *Agenda Conmemorativa,* published every month and packed with information, cultural events, exhibitions, concerts, and photos. There are also offices in the bus terminal and the airport.

The **Ministerio de Turismo** (Bolívar and Tomas Ordóñez, tel. 7/282-2058, 9 A.M.–5 P.M. Mon.–Fri.) has an office with maps and brochures. For information on Azuay Province, the **Camara de Turismo del Azuay** (Larga and Huayna Capac, 9 A.M.–5 P.M. Mon.–Fri., tel. 7/284-5657) has a new office near the Museo del Banco Central.

Money Exchange and Communications

Most *casas de cambio* are found east of Parque Calderón. **Vaz Cambios** (Gran Colombia 7-98 at Cordero, tel. 7/283-3434) has a branch with Western Union money-transfer service available. **Delgado Travel** (Gran Colombia and Mariano Cueva, tel. 7/283-3673) is another dependable option.

If you'd rather deal with a bank, the **Banco del Pacífico** (Malo 975 at Gran Colombia) makes cash advances on credit cards. Most

Health Care

The 24-hour **Clínica Santa Inés** (Córdova 2-67 at Agustín Cueva, tel. 7/281-7888) is just across the river from the center and employs a few English-speaking doctors. **Clínica Hospital Monte Sinai** (Miguel Cordero 6-111 at Solano, tel. 7/288-5595) is another highly regarded hospital in the city.

GETTING THERE AND AROUND

Buses

Cuenca's *terminal terrestre* is probably the most orderly and pleasant bus terminal in the country. It is two blocks northeast of the traffic circle at España and Huayna Capac. Several companies run luxury bus services to Guayaquil (4 hours, $8), which recently increased in price, and Macas (7 hours, $8.50). Panamericana (España 5-24) has an office just beyond the bus station and sends luxury buses to Quito (10 hours, $12) daily at 10 P.M. Buses to Loja (4.5 hours, $7.50) travel via Saraguro, and Transportes Cañar has direct buses to Ingapirca ($2.50) at 9 A.M. and 1 P.M. daily. Jahuay has more regular buses to Tambo ($1.80), where you change for Ingapirca. For El Cajas National Park (45 minutes, $2), take a Guayaquil bus and ask the driver to let you off at the entrance.

For Gualaceo, Chordeleg, and Sigig, buses run every hour. Buses to other small towns and villages around Cuenca leave from Terminal Sur, close to the Feria Libre outdoor market on Avenida de las Américas. Local city buses cost $0.25.

Taxis and Car Rental

The minimum taxi fare in Cuenca is $1.25, which will get you to most places in town (taxis don't have meters). The bus station and airport are each a $2 ride from the city center. Reputable, prebookable companies include **Ejecutivo** (tel. 7/280-9605) and **Andino** (tel. 7/282-3893). For car rental, try **Localiza** (tel. 7/408-4631) at the airport or bus terminal.

Air

Planes leave from Cuenca's Mariscal Lamar

CONSULATES IN CUENCA

- **Brazil:** Ramírez Dávalos 1434 at Turuhuaico, tel. 7/408-9054

- **Chile:** Paseo 3 de Noviembre 2406 at Escalinata, tel. 7/284-0061

- **France:** Gran Colombia 661, Ed. Gran Colombia, tel. 7/283-4644

- **Germany:** Bolívar 9-18 at Malo, tel. 7/282-2783

---

banks also have **ATMs** for up to $500 daily in cash withdrawals.

Cuenca's **post office** (Borrero and Gran Colombia) is in the center of town.

Language Schools

Cuenca is a very popular city to study Spanish for extended periods, which explains the many high-quality language schools in town. The **Centro de Estudios Interamericanos** (Cordero and Jaramillo, tel. 7/283-9003, www.cedei.org) offers Spanish classes ($6 per hour) as well as courses in Kichwa, colonial Latin American history, and Andean literature. It can also arrange positions teaching English.

Nexus Lenguas y Culturas (3 de Noviembre 2-47 at Jacarandá, tel. 7/283-4677) offers Spanish classes ($5 per hour) and has positions teaching English locally. The **Centro Cultural Ecuatoriano-Norteamericano Abraham Lincoln** (Borrero 5-18 at Vásquez, tel. 7/284-1737, tel./fax 7/282-3898, www.cena.org.ec) is recommended ($7 per hour). It can also arrange homestays with local families.

The **Si Centro** (Borrero and Sucre, tel. 7/282-0429) language school comes recommended as well. **Fundación Amauta** (Miguel and Córdova, tel. 7/284-6206) is highly recommended by the tourist office, as it also works with local communities and development.

THE ECUADORIAN ANDES

CUENCA AIRLINE OFFICES

- **Aerogal:** España 1114, tel. 7/286-1041 or 7/281-5250, www.aerogal.com.ec

- **Air Cuenca:** tel. 7/408-4410 or 7/408-3381, www.postges-ec.com

- **Avianca:** Córdova 8-40 at Luis Cordero, tel. 7/245-5563, www.avianca.com

- **Copa:** Lamar 989 at Aguirre, tel. 7/284-2970, www.copaair.com

- **LAN:** Bolívar 9-18 at Malo, tel. 7/282-2783, www.lan.com

- **Lufthansa:** Bolívar 9-18 at Malo, tel. 7/282-2783, www.lufthansa.com

- **TACA:** Sucre 7-70 at Cordero, tel. 7/283-7360, www.taca.com

- **TAME:** Astudillo 2-22 at España, tel. 7/410-3104, www.tame.com.ec

airport, two kilometers northeast of the town center on Avenida España. It's a 10-minute walk from the *terminal terrestre* or a short hop by taxi or local bus.

TAME has offices in town (Astudillo 2-22, tel. 7/288-9581 or 7/410-3104) and at the airport (tel. 7/286-6400) and flies to Quito (Mon.–Sat., $85 one-way) and Guayaquil (Mon.–Sat., $70 one-way). For similar prices, **Icaro, Aerogal,** and **Air Cuenca** also regularly fly to Quito and Guayaquil.

BAÑOS

Don't confuse this tiny town eight kilometers southwest of Cuenca with its larger namesake in Tungurahua Province. It's not as impressive as a spa resort but nevertheless offers the best opportunity for a relaxing few hours to ease those limbs after days of hikes and sightseeing.

While the benefit of the mineral content of the waters is debatable, there are several commercial warm baths. The most attractive is at

Hostería Durán (tel. 7/289-2485, www.hosteriaduran.com, $58 s, $85 d, baths only $5.50) which has two warm pool heated to 38°C. This full resort boasts tennis courts, a gym, waterslides, and plush guest rooms with all the amenities. The *hostería* **Rodas** (tel. 7/289-2161, www.hosteriarodas.com, $50 s, $70 d, baths $2) has a less appealing outdoor pool, but inside the small hot pool is the hottest in town. A third set of baths is found at **Agapantos** (tel. 7/289-2493, www.agapantos.com, $2.25), which has two warm pools.

Take a taxi from Cuenca ($4–5), or catch a local bus at the intersection of 12 de Abril and Solano, south of the river, which then passes the Plaza San Francisco on Córdova. Buses run from Cuenca to the top of the hill, where a baby-blue church with tiled domes is worth a look. Hostería Durán is a short distance below, surrounded by a billiards hall, discos, and restaurants.

◖ EL CAJAS NATIONAL PARK

If you're longing for fresh air and rugged landscapes after a few days' sightseeing in the city, this huge national park on Cuenca's doorstep is the best place to go. It's only an hour from the city by bus, so it is easily visited on a day trip. With dramatic open rolling land and jagged rocks, Cajas feels almost like the Scottish Highlands. Among the park's 28,000 hectares there are more than 200 lakes here and a variety of trails, ranging from a gentle hour-long stroll to two-day hikes. It's also an excellent place for trout fishing, and even though it's popular among locals, the park is big enough to find solitude.

Most of El Cajas lies above 3,000 meters elevation, with *páramo* covering most of the rugged terrain. Frost and ice above 4,000 meters try their best to deter the thriving of hardy vegetation, such as the tiny quinoa tree, which clings to life higher than any other tree in the world. The park straddles the continental divide, so rivers rush both east to the Amazon and west to the Pacific Ocean. El Cajas is the continental divide's most westerly point in South America.

THE ECUADORIAN ANDES

© BEN WESTWOOD

Cerro San Luis rises above Laguna Toreadora at the entrance to El Cajas National Park.

Visitors stand a good chance of seeing the wild llamas that were reintroduced to the park in the late 1990s. The park's other animal inhabitants, such as spectacled bears, pumas, and oncillas, are more elusive. A long bird list includes hummingbirds, toucans, and Andean condors.

Archaeology

Fragments of Inca roads throughout the reserve link numerous *tambos*—ruins of way stations along the royal highway, which ran through here all the way to the coast. Traces of the roads connect Laguna Luspa to Laguna Mamamag, and Laguna Ingacocha to Laguna Ingacarretero. The area near Molleturo Hill has the highest concentration of ruins in El Cajas, where great views of Chimborazo and El Altar give evidence of the Inca skill at picking sites that were both scenic and easily defended. Other ruins can be found near Laguna Toreadora and Laguna Atugyacu.

Visiting the Park

The main route to El Cajas from Cuenca is along the main road down to Guayaquil, which climbs to 4,000 meters before dropping down dramatically to sea level in just 1.5 hours. Just 34 kilometers from Cuenca is the main entrance to the park at the Laguna Toreadora **visitors center** (6 A.M.–5 P.M. daily, park entry $2 pp).

Buses heading to Guayaquil every hour from Cuenca's main *terminal terrestre* take about 45 minutes to reach Laguna Toreadora ($2). There are also buses run by Occidental leaving from their bus terminal (Mariscal Lamar and Miguel Heredia). To return, simply flag down a bus on the main road outside the entrance.

Ask to be dropped at the *refugio* (tel. 7/237-0126), where you can pay the recently reduced entrance fee ($2 pp), which includes a free map and an information sheet. You can stay overnight here, but there is only capacity for six people, so advanced booking is advisable. There are kitchen facilities and electricity but no hot water.

You'll certainly work up an appetite hiking here, and the restaurant just up the hill

© BEN WESTWOOD

Llamas were reintroduced into the high plains of El Cajas in the late 1990s.

from the refuge serves great meals, including delicious *locro de papas* (potato soup, $2), trout ($4), and a three-course set lunch ($7.50).

El Cajas is full of hiking trails; eight are clearly marked, ranging from three hours to two full days. Note that groups numbering eight or more must be accompanied by a guide. Around Laguna Toreadora is the most popular short hike, the trail to Laguna Totoras and Laguna Patoquinuas takes about six hours, and climbing Cerro San Luis, the highest point in the park at 4,200 meters, takes about four hours. Another popular day hike is the trail from the Tres Cruces hill, four kilometers west of the information center, up over the continental divide (4,103 meters) and past Laguna Larga, Laguna Tagllacocha, and Laguna Luspa.

Overnight hikes include a trek to the Inca ruins by Lago Osohuayco and the hike from Miguir to the southern park guard post at Soldados. Be warned that trails have a tendency to peter out, and the weather can turn on you in a minute. Whatever time of year, the high elevation means it gets cold. Night temperatures can drop below freezing, and deaths from exposure have occurred here. Even during the day it's cold, although it heats up considerably when the sun breaks through. The solution is to bring plenty of layers—ideally a thick sweater or jacket as well as waterproof clothing. Also bring maps, a compass, and waterproof boots. Consider fishing gear and a compass if you plan to wander far afield. Four IGM 1:50,000 maps cover the area: *Cuenca, Chaucha, San Felipe de Molleturo,* and *Chiquintad,* although the map included in the entrance fee is usually good enough.

The August–January dry season is the best time to visit, promising the most sun and regular but short rain showers. The rainy season, February–July, has the highest average temperature but more precipitation. The entire park is at 3,000–4,000 meters elevation, and high elevations make acclimation essential—hike high and sleep low. If you're not adjusted to Cuenca's elevation (2,500 meters), you'll find hiking in Cajas very difficult. If traveling up from Guayaquil, you should ideally take a day or two to adjust before coming to El Cajas.

Tour companies in Cuenca organize excursions to El Cajas (from $40 pp). Try **Expediciones Apullacta** (Gran Colombia 11-02 at General Torres, Suite 111, tel. 7/283-7815, www.apullacta.com). Overnight tours (from $150 pp) include a guide, food, transportation, and camping gear.

EAST OF CUENCA

The hills above Cuenca to the east contain several villages renowned for their crafts, especially jewelry and hats. Sunday is market day and easily the most interesting day to visit, but plenty of stores open throughout the week. There are several buses per hour from Cuenca running regularly to Gualaceo ($0.60), Chordeleg ($0.75), and Sígsig ($1.25), so it's quite easy to visit all three on a day trip. The trip can also be done as a loop by returning through the hillside village of San Bartolomé, where generations of craftspeople have made guitars by hand, then crossing over the *páramo* to El Valle and Cuenca. Alternately, if you have the extra cash, most Cuenca tour operators offer guided trips ($45 pp) to the villages on weekends.

Gualaceo

On the banks of the Río Gualaceo, 34 kilometers from Cuenca, this small town hosts the largest indigenous market in the area every Sunday. Three separate markets—fruits and vegetables, crafts and clothes, and produce and household goods—blend effectively into one. Visitors come for the fine woven and embroidered textiles, such as the *macana* shawls with macramé fringe, and for the impressive surrounding scenery that has earned Gualaceo the nickname "the garden of Azuay." Gualaceo's **Peach Festival** in early March features exhibitions of flowers and crafts. The center of town itself is not quite as picturesque as the name suggests, however, and shopping aside, Chordeleg and Sígsig are actually prettier.

Most visitors just pass through, but if you decide to stay, the budget **Residencial**

Gualaceo (Gran Colombia, tel. 7/225-5006, $6 s, $10 d), a few blocks northwest of the main plaza, has adequate guest rooms. Inexpensive **Restaurant Don Q** (Gran Colombia and 9 de Octubre, no phone, lunch daily), on the northwest corner of the main plaza, does the usual staples well and is popular with locals.

Buses for Gualaceo leave every 15 minutes from Cuenca's *terminal terrestre* (45 minutes, $0.60). Gualaceo's bus station is on the east side of Roldos between Cordero and Reyes, southeast of the main market plaza.

Chordeleg and South

Just five kilometers south of Gualaceo, a pleasant two-hour walk if you're feeling energetic, this small village has specialized in jewelry for centuries, turning silver and gold from nearby mines into finely wrought rings, bracelets, necklaces, and earrings. On the main square and dotted around town are scores of *joyerías* (jewelry shops), and it's also a good place to shop for clothing, including Panama hats. It gets very busy on Sunday, with a wider range but slightly higher prices. A small **Museo Comunidad** (23 de Enero 4-21, tel. 7/222-3095, 8 A.M.–5 P.M. Tues.–Sun., free) on the main plaza has displays on the history and techniques of making jewelry and other local crafts such as ceramics, hat weaving, and textiles.

Grab a bite to eat on the main square at **El Yugo** (Plaza Central Chordeleg, no phone, breakfast, lunch, and dinner daily, $2–4), which does good lunches.

Sígsig

Some 26 kilometers by bus south of Chordeleg (20 minutes, $0.25), this pretty town hosts a smaller Sunday market but is known more for the Panama hat factory just outside town, **ATMA** (Associación de Toquilleras María Auxiliadora, tel. 7/226-6377). It's worth making the trip out here for the best-quality hats. *Superfinos* sell for $50–80, less than half the price of many stores in Cuenca, and even the cheapest standard hats are of better quality in Sígsig. It's not that easy to find the factory on foot, so it's better to take a taxi from the center ($1).

© BEN WESTWOOD

Traditional indigenous cultures thrive in the villages around Cuenca.

Sígsig has an attractive main square and is surrounded by impressive scenery, good for hiking, and there are some archaeological sites: 10 kilometers south of town are the famous pre-colonial caves of Chobshi, and nearby are the Inca ruins at Shabalula. Other impressive areas nearby include the mountain of Fasayñan, the hills of Huallil, the lakes of Ayllon, the shore of the Río Santa Bárbara, and the lake at San Sebastián. For longer hikes, the Chaquiñan walking road southeast to Gualaquiza in the Amazon lowlands takes 2–3 days.

The surrounding attractions mean that staying in Sígsig makes more sense than in the other towns. There is a decent mid-range hotel opposite the bus station, **Fasayñan Hotel** (tel. 7/226-7021 or 8/673-8366, $12.50 pp, breakfast included), which has guest rooms with private baths and a restaurant downstairs.

SOUTH TO LOJA
Girón and El Chorro
The Panamericana highway splits 15 kilometers south of Cuenca. The western branch

makes its way downhill to Machala, reaching Girón after 27 kilometers. This is a spot relatively untouched by tourism. The town itself has a pretty central square with a museum, **Museo Casa de los Tratados** (Bolívar and Andrés Córdova, tel. 7/227-5061, 8 A.M.–6 P.M. daily, $1.25), which commemorates a treaty signed in 1829 between Gran Colombia and Peru shortly before the emergence of the Ecuadorian nation.

About 5 kilometers out of town is **El Chorro,** a long waterfall tumbling down a cliff surrounded by lush vegetation. It's a two-hour hike, but the scenery is well worth it. There's a refuge right next to the waterfall, **El Chorro de Girón** (tel. 7/227-5783, $5 pp) that offers guest rooms and camping as well as a restaurant, although it's mainly open on weekends and is often closed during the week.

Jima
This village, about 20 kilometers southeast of Cuenca, has a small amount of community-based tourism thanks to U.S. Peace Corps volunteers who helped to set up the nonprofit **Fundación Turística Jima** a few years ago. The town has some very good day hikes and is the starting point for a 3–4-day trek through San Miguel de Cuyes and La Florida to the edge of the rainforest. Guides can be hired through the foundation, and hikes (about $60 per group per day) include lodging and food. Contact Nancy Uyaguari at **Fundación Turística Jima** (Amazona, tel. 7/241-8278, caritas2011@gmail.com) for further information on tourism and volunteering.

There are very limited accommodations in town, but **Hotel Jima** (Benigno Torres, tel. 7/241-8003, $6–10 pp) has guest rooms with shared and private baths and provides meals. In town, **El Pucón** (Amazona, tel. 7/241-8278, lunch and dinner daily, entrées $2–3) restaurant is a good place to eat.

The biggest event in town is the rowdy **Festival de la Chicha de Jora,** held on the first Saturday in October, which includes a contest to judge the best *chicha* (a bitter alcoholic drink made from maize), along with dancing and presumably lots of drinking.

Transportes Jima buses leave Cuenca (2 hours, $2) every couple of hours 8:30 A.M.–5 P.M., boarding opposite the Feria Libre outdoor market on Avenida de las Américas.

Saraguro

The eastern branch of the Panamericana climbs over the Tinajilla Pass (3,527 meters) before reaching this village, which is home to the famous Saraguro *indígenas*. Walk down the hill from the highway to the main square, handsome church, and indigenous artisanal shops. The town is busiest during the **Sunday-morning market,** when most of the Saraguros from surrounding villages flood the town. Ask directions to the home workshop of **Manuel Encarnación Quishpe,** who weaves dozens of different kinds of textiles.

There is good **hiking** in the area, and suggested hikes nearby include the Hizzikaka (Sinincapa) Caves, the Virgen Kaka Waterfall, Puglla Mountain, and the Washapamba Cloud

THE SARAGUROS

The indigenous Saraguros, whose name means "corn germination" in Kichwa, are a unique indigenous culture in Ecuador, originating from Lake Titicaca on the border of southern Peru and Bolivia. They were brought here in the 16th century by the Inca *mitma* system (a policy of relocating colonies), and over 30,000 thrive in the town of Saraguro and nearby mountain villages of Oñacapa, Lagunas, Quisuginchir, and Tuncarta.

The Saraguros are known for their distinctive dress, which is most commonly black. Men wear black pants, leather belts decorated with silver, sleeveless shirts known as *cushma*, and a poncho. Women wear long, black pleated skirts, embroidered blouses, black wool shawls, and elegant beaded necklaces. Both sexes wear wide-brimmed hats, usually black or white, and wear their hair in a single braid running down their backs.

The predominance of black has led to a common misconception that the Saraguros are in perpetual mourning for the death of Inca leader Atahualpa, but you'll be dismissed if you mention this locally. In fact, Saraguro also wear dark blue and other colors.

The financially successful Saraguros began as crafts makers, but they've since moved on to herding cattle as far as the Amazonian province of Zamora-Chinchipe in search of grazing land. Nowadays, crafts and farming remain common professions, but education has increased markedly in the community in

© BEN WESTWOOD

The Saraguros were moved by the Inca from Bolivia to Ecuador.

the past 30 years, and many Saraguros are now doctors, lawyers, and teachers. Some of the younger generation cast off their official dress, and many have migrated to other parts of Ecuador and even Italy and Spain, but local community groups are working hard to preserve their unique heritage.

For further information on the Saraguros, visit www.saraguro.org.

Forest. Local guides are available to lead the 3–4-day hike to the rainforest as well as several other routes. Local tourism association **Operadora de Turismo Saraurku** (10 de Marzo, tel. 7/220-0331 or 8/594-7476, www.turismosaraguro.com) has an office on the main plaza and can arrange family homestays ($27 pp), including three meals, and also three-day tours to Amazon communities ($250 pp). Horseback riding and cycling is also available. For further information on community tourism, contact **Fundación Jatari** (Loja and Guayaquil, tel. 7/220-0071, www.jatari.org), which was constructing a Saraguro community museum at the time of this writing.

Most travelers visit for a couple of hours, but if you want to stay, there are a few simple hotels in town. The best in the center is **Samana Wasi** (10 de Marzo and Panamericana, tel. 7/220-0315, $10 pp). On the outskirts of town toward the peak is the best place to stay in the whole area: The adobe and wood **⟨ Hostal Achik Wasi** (near Saraguro, tel. 7/220-0058, $15 pp, breakfast included) has clean, comfortable guest rooms, hot showers, and balconies with great views over the town.

Outside the hotels, **Mama Cuchara** (Parque Central, no phone, breakfast, lunch, and dinner daily, $2–3) is the best place to eat in town. True to its name (Mother Spoon), it serves up traditional meals washed down with *horchata,* a refreshing pink drink made with 19 herbs and flowers. Profits go to a local women's association.

Buses to Loja (1.5 hours) and Cuenca (3 hours) pass every half hour and stop in front of the bus companies' offices on Calle Azuay; some also loop through the plaza before leaving.